UNSTUCK YOURSELF

THRIVE BEYOND
BURNOUT
&
DISCOVER YOUR
TRUE PURPOSE

LAURA CARDWELL
MEGHAN O'MALLEY, M.S.

Copyright © 2025 by Meghan O'Malley and Laura Cardwell

Unstuck Yourself
Thrive Beyond Burnout & Discover Your True Purpose

All rights reserved.

No part of this work may be used or reproduced, transmitted, stored, or used in any form or by any means graphic, electronic, or mechanical, including but not limited to photocopying, recording, scanning, digitizing, taping, Web distribution, information networks or information storage and retrieval systems, or in any manner whatsoever without prior written permission from the publisher.

In this world of digital information and rapidly-changing technology, some citations do not provide exact page numbers or credit the original source. We regret any errors, which are a result of the ease with which we consume information.

Without in any way limiting the author's and publisher's exclusive rights under copyright, any use of this publication to train generative artificial intelligence (AI) or Large Language Model (LLM) technologies to generate text is expressly prohibited.

The information provided in this book is strictly for informational purposes and is not intended as a substitute for advice from your physician or mental health provider. You should not use this information for diagnosis or treatment of any physical or mental health problem.

Editor: Anna Paradox
Senior Editor: Laurie Knight

An Imprint for GracePoint Publishing (www.GracePointPublishing.com)

GracePoint Matrix, LLC
624 S. Cascade Ave, Suite 201
Colorado Springs, CO 80903
www.GracePointMatrix.com
Email: Admin@GracePointMatrix.com
SAN # 991-6032

A Library of Congress Control Number has been requested and is pending.
ISBN: (Paperback) 978-1-966346-04-3
eISBN: 978-1-966346-64-7

Books may be purchased for educational, business, or sales promotional use.
For distribution queries contact Sales@IPGbook.com
For non-retail bulk order requests contact Orders@GracePointPublishing.com

Printed in U.S.A

Table of Contents

Foreword III
Introduction: Welcome to the Journey 1

SECTION 1:
HUMAN DESIGN 101: THE BLUEPRINT TO BURNOUT

Chapter 1: Human Design: Your Blueprint for Purpose-Full Thriving 21
Chapter 2: The Power of Knowing Your Type: An Invitation to Align 37
Chapter 3: Innovating Catalyst 47
Chapter 4: The Master Builder 55
Chapter 5: The Accelerated Builder 63
Chapter 6: The Possibilitarian Guide 73
Chapter 7: The Reflective Evaluator 81
Chapter 8: Storytime: The Messy and Magical Path of Living Our Design 89

SECTION 2:
INTRODUCTION TO "THE GRIND"

Chapter 9: G—GREED: Money, Capitalism, and Value, Oh, My! 107
Chapter 10: R—RIGIDITY: The Limits of the Linear Life 115
Chapter 11: I—ISOLATION: Competition, Hierarchy, and the Individualization of Success 123
Chapter 12: N—NEGLECT: The Martyrdom of Success: Betraying Our Needs to Belong and Be Valued 133
Chapter 13: D—DISCONNECTION: Top-Heavy Living Versus Fully Embodied Leadership 143
Chapter 14: Storytime: Living Through the GRIND 151
Chapter 15: Okay, So You See the GRIND More Clearly... Now What? 161

SECTION 3:
THE BRIDGE FROM GRIND TO PROSPER

CHAPTER 16: THE PROSPER FRAMEWORK: BUILDING YOUR PERSONALIZED TOOLBOX FOR THRIVING 169

CHAPTER 17: P—PURPOSE: THE TRUTH OF WHO WE *BE* 177

CHAPTER 18: R—RESPONSE-ABILITY: RECLAIMING YOUR POWER TO CHOOSE 195

CHAPTER 19: O—OPENNESS: THE COURAGE TO EXPAND 203

CHAPTER 20: S—SELF-WORTH: RECLAIMING YOUR INHERENT VALUE 211

CHAPTER 21: P—PLEASURE AND PLAY: THE JOYFUL PATH TO PRESENCE AND RESILIENCE 221

CHAPTER 22: E—EMBODIED ALIGNMENT: THRIVING AS YOUR AUTHENTIC SELF 229

CHAPTER 23: R—RESONANCE: TAPPING INTO ABUNDANCE 235

CHAPTER 24: STORYTIME: BRINGING PROSPER TO LIFE 245

SECTION 4:
FROM INSIGHT TO INTEGRATION

CHAPTER 25: EMBODIED PURPOSE AND CHOICE: THE PRACTICE OF INTEGRATIVE SOMATIC EXPERIENCE 269

CHAPTER 26: QUICK ISE STRESS MANAGEMENT AND DECONDITIONING GUIDE 277

CHAPTER 27: FINAL STORYTIME: THE MAGIC OF COCREATING IN ALIGNMENT 291

CHAPTER 28: YOUR ISE RESOURCES 295

RESOURCE GUIDE 306
ACKNOWLEDGMENTS 311
ABOUT THE AUTHORS 315

Foreword

There comes a moment in nearly every life when we find ourselves standing at the edge of something invisible yet immovable. It is not a wall in the traditional sense, but something felt—heavy, quiet, and persistent.

You cannot knock it down. You cannot go around it. You cannot logic your way through it. But you feel it in your body, your thoughts, your relationships, your work, and in the silence of your own heart.

It is the sensation of being stuck.

"Stuckness" is not simply confusion or indecision. It is not just a pause or a temporary stillness. True stuckness is an ache in the soul. It is the echo of something long buried beneath obligation, adaptation, and fear. It is a call from within that longs to return to the center of truth, to recreate and rebuild a life that is filled with purpose and meaning.

This book is written for those who have felt that ache.

It is for those who have tried to "think positive" their way out of burnout, only to return again and again to the same patterns. It is for those who have followed every mindset tool and productivity system, only to feel even more disconnected from their core self.

It is also for those who know, deep down, that there is another way to live. It is for those who can sense that way but have no clear map to get there. It is for those who have inherited patterns, absorbed conditioning, or repeated stories that never belonged to them in the first place.

This is not a book of strategies or formulas. What Laura and Meghan have created is a reclamation. It is a reclamation of body, truth, voice, and inner knowing. It is an invitation to return to a life that feels deeply and uniquely your own.

By integrating Human Design with a grounded process of inner healing, this book does more than offer information. It provides a compassionate and clear path back to the self. It reminds us that transformation does not begin in the mind alone but in the alignment between truth and embodiment. It is a courageous and gritty journey that requires you to shed everything you've picked up and felt responsible for that was never yours to carry. It asks you to stand naked in front of yourself and find all the bits and pieces you love and accept, even when others will judge you. It is an adventure that calls in your spirit, aligns it with your body, and pushes you to take bold action as a conscious, creative leader.

We live in a culture that often treats the body as something to fix, manage, or optimize. Rarely do we treat the body as a collaborator in the unfolding of our lives. But your body has been listening all along. It has recorded every choice, every silence, and every *yes* that was meant to be a *no*. It remembers what your conscious mind has forgotten.

It remembers trauma and triumph. It holds the weight of what has not been said and the truth of what still longs to be heard. It carries both the memory of your lineage and the code of your potential.

This book will teach you how to listen, both to your body and your soul. You will learn how to read the body's signals. You will begin to hear the subtle ways it speaks "yes" and "no." You will learn to meet discomfort with compassion and to stop doubting the wisdom that lives inside you.

You will be guided back to yourself, not as an idea or concept, but as a felt, integrated experience. You will begin to rebuild the connection that was never truly lost, only overlooked.

But this return requires more than awareness. It requires direction. That direction comes in the form of Human Design. Human

Design is not a belief system. It is a practical map that helps you understand how you are meant to make decisions, move through life, and respond to the world.

It offers insight into your resilience, boundaries, and unique rhythm. It reminds you that you are not here to live like anyone else; you are here to live in accordance with your own design and the story that only you can fulfill.

When combined with healing practices, Human Design becomes more than a chart. It becomes a living compass. It can help you navigate life with clarity, compassion, and courage.

This book will not just tell you what Human Design Type you are. It will show you how to feel the difference between alignment and adaptation. It will help you notice when you are acting from fear rather than truth. It will help you trust your decisions and recognize when you are being pulled away from your core self.

You will learn to lead yourself—not just intellectually, but energetically and emotionally. *That* is the beginning of real change.

One of the most profound truths in this book is that healing is not about becoming more. It is about releasing what was never ever yours.

It is about unbecoming the shame, the guilt, the pressure, and the performance. It is about shedding the masks that once kept you safe but now keep you stuck. It is about letting go of the expectations that silence your voice and distort your intuition.

This is not a call to perfection. This is not about rushing toward resolution. It is an invitation to meet yourself, as you are, with compassion and curiosity.

You will learn how to hold boundaries with integrity. You will learn how to say no without resentment and yes without fear. You will begin to understand how to let go of old roles and step into new ones—not from obligation, but from resonance.

Laura and Meghan do not avoid difficult topics. They write openly about the challenges that shape us—disconnection, rigidity, emotional neglect, inherited pain, and the pressure to conform.

They also write with courage, hope, and unwavering trust in the human capacity to heal. They show you how to reclaim the space between stimulus and response—the space where personal power lives. From their own raw stories and vulnerable shares, they truly embody the leadership they are calling forward for you. You will walk this path with their loving guidance and embodied wisdom.

Healing does not require erasing the past. It requires reclaiming the capacity to choose what comes next. This is how you become the author of your own story. This is also how you begin to lead—not in title, but in presence. True leadership is not based on performance, status, or authority. It is rooted in clarity, embodyment, and self-responsibility.

It begins with a willingness to *feel* your life, not just think about it. It requires the courage to live according to your inner truth, even when it contradicts the noise around you.

It is the ability to stand firmly in yourself without the need to explain or defend. It is the practice of living from your values, your design, and your vision.

When you lead from that place, you give others permission to do the same. You create coherence. You change the field.

This is not abstract work. It is what the world needs now.

We are witnessing the consequences of unhealed leadership on a global scale. Too many decisions are being made from fear, scarcity, and disconnection. Too many leaders are operating from unexamined conditioning.

If we are going to build a just, equitable, and sustainable future, we must begin with leadership that is aligned, embodied, and healed. We need people who are willing to do their own work first. We need people who can hold power without perpetuating harm.

Healed leaders make sustainable choices. They create impact without destruction. They serve from integrity rather than image. They shape communities and cultures that are rooted in dignity, equity, and care.

This book is a guide for becoming one of those leaders.

It is not a quick fix. It is not a step-by-step program. It is a companion for the journey inward.

It will meet you in your hardest moments. It will walk beside you through uncertainty. It will celebrate your quiet victories. It will remind you that you are not broken, only becoming.

It will teach you how to live from your center. It will show you how to rebuild trust with yourself. It will help you clear what is no longer aligned and reclaim what has always been yours.

If you are here at the edge of something unnamed, you are not lost. If you have felt a stirring inside, asking for more than survival, you are not alone.

Laura and Meghan are here to walk *with* you—through story, through truth, and through the radical act of remembering who you are.

You are not too late. You are not too much. You are not behind.

You are ready.

I'm so excited for you to let this vital journey begin!!

From my Heart to Yours,
Dr. Karen Parker

Introduction: Welcome to the Journey

Let us start with a confession: We didn't write this book because we've always had it figured out. We wrote it because, like you, we've walked the path of burnout, overwhelm, and "stuckness." We've hustled until the magic of life seemed to evaporate and we found ourselves living beneath the heavy, wet blanket of "should-dom." We've checked all the boxes—taking the classes, reading the books, investing in the coaching, pleasing, proving, and chasing fulfillment—and still found ourselves wondering, *Is this it?*

Good-bad news: This book is not a prescriptive one-size-fits-all formula. It's a map we created to help *you* uncover *your* unique path to purpose, well-being, sustainable success, and impact. Why? Because we were once in your shoes. We lost our spark trying to keep up with life's relentless "shoulds," pouring ourselves into supporting others, and unknowingly running ourselves into the ground. Through trial, error, and a lot (like a *lot*) of soul-searching, we discovered the way back—not to someone else's idea of success, but to our very own version of thriving.

So, hey! We're Meghan and Laura: two recovering hustle-aholics equipped with a vast mix of personal growth tools, big dreams of creating a better world, and a stubborn belief in the magic of purpose-driven, authentic living. Between the two of us, we bring decades of professional expertise, loads of "brutiful" hard-earned life lessons, and an ongoing commitment to figuring out how to stop settling and start really and truly living.

Why We Wrote This Book

We spent years trying to follow other people's road maps. We chased success, fulfillment, and expanded impact the hard way. We read the books, joined the programs, hired the coaches. When it comes to doing the work, one might even say we got a little addicted to it at times. (Did you know that control, perfectionism, and avoidance can hide in personal growth costumes?) But we realized—after investing more hours and dollars than we'd like to admit—that most approaches were missing something critical: *us!* They were built on someone else's success story, not on *our* unique design. They homogenized an inherently individual process. So, of course those frameworks, strategies, and approaches worked for them, but they only kind of worked for us—at best. And the very things we were investing our time, energy, and money in, with the hopes of finding more ease and relief (finally!), just became another thing driving our misalignment-flavored burnout! Ugh.

After repeating this hope-burnout-hope-disappointment process a ridiculous number of times—and watching countless others do the same—we knew we had to create a framework that honored human diversity at its core. We knew the purpose-driven people of the world needed a holistic, individualized, personal growth framework—*not* another one-size-fits-all approach but a path to design the one-size-fits-*you* approach. This book, and the framework it introduces, is the result of that humbling, decades-long scavenger hunt. We have blended science and loads of lived experience into a process that we hope you make powerfully and uniquely yours.

We knew that in order to write this book and share this work with integrity, we had to live it first. Every chapter, every tool, every insight has been hard-earned, test-driven, and well-practiced through our own journeys of burnout, overwhelm, and the humbling process of investing our time, energy, and money into paths that simply weren't right for us. It's been a messy, often exhausting road, but our hope is that by sharing it with you, we can help you skip some of the pain, disheartening trial-and-error, and overwhelm that we faced.

This book is the guide we wish we'd had decades ago—a map to re-story our lives, live our design, and thrive in alignment with our purpose. It's a guide to making choices that reflect who you really are, not who the world expects you to be. We've spent years questioning, failing forward, gathering insights, and building this framework, not just for ourselves but for you, in the hope that your journey can be a little less daunting and a whole lot more joyful.

We have also learned to offer our younger selves boatloads of compassion, knowing they were doing the best they could with what they had. They hustled, overgave, ignored their own needs, and fell into cycles of burnout—not out of failure, but out of conditioning. And just like we've learned to meet those past versions of ourselves with grace, we invite you to do the same. Offer compassion to the part of you that bought into the hustle, that chased external validation, that invested time, energy, and money into things that didn't truly serve you. That version of you wasn't wrong—they were just following the only map they were given. But now, we're here to hand you a different map, one rooted in alignment, purpose, and sustainability. This is our gift to you—an invitation to release the struggle, write a new story, and embrace the wisdom and truth that is already within you, just waiting to be unlocked.

MEET YOUR TOUR GUIDES

We know that before you dive into this adventure with us—exploring burnout, purpose, alignment, and the inherently vulnerable work of real-deal personal growth—you need to know *who* is asking you to trust them. And honestly? You *should* want to know. Your brain is wired to seek both logical and relational buy-in. Logically, you want to know we have the training, experience, and expertise to guide you. Relationally, you want to feel that we're not just more voices spewing sparkly solutions from some unattainable pedestal. We believe in "authentic humaning"—in sharing not just our hard-earned wisdom but also our real, messy, beautifully imperfect humanity. There are already too many polished, overly perfected thought leaders out there. That's not us. We live this work. We've stumbled, burned out, rebuilt, and learned the hard way so that you, hopefully, don't have to. Before we get started, let's do this the way we do best—not with a list of credentials, but with a story—because all the best journeys begin that way.

The Embodied Leadership by Design Origin Story

Once upon a time...

Two women—fueled by caffeine, good intentions, pockets full of supplements, and (on a good day) some meditation—found themselves in a small, mirrored studio in downtown Asheville, NC, on a weekday morning, surrounded by hip-hop beats and a room full of dancers. There was nothing networking or professional about their weekly meetings in the dance studio. There, they were just two humans, dropping responsibilities for an hour to laugh, unleash some closeted sass, and embody joy.

They found their way to this studio for similar reasons. Meghan came to escape the grind of her perfectionist, hyperintentional life of achievement and personal growth, seeking movement and a chance to just let loose. Laura arrived looking for the music to drown out the heavy drive of overachievement, intellectualization, and the familiar weight of always being "fine." Neither of them could have imagined the long-term magic they were stepping into.

For over a year, they danced and laughed (a lot!). And for over a year, they had no clue what the other did outside of those walls. This was their shared sanctuary—a place where joy wasn't just welcome, it was *the* goal. It was a break from the hustle, the expectations, and the limiting stories they were still trying to untangle in their lives.

And then came the moment that would change everything. One day after class, Laura casually mentioned something about neuroscience and her brain integration clinic. Meghan's ears perked up. As someone trained in neurofeedback (brain-based EEG biofeedback) and applied neuroscience herself, Meghan couldn't believe it. She looked at Laura with wide, knowing eyes and intuition fully lit up, and said, "We should definitely get tea sometime."

That one sentence was all it took to open the door to a connection neither of them could have planned. Over cups of tea, they discovered that Meghan—a licensed psychotherapist turned transformational and relationship coach—had been using applied neuroscience and somatic practices to help people come home to themselves and create more magical lives. At the same time, Laura—a holistic health expert with over fifteen years of experience in applied neuroscience, energetic kinesiology, and transformational coaching—had been helping people zoom out, recalibrate their perspectives, and align with their authentic selves.

What started as a casual tea date quickly became something much deeper—an unshakable best friendship, a partnership in purpose, and a mirror for the places they were each still learning to see within themselves. They challenged each other's old stories, illuminated blind spots that had gone unnoticed, and lovingly held space when the other was called to take (yet another) terrifying leap of faith.

It wasn't just about business. It wasn't just a great friendship. It was about learning—over and over again—how to live in the nuanced dance of joy and true alignment while learning to embody their (capital P) Purpose in the world. They wrestled with their own conditioning, experimented with what it meant to live and lead by their unique design, and walked each other through the messy, beautiful process of untangling from the hustle to reclaim a way of working, creating, relating, and pursuing success and impact… that actually *felt good.*

Best friends. Business partners. Guides in growth. Allies in expansion. And above all else—two humans committed to walking their talk, so that when they invited others into this work, they could do so with full-bodied, soul-deep integrity.

The End (but really, just the beginning).

***

That day in the dance studio, when our work worlds collided, we had no idea where this connection would take us. But the resonance between us was undeniable. From tea to podcasts, from brainstorming sessions to a full-fledged business partnership, our collaboration grew organically. Today, that connection has evolved into three business ventures, a book, and a friendship that feels grounding, illuminating, and always guiding us back to our true purpose.

Looking back, the dance studio feels like the perfect metaphor for what we've built together. It was never about perfection. It was about showing up, moving through the messiness, and letting joy lead the way. That's what this book is all about, too—a celebration of the serendipitous magic that happens when you follow the breadcrumbs of your truth.

We're not here as gurus with all the answers. We're here as your guides—two recovering burned out overachievers—who've navigated the messy, beautiful adventure of coming home to ourselves, over and over again. We've created a framework that honors the whole person—mind, body, and spirit. And we're still walking this journey *with* you, every day.

What You'll Find in This Book

This book is for the purpose-driven humans of the world—the dreamers, doers, and visionaries who want to create impact without losing themselves along the way. It's for anyone who has ever felt like they were carrying the weight of the world, trying to keep up with life's expectations, while their own needs got lost in the shuffle. It's for people who are ready to stop settling for overwhelm, barely enough, and simply surviving… and who are ready to live into their unique path toward success, purpose, and impact without sacrificing their well-being.

Throughout the book, you'll be introduced to two powerful frameworks: **GRIND** and **PROSPER**. Together, these frameworks will help you:

- reflect on the cultural narratives and conditioning keeping you stuck in cycles of burnout
- reconnect with your purpose, self-worth, and capacity to choose (to lead your life based on your unique design instead of defaulting to following others)
- learn to align with your unique design for sustainable success and well-being

But awareness alone isn't enough—because knowing what needs to change and actually making that change are two very different things. That's where embodiment comes in. Through years of practice, research, and working with real people navigating real transformation, we developed ISE™ (Integrative Somatic Experience)—a tool designed to bridge the gap between insight and lasting change. ISE weaves together the most effective, science-backed, and time-tested approaches to healing, transformation, and personal growth into one accessible, comprehensive, and wildly effective method. This book isn't just about shifting your mindset—it's about retraining your nervous system, rewiring deeply held patterns, and teaching your body to fully embody new, empowering stories instead of defaulting to the conditioned loops that have kept you stuck.

With ISE™, you'll learn to work with your nervous system, process emotions, manage stress more effectively, and create real-deal change so you're not just understanding your growth—you're actually living it. This whole-self integration piece is what makes transformation sustainable—helping you move beyond fleeting *aha* moments and into a life where well-being, success, and purpose are a way of life.

This journey isn't about abandoning ambition or playing small… *far* from it! It's about crafting *your* path to build a beautiful, meaningful life that you don't want to escape.

Why You Can Trust This Process

We're not here to sell you the idea that life will magically transform overnight. (Spoiler alert: It won't.) What we're offering is a grounded, practical, and deeply personal process for creating empowering change—one that feels right even when it feels challenging. Our framework combines the foundational understanding of applied neuroscience, the embodied wisdom of somatics (the study of sensations in the body), our lived experience, and the intuitive guidance of Human Design (an archetypal system of self-understanding). It's not just theory; it's a way of living that we've tested, tweaked, and refined in our own lives and with our clients for years.

And through it all, we've learned that holistic success isn't about trying to win at someone else's storyline—it's about finally stepping into our own. And you can too.

This is more than a book; it's an invitation. An invitation to reconnect with your magic, rediscover your spark, and create a life that feels as good as it looks. We'll be your tour guides, offering tools, stories, and a whole lot of heart as we walk this path together.

So, it's time for you to decide: Are you ready to stop hustling for your worth? To stop pretending you're fine, fulfilled, and happy when, deep down, you know you're not? Are you ready to release your attachment to fitting in so that you can finally claim your role as the powerfully wise creator of your life, your story, and your path to purpose?

If so, you're in the right place, and we're so glad you're here.

Unpacking Your Toolbox

Every great adventure requires the right tools, and this journey toward rising above burnout, clarifying your purpose, and reclaiming your authentic self is no different. While we wish transformation were as simple as snapping your fingers or finding that one magic answer, the truth is that real, lasting change comes from a blend of unsexy daily practices, compassionate curiosity, and countless brave choices.

The tools we'll be using are not about fixing you—because *you are not broken.* (Read that again.) Instead, these tools are meant to support you in uncovering the layers of conditioning, fear, "not-you-ness," and outdated stories that keep you from living the life you're actually designed to live. These tools are your allies, here to support you in breaking up with burnout, and coming home to your most authentically brilliant self.

So, let's unzip our metaphorical backpack and unpack the tools we'll be exploring on this journey....

Human Design: Your Blueprint for Alignment

You may have read other personal growth or leadership books, but you may be new to Human Design. We'll talk more about Human Design later, but for now, think of it as a brilliantly complex cosmic map that reveals your unique energetic blueprint. Based solely on your birth data (date, time, and location), Human Design shows you how you're uniquely designed to embody your purpose, navigate challenges, make choices, serve humanity, and truly prosper. Your Human Design chart highlights your unique strengths, strategies to find alignment, and the gifts you're here to bring to the collective.

When we first discovered this tool, we had a strong push-pull response to it. On one hand it felt like a powerful mirror for some key aspects of ourselves that had been suppressed, denied, or devalued, *but* on the other hand, it was often presented in a way that felt overly complicated, exclusive, painfully intellectualized, and hard to apply to real life. And in some cases, it was just too damn "out there." We're both pretty transparent about our mystical leanings, but we live real lives; we like science and prefer more grounded approaches to our spiritual adventuring and personal growth.

Thankfully, there are some amazing teachers sharing Human Design in a way that's more humanized and digestible these days. But even so, learning about your specific design without having to decode the whole damn system can still feel overwhelming. And let's be real—if you picked up this book, you're probably already moving through life with less time, energy, or bandwidth than you'd prefer. You likely don't have hours upon hours to dive into the depths of learning a complex framework on top of all you have going on. That's where we come in. We're deeply invested in helping you understand *your* design in a way that's practical, clear, and immediately applicable—without requiring you to become a Human Design expert in the process.

As two self-proclaimed personal growth nerds, with multiple degrees, certifications, and neuroscience backgrounds—evidence of how much we love a good, complex, never-ending, growthy deep dive—we were still overwhelmed early on in our learning of the system. That being said, we stuck with it and have yet to find an archetypal tool or assessment that is more efficient in helping to rise above burnout, clarify one's authentic needs, and chart the course toward purposeful, truly aligned living, leading, and relating. It has completely transformed how we navigate our own lives—helping us break free from outdated conditioning, make decisions with more ease, and finally experience the kind of success that feels more nourishing than depleting. And we're determined to make it wildly accessible, because we think, now more than ever, it's time for people to find their way home to who they really are. Consider this book a foundational taste—the tippy top of the iceberg, really—of what learning about your unique design can do for you.

Applied Neuroscience: Rewiring Your Brain for Success

Self-awareness and new insights are super cool, but how often do they really stick? How often does learning something new really translate into sustainable, lasting change? The thing is, change isn't just a mindset shift—it's a full-on neurological shift. Applied neuroscience gives us practical tools to literally rewire our brains, regulate our nervous systems, and break free from old patterns of stress and reactivity. Understanding how the brain works—and how to work with it—is a game-changer in creating sustainable well-being. And *that's* what we're about around here!

Through simple, science-backed practices, we'll help you shift out of chronic stress and tension and into an expanded state of creativity, connection, and possibility. This isn't about pushing through—you've probably done enough of that for a lifetime already. It's about creating a foundation of inner safety, harmony, and aligned choice that allows you to naturally expand into your full potential and increase your sense of holistic well-being.

Somatics and Embodiment Practices: Rewiring Your Story from the Inside Out

Your body is a profound source of wisdom. It knows the unfiltered truth of what's aligned for you and what isn't, what's healthy and what's not. But here's the kicker: Your conscious mind only has access to about 5 percent of what's really going on in your brain and body. Read that sentence again. For anyone who still thinks they should be able to be completely aware, on a conscious level, of why they're stuck, what the plan should be, etc., read… that… again. There's an abundance of emotions, stories, patterns, and knee-jerk motivations that fly under the conscious radar in that remaining 95 percent. That means a lot of what's keeping you stuck—those inherited stories, anxieties, and fears that are looping in the background, keeping you stressed, stagnant, or settling—are literally outside of your "thinking life."

Somatics bridges that gap, helping you bring your awareness out of your head and into the rich, often suppressed, and overlooked wisdom of your body. These practices are about more than just releasing tension (though that's a great perk). Somatics invites you to partner with your body to rewrite the stories that shape your life—not just to release the old, inherited ones that no longer serve you, but to actively embody and move toward the unseen potential you're ready to live into.

Your body is your most powerful source of intuition. Intuition isn't some mystical gift reserved for good witches, roadside psychics, or mystics—it's a system of resonance hardwired into every human body. Yes, even yours. Through subtle sensations, gut feelings, and quiet urges, your body lets you know what is truly aligned for you. While the mind can get tangled in loud, conditioned stories of fear, expectation, and "shoulds," your body holds unfiltered wisdom.

Somatics helps you tap into this wisdom by bringing you back into a state of embodied awareness. When you trust the sensations and signals your body provides, you connect with an inner compass that bypasses the conditioned noise of the brain and guides you toward decisions and actions that resonate with your deepest truth, your undiluted purpose, and the path of least resistance. Intuition, which often speaks in somatic sensation and subtlety, becomes a reliable and empowering guide pointing you toward the life you're actually meant to live.

Here's the thing that makes it tricky: Your body-brain system (it's all connected) is hardwired to prioritize safety. Unfortunately, the nervous system tends to confuse *safety* with *sameness*. That's why, even when you consciously want positive change—whether it's a new career, a healthier relationship, or showing up as your most authentic self—your body often resists, pulling you back to what feels familiar. It's not your fault; it's your body's protective programming. But here's the good news: That programming isn't fixed. You can work intentionally *with* your body to redefine what feels safe, anchoring yourself in the new and aligned story you want to live.

In this book, we'll guide you through somatic practices that help you tune into your body's signals, uncover and release old patterns, and consciously rewire yourself for growth and possibility. These techniques allow you to not only navigate challenges and make aligned choices but also to embody your true self in a way that feels deeply anchored, authentic, and free. When your body is on board with your vision, it becomes a powerful ally—not just holding your intuitive wisdom but helping you practice living the life you're truly meant for.

DECONDITIONING WORK: RECLAIMING YOUR AUTHENTICITY AND PLANTING NEW POSSIBILITIES

We all carry layers of conditioning—the beliefs, behaviors, and expectations we've absorbed from family, culture, and society. Some of these layers have served us in navigating the world, but many are responsible for keeping us stuck in burnout cycles, overachievement, chronic stress, people-pleasing, or self-doubt. Deconditioning is the process of peeling back these inherited layers to reveal the unfiltered truth of who you are underneath—the version of you that feels inspired, on purpose, and fulfilled.

This isn't just about you. Your personal growth is bigger than just your story—it's a quiet form of heart-centered service that ripples out into the world. Deconditioning isn't just liberating yourself from what no longer serves you; it's an act of honoring your unique voice, perspective, and contribution to the collective. Think of it as the natural abundance that comes from embracing human diversity. When you show up fully as yourself, you add your irreplaceable energy and gifts to the beautiful mosaic of humanity. You become a catalyst for solving complex problems, imagining new potentials, and creating a world that thrives on diversity.

When you live authentically, you stand as a billboard for diversity—not just in mental concept but in action. In a world that talks a big game about inclusivity yet clings to the idea of fitting into a narrow mold, being fully, unapologetically *you* is an act of true leadership. It challenges the homogenized model of "success" and reminds the world that authentic progress is born from the bold, expansive spectrum of what it means to be human. This work matters—for you, for us, and for the world we're all dreaming into being.

The tools in this book pave the way for your journey of deconditioning, making it the final, integrative piece of your toolkit. Human Design invites you to question what you've been told about who you should be, how you should live, and what's possible for you. It reveals where you've inherited stories that are not yours to carry, and it guides you toward your authentic essence—the version of you that thrives when aligned with your unique blueprint. Applied neuroscience supports you in navigating the very real nervous system discomfort that arises when stepping beyond the burnout-flavored comfort zones you've grown accustomed to. Your body-brain system often mistakes familiarity for safety, and even the most positive change can feel terrifying. Applied neuroscience helps you rewire these patterns, enabling you to lean into growth, take aligned risks, and build a new sense of inner safety. Somatic practices, on the other hand, bring you into connection with your body's unfiltered truth—the deep wisdom and intuition often buried beneath conditioned fears and familiar stories. These tools, when combined, allow you to release what's holding you back while planting the seeds of new possibilities, empowering you to thrive as you embody your design, rather than defaulting to the life you've been told you should settle for.

Deconditioning brings all these tools together, helping you reclaim the most aligned and authentic version of yourself. It's a process of remembering who you are beneath the noise of external expectations, reconnecting with what truly matters to you, and creating a life that feels deeply nourishing, inspired, and alive. Through this work, you can build a life that doesn't just look good on paper but feels profoundly right in your body—a life that honors your humanity, celebrates your uniqueness, and allows you to contribute to the collective from a place of wholeness, joy, and alignment.

One last thing before we begin: This is *your* journey. While we'll offer guidance, practices, and insights, you are the expert on your own experience. There's no one "right" way to move through this process, no gold star for getting it perfect on the first try—or even the hundredth. Personal growth isn't about ticking off a list or achieving some final destination. It's a process, an unfolding, an adventure. Some days will feel clear and inspired, and others might feel murky or challenging—and that's okay. In fact, that's actually a sign that you're on the path to true purpose, authentic growth, and lasting transformation.

As you move through this work, we invite you to practice radical compassion, childlike curiosity, and complete permission to be gloriously human. Dismiss any tendency to grade yourself on how well you're doing or to view transformation through a pass-fail lens. This isn't about perfection; it's about progress, about showing up for yourself with a willingness to explore, experiment, and uncover what's true and aligned for *you*. Every step you take—no matter how big or small—is significant. We're often taught to seek shiny, sparkly, and impressive outcomes, but what we've learned over years and years of walking this path and guiding others through it is that the path toward really and truly transforming your life for the better requires countless, incremental, unsexy investments in creating that change.

Trust yourself and the wisdom within you.

We've all been taught to focus on some sort of elusive finish line, but the journey itself is the gift.

Okay, we've officially laid the foundation for our adventure together.

But first, we'd like to formally offer you a permission slip.

As I begin this process, I give myself permission to release the need to have it all figured out or get it "right" the first time. I let go of perfectionism, self-judgment, and the fear of doing it wrong, choosing instead to approach this journey with curiosity rather than criticism. I give myself grace to stumble, recalibrate, and try again, knowing that even the messy steps move me closer to alignment. I will celebrate the small wins, the quiet moments of clarity, and the courage it takes to keep showing up. On hard days, I will hold space for all the feelings that arise, offering myself compassion and understanding. I give myself permission to experiment with new possibilities and trust my inner wisdom to discern what feels right for me. Above all, I embrace this journey as an adventure, not a test, allowing joy, ease, and compassion to guide the way. I am worthy of this process, and I trust myself to grow in my own way, in my own time.

X _____

Okay, *now* you're ready.

Section 1
Human Design 101: the Blueprint to the Burnout

Chapter 1
Human Design: Your Blueprint for Purpose-full Thriving

Let's start with a foundational truth: You are not a random collection of quirks, traits, and preferences. You are a divine masterpiece in motion, uniquely encoded with a cosmic blueprint that knows exactly how you're designed to thrive. *Wait. What?!* If that sounds a little mystical and out there, stick with us—it's a statement rooted in both ancient wisdom and modern science. Think of this blueprint as a bridge between the stars and your cells, guiding you back to the truth—the actual truth—of who you are.

For most of us, the journey of self-discovery begins with reflection tools: personality tests, career assessments, or even the occasional "What Type of Dog Are You?" magazine quiz. These tools can be illuminating and fun, and they can help us see parts of ourselves more clearly, but they rely on something inherently flawed: our own perception of ourselves. Our egos love to sneak into the process, bringing biases, blind spots, and the weight of years of societal conditioning, fears, calcified identities, shoulds, and inherited narratives. That's where Human Design takes a completely different route—one that bypasses the ego and taps straight into the cosmos.

Human Design is often referred to as the science of differentiation—a fancy way of saying that it shows us what makes each of us unique. But it's so much more than a personality assessment. While personality tests ask, "Who do you think you are?" Human Design says, "Here's who you've always been, and *how* you are meant to thrive." It definitely gives us some clues about *who* we are, but it's a system that shows us much more about *how* we're meant to find alignment, grow toward wholeness, embody our purpose, and serve humanity.

Based on your birth data (date, time, and location), Human Design generates your energetic blueprint: a map of your strengths, challenges, purpose, and potential. It blends ancient wisdom systems—like the I Ching, astrology, and the chakra system—with cutting-edge insights from quantum mechanics and genetics. It's not a system that's interested in how you've conformed and contorted yourself to fit in or succeed in this world. Instead, it's a powerful mirror that reflects your authentic essence—your energetic DNA, your soul map, *your* success blueprint.

Wait. What? A cosmic blueprint?

Bear with us. We will get to more science a bit later, but for now, picture a cosmic polaroid taken the moment you entered this world. That's your Human Design chart. It reflects the energetic imprint of the cosmos (the quantum field, really), mapping out your strengths, challenges, and purpose, and reflecting them back in ways that feel less like finding yourself and more like settling into a sense of remembering who you've always been.

When you understand your design, life begins to make more sense. The patterns that felt like roadblocks reveal themselves as purposeful lessons. The relationships or jobs that drained you start to make sense within the context of misaligned energy. And the choices that once felt cloudy come into sharp focus because you're no longer working against your natural flow.

Human Design doesn't ask you to change who you are in order to succeed or fit in more seamlessly. Instead, it invites you to reclaim your uniqueness, embrace your gifts, and lean into the challenges that refine and grow you on your path of becoming. It's about stepping into the fullest expression of your (capital P) Purpose and owning your contribution to the collective whole.

> Because when you're thriving as yourself—your true self—you give others permission to do the same, and that's when the magic truly begins.

UNLOCKING YOUR UNIQUE LEADERSHIP BLUEPRINT

We've been talking a lot about the journey back to your truest self—the version of you that's aligned, energized, and fully tapped into your purpose. But let's be honest: The road to clarity is often paved with shoulds, outdated identities, and the stories we tell ourselves about who we *think* we need to be.

That's exactly why we love Human Design.

Unlike personality tests where you can (intentionally or not) skew your answers based on who you *wish* you were, Human Design doesn't ask for your opinion. There's no room for overthinking, self-editing, or answering as the "more evolved" version of yourself. Instead, it gives you a cosmic snapshot—a blueprint based purely on the moment you were born. No filters. No fluff. Just the energetic truth of how you're designed to operate in the world.

And now, we bet you're wondering: "Okay, but how do I find mine?"

How to Get Your Human Design Chart

Getting your chart is simple. You just need three things:

1. your **birth date**
2. your **exact birth time** (or as close as possible)
3. your **birthplace**

Once you have those, head over to embodiedleadershipbydesign.com to generate your chart. We've made it easy—when you run your chart with us, you'll see your Leadership Type right away, using the language and framework we'll be diving into throughout this book.

If you'd rather use a traditional Human Design site, that works too. Just Google "free Human Design chart," and you'll find plenty of options. The only catch: Traditional Human Design uses different names for the five types. No worries, though—we'll include a simple reference chart so you can swap in your Leadership Type and keep rolling.

So go ahead—get your chart, make a note of your Type, and let's dive in. We can't wait to show you what's possible when you align with the way you're *actually* designed to lead, thrive, and prosper.

Traditional Human Design	**Embodied Leadership Type**
Manifestor	Innovating Catalyst
Generator	Master Builder
Manifesting Generator	Accelerated Builder
Projector	Possibilitarian Guide
Reflector	Reflective Evaluator

A Note on Language

Before we go any further, we want to take a moment to acknowledge something important. One of the leadership types we name in this book is the **Master Builder**—our term for the Human Design type traditionally known as the Generator.

We recognize that the word *master* can carry painful and oppressive connotations, especially within the context of slavery, systemic racism, and colonial power structures. For readers whose identities or family histories have been impacted by these systems, we want to be clear: Our use of this word is *not* rooted in those harmful histories.

Instead, we chose the term *Master Builder* from the original meaning of *mastery*: the process of cultivating deep skill, joyful devotion, and aligned excellence over time. As you'll see when we explore this type more fully, the theme of mastery is central to how this leadership style thrives—through building a life, craft, or path that is deeply satisfying and sustainably energizing.

We share this note with care, especially for those attuned to the nuances and weight of language. We believe that conscious leadership includes conscious word choice—and we're committed to using language that honors both clarity and compassion.

Okay, you've got what you need. Let's go a little deeper....

The Quantum Magic and Mechanics of Human Design: How It Works

At its foundation, Human Design is rooted in the principles of quantum physics—the science that reveals the universe as a dynamic field of energy in constant motion. But to really appreciate what that means, let's rewind for a moment.

For centuries, most of science operated from what's called *Newtonian physics*, named after Sir Isaac Newton. In Newton's world, the universe was like a giant machine: orderly, predictable, and made up of solid objects moving through empty space. Everything was thought to operate through cause and effect. If you knew where something started, you could calculate where it would go. This view worked beautifully for understanding things like gravity, motion, and planetary orbits. And for much of daily life, it still does.

But as scientists quested to understand the deeper building blocks of our reality—zooming in past molecules, past atoms, and into subatomic particles—they began to discover something surprising. The deeper they looked, the less solid things became. Instead of finding tiny billiard balls at the core of matter, they found waves of energy. Particles would appear and disappear. They could exist in multiple places at once. They could even seem to communicate across vast distances, as if everything was somehow connected.

In other words: Even at its most solid, reality is made of energy.

This is where quantum physics enters the conversation. Instead of seeing you (or anything else) as fixed and separate, quantum physics shows that everything—every object, every person, every interaction—is part of a vast web of vibrating energy fields. You are not simply a solid body moving through space; you are a living, breathing field of energy constantly interacting with everything around you.

Everything in existence—from the stars in the sky to the cells in your body—vibrates at a unique frequency, literally measured in hertz (yes, it's the same measurement as the lightbulbs in your house or the musical notes of a piano). Frequency simply refers to how fast something vibrates—how many cycles of energy it completes per second. You, too, are a living, breathing part of this energetic symphony, carrying your own distinct frequency.

This energetic imprint, formed at the moment of your birth, is like a cosmic fingerprint—a unique blueprint that Human Design translates into your personal chart.

Quantum physics introduces us to the concept of resonance, the natural alignment of frequencies that creates harmony and amplifies energy. Imagine tuning a musical instrument: When one note is perfectly in tune, it effortlessly vibrates in harmony with the others. This happens because frequencies that match or complement each other create what's called *constructive* interference—where the energies combine and amplify one another. When frequencies are mismatched, they create *destructive* interference, leading to dissonance, resistance, and depletion. Human Design operates on this same principle. Your chart captures your unique energetic resonance, not as a reflection of self-perception or subjective personality traits, but as the science of how your energy aligns with the world around you—and how the world interacts *with* you. It's literally about how you vibrate and resonate with the vastness of the quantum universe.

Is your mind blown yet? Yes? No? Okay, onward, nonetheless.

When you're out of alignment with your design—and thus out of resonance—life can feel like grinding gears or swimming upstream. It's exhausting, full of resistance, and often frustrating, as though you're trying to play an instrument that's hopelessly out of tune. On a practical level, this sense of being "out of tune" with life can manifest as money, health, or relationship problems—really, all types of stuckness.

And there's a physiological cost to this misalignment.

Chronic stress, exhaustion, burnout, and overwhelm aren't simply emotional states—they are the biological consequence of prolonged energetic incoherence.

When you're pushing against your natural design, your nervous system remains in a state of hypervigilance, flooding your body with stress hormones, disrupting your immune system, and draining your vital life force over time.

This misalignment happens because the stories and conditioning you've absorbed over time pull you away from your natural resonance with life. But here's where the magic—and science—come into play. When you align with your design, you shift from resistance into flow. The energy you once spent forcing or fighting against your nature becomes available for what truly lights you up, feels purposeful, and aligns with your unique gifts. Life becomes less of an uphill battle and more of a purposeful, flowing adventure.

To be clear, your Human Design chart is not a rigid set of rules. It doesn't box you in or dictate a fixed path or identity. Instead, it illuminates your potential—the most authentic and aligned way for you to thrive. In a way, Human Design mirrors what quantum mechanics teaches us about probability: You are not locked into a single fixed reality, but instead you exist within a field of possibilities. Your design helps you navigate these possibilities and choose the path of least resistance, the path that resonates most deeply with your nature.

It reveals how you're naturally wired to make decisions, nurture relationships, contribute to the world, and navigate challenges. This is the essence of resonance: aligning with the frequencies that amplify your gifts, creating a sense of coherence and harmony within yourself and with the world around you.

Quantum Mechanics 101

Take a deep breath. That's a lot of brain-bending science—and there's still a bit more. Since we're going to be talking about the stories we choose to focus on, we need to talk a bit more about quantum mechanics.

We discussed how your ability to live into your cosmic blueprint creates a unique frequency. In addition to that, every thought, emotion, and action carries a frequency. This is where conscious choice comes in. Your state of being plus the quality of your thoughts, emotions, and actions create (equal) your overall frequency. And when these frequencies align with your authentic design, you stop wasting energy trying to be someone you're not. Instead, you amplify your natural strengths, harmonizing with the larger energy field of life. This creates a ripple effect, not just within your own life but in the lives of those around you, as your aligned energy contributes to the collective symphony.

And here's where it gets even more fascinating: In the quantum world, simply paying attention changes things. This is known as the *observer effect*—the discovery that when scientists tried to measure subatomic particles, the particles actually behaved differently depending on whether they were being observed. Mind blowing, right?!

In some experiments, particles acted like tiny bits of matter when measured, but like waves of energy when left alone. It was as if the act of observation caused the particle to "decide" how to behave. What this means—at least in the simplest way we can put it—is that *conscious attention influences practical outcomes.*

In your life, this translates to something both profound and practical: Where you place your focus helps determine which version of reality takes form. Every moment holds countless possibilities (think of it like multiple potential songs waiting to be played), but your focus acts like a kind of tuning dial, helping certain potentials become the one you actually experience.

You are not just floating through life reacting to circumstances; you are actively participating in which version of reality you experience based on what you're paying attention to, how you feel, and how you engage. Your focus and awareness are a powerful part of the creative process.

Think of life as an orchestra, with each person playing their own unique instrument. When you're playing your true part, your music blends seamlessly into the larger composition, creating harmony. But when you try to play someone else's part, the entire symphony feels discordant. Human Design helps you identify your instrument and teaches you how to play it beautifully and collaboratively with life. The result is harmony—within yourself and with the collective.

By aligning with your Human Design, you harness the power of resonance. You shift from grinding and pushing through resistance to embracing natural flow. The struggles that once felt insurmountable begin to dissolve, replaced by a sense of ease, clarity, and natural momentum. This isn't just philosophy or wishful thinking; it's the quantum mechanics of energy in motion. When you live in alignment with your design, you're no longer wasting energy fighting the current. Instead, you're riding the wave of your unique frequency, supported by... well, the whole universe!

THE THEATER OF LIFE

Imagine life as a grand theater production. The curtain rises, the lights dim, and each person steps into their role—actors, directors, playwrights, stagehands, audience members—all working together to create a masterpiece. Now, imagine what would happen if one person tried to do it all: write the script, direct the cast, perform every role, manage the stage lights, and critique the performance. Chaos, right? Not to mention burnout.

Yet this is exactly what modern culture asks of us. We're told to be everything to everyone—visionary creators, tireless workers, sharp strategists, and empathetic supporters—all while somehow maintaining balance and joy. It's no wonder we're so often left feeling exhausted, overwhelmed, and deeply disconnected from ourselves.

Human Design offers a different approach. It helps us understand our unique role in the theater of life and invites us to play that role fully, intentionally, and unapologetically. When we do, something magical happens. We stop trying to be everything, and instead, we become *ourselves*. We work with others, not against them, contributing our gifts to the collective without depleting ourselves in the process. The result? Less burnout, more joy. Less resentment, more inspiration.

In this theater metaphor, each Human Design Type—what we renamed as the five Leadership Types—represents a different role in the grand production. No role is more important than another, and each is essential to the success of the performance.

- **Innovating Catalysts** (Manifestors in traditional Human Design) are the playwrights. They initiate the story, spark the new idea, and create something where there was nothing before.
- **Master Builders** (Generators in traditional Human Design) have a singular role that they choose to master—the actor, the stagehand, or the costume designer. They bring the story to life with their steady, reliable energy, investing themselves in their unique role with dedication and presence. They are the lifeblood of the production, infusing it with vitality and joyfully bringing the idea into form for others to enjoy.
- **Accelerated Builders** (Manifesting Generators in traditional Human Design) are the actors, multitasking stagehands, and creative problem-solvers. They hold multiple roles—act, direct, and adjust on the fly—seamlessly weaving efficiency and innovation into the production. Their energy is dynamic and contagious.
- **Possibilitarian Guides** (Projectors in traditional Human Design) are the directors. They stand outside the scene, observing and offering guidance to ensure that everything flows harmoniously. They amplify the talents of others and provide clarity and direction when the cast and crew lose sight of the vision.
- **Reflective Evaluators** (Reflectors in traditional Human Design) are the audience and critics. They mirror the performance back to the cast and crew, showing how well

the production resonates with its intended purpose. Their feedback offers profound insights into the health and harmony of the entire endeavor.

Each role is distinct, yet interdependent. Together, they create something extraordinary—a cocreative ecosystem where everyone thrives by doing what they do best.

Sure, you CAN play every role—but the question is, should you?

Let's be clear: This isn't about telling you what you *can't* be or do. We're here to liberate, not limit. But we've seen far too many people try to play all of the roles (and maybe we've even fallen into that ditch a few hundred times ourselves) and it always leads to some experience of disappointment, overwhelm, stress, or burnout. And we don't want that for you.

Everyone *can* step into any role in this metaphorical theater. Sometimes life calls on you to act like an Innovating Catalyst, to boldly initiate something new. Other times, you may channel your inner Master Builder to sustain effort and keep things moving. But just because you *can* play every role doesn't mean you should make a habit of it or build an identity or life that expects you to be all of the things all of the time.

When you try to do it all—you spread yourself thin. Your energy becomes fragmented, and instead of excelling in one area, you struggle to keep up in all of them. You lose sight of your true inspiration and joy. You end up living countless shoulds instead of making decisions rooted in true alignment. Over time, this leads to exhaustion, frustration, and a creeping sense of failure and disappointment. Burnout isn't a personal flaw; it's often just an indicator that you're playing roles that actually aren't authentically yours to play.

Your Leadership Type reveals the role you're naturally suited to play—the one that feels energizing, purposeful, and aligned with your essence. When you lean into this role, you unlock a new level of ease and flow. You have more energy for what lights you up and less resentment from choices, roles, and relationships that drain you. And because you're not trying to be all things to all people, you create space for others to step into their roles, too. The entire production becomes more joyful, more inspired, and far less depleting.

The world we live in doesn't make this whole collaborative orchestra approach to life easy. We're bombarded with messages that equate worthiness with productivity, and independence with success. We're told to hustle harder, grind longer, and prove our value by doing... it... ALL. This be-all-the-things mindset creates a cultural trap: We end up resentful, depleted, and disconnected from ourselves *and* each other—not because we're failing at life, but because we're trying to thrive in ways we simply weren't designed to.

Here's the truth: When you play your role fully and with intention, you thrive. Naturally. The work you do feels meaningful, not exhausting. Your contributions ripple out into the collective, creating harmony instead of competition. You don't get burned out, overwhelmed, or wet-blanketed from chronically doing things that are out of your nature. And the "ah-mayzing" thing about this collaborative approach is that when everyone embraces their unique role, the metaphorical theater of life becomes full of ease, inspiration, and *collective* thriving.

Each role is honored.

Each contribution is valued.

And each person feels seen, nourished, and inspired.

Sounds dreamy, right?! We think so too.

***

As we journey through this book, you'll explore your unique Leadership Type and role in the collective ecosystem, gaining clarity on how you're designed to thrive. You'll learn to spot the conditioned stories that pull you away from your natural gifts (through the GRIND framework), you'll discover how to practically realign with the stories you choose (using the PROSPER framework), and you'll be guided through a process of re-storying your life both consciously and unconsciously through our ISE process. Because this isn't just about intellectual insight, it's about real, lived embodiment and sustainable change. When we shift from forcing ourselves into someone else's success model to fully inhabiting our own, when we stop battling burnout and start working *with* our energy, when we regulate our nervous systems and trust the role we were born to play, burnout, overwhelm, and the chronic "meh-ing" of life naturally begin to dissolve. So, as you move through these pages, let this metaphor sink in: You are part of a collective production, and the role you were born to play is not only enough—it's essential.

***

You don't need to be all of the things to all of the people.

Again… You *don't* need to be *all* of the things to *all* of the people.

It's officially time to pack up your superachiever cape and trade it in for something much more sustainable and comfy.

You just need to be *you*—fully, unapologetically, and intentionally. When you do that, you will begin to really thrive, your relationships will flourish, you will have the clarity you need to feel authentically confident. Instead of exhausting yourself by forcing and pushing life, aligned collaborations and opportunities will find you. You will make decisions with clarity, your enoughness and sense of purpose will rise, and that life of normalized burnout will become a thing of the distant past.

All of that sounds great. So why aren't we already living into our authentic design, you ask?

Well, for generations, we've been taught to adapt, to fit into systems and structures that weren't built to honor the full spectrum of human diversity. This pressure to conform has left many of us burned out, disconnected, and questioning our worth. Human Design offers a powerful alternative. It invites you to embrace your inherent value, lean into your unique gifts, meet challenges with greater insight and purpose, and release the conditioned stories that keep you stuck and small.

When we operate from alignment with our design, we don't just thrive individually—we elevate the whole collective. Imagine a world where every person understood and honored their energetic blueprint and stepped into their role with confidence and ease. Instead of competing for success, we'd cocreate a reality where every contribution is valued and celebrated.

Human Design facilitates this paradigm shift.

It's not about fixing you to fit the world—it's about freeing you to be yourself so you can positively impact and transform the world.

Think of it as an instruction manual to embody the most empowered, inspired, and successful version of yourself. And isn't that what we're all searching for? Not just success, but a sense of deep purpose. Not just surviving, checking boxes, and going through the motions of adulting, but truly thriving in a way that feels authentic and sustainable.

Human Design isn't just another tool; it's an invitation. It invites you to see yourself more clearly, beyond the layers of conditioning and expectation. It invites you to reclaim your gifts and step into your unique role in the collective dance. Most of all, it invites you to trust that you are perfectly enough—exactly as you were designed.

For now, take a breath.

You are not broken.

You are not behind.

You're standing at the edge of an epic adventure guiding you home to yourself, holding a map that only you can read.

Exciting, right?!

Chapter 2
The Power of Knowing
Your Type: An Invitation to Align

Have you ever wondered why some people seem to move through life with effortless ease while others struggle against invisible currents? Or why certain opportunities seem to land in one person's lap while another works tirelessly to no avail? Or why some relationships thrive while others feel like constant friction? Beyond the obvious issues of unearned privilege and compromised access to resources (which we will discuss in the GRIND framework), the vastly underexplored answer to stuckness is that it lies in energy: specifically, your unique energetic blueprint.

Your Human Design chart is like a multifaceted gem—each facet offering a new perspective, a reminder, a clue, or a piece of guidance about who you are and how you're designed to thrive. It's not just about how you lead in the traditional sense; it's about how you live, work, love, and embody your most authentic self. Your chart reveals insights into your ideal living and working environment, the dynamics that shape your relationships, your natural ways of making decisions, and even how your body processes energy. It's a road map for understanding the nuances of your gifts, challenges, and purpose, showing you how to create a life that feels uniquely and unapologetically yours. While this book focuses on just one foundational aspect—your Type—know that this is just the beginning of what Human Design can offer as a tool for transformation and alignment.

Earlier we introduced the foundational concept of Human Design and the five Leadership Types, exploring how they create an interdependent ecosystem that thrives on diversity and collaboration. But understanding your Type isn't just a curiosity or a tool for self-reflection—it's the foundational key to unlocking your unique frequency, the one that the quantum field recognizes and responds to. This frequency is your signature, and when it is clear and aligned, it creates a ripple effect that impacts not only your own well-being but also the collective harmony of the groups, systems, and relationships you are part of.

Each Leadership Type carries a specific energetic role, a distinct way of contributing to the collective good. Whether you're here to guide, sustain, innovate, reflect, or catalyze, your Type holds the key to a life of aligned opportunities, meaningful success, and sustainable well-being. The sections ahead will dive deeply into each of the five Leadership Types, revealing their purpose, design, and challenges. But first, let's talk about *why* this matters.

> Understanding your Type isn't about limiting yourself to a label—it's about liberation. It's about freeing yourself from the cultural conditioning that tells you to be all things to all people, to hustle for worthiness, or to force outcomes that drain your vitality.

It's about stepping into the truth of who you are and operating from your natural strengths rather than your perceived weaknesses. Knowing your Type provides a map back to your authentic self and a strategy for navigating life with clarity, ease, and flow.

The Rhythm of Energy: Sacral Versus Non-Sacral Types

In a world that worships productivity and external metrics of achievement as signs of worthiness, we've all been conditioned to believe the lie that more *doing* is always better. Work harder. Do more. Hustle. Rest *only* after you've earned it. Sound familiar? Most of us got that memo. But here's the truth: Energy isn't a one-size-fits-all sort of thing. In Human Design, your energy flow is as unique as your fingerprint, and there's a lot of wisdom to be found when we look at the Sacral Center—the literal engine of creation and action in your chart.

Connected to the chakra system, there are nine energy centers in every Human Design chart. Each of those centers is either "defined" (colored in) or "undefined" (not colored in). We won't go into all of the energy centers in this book, but since we're talking about burnout, we need to discuss the Sacral Center before we dive fully into introducing the five Leadership Types, because it creates a foundational understanding of how you're actually designed to "do" life.

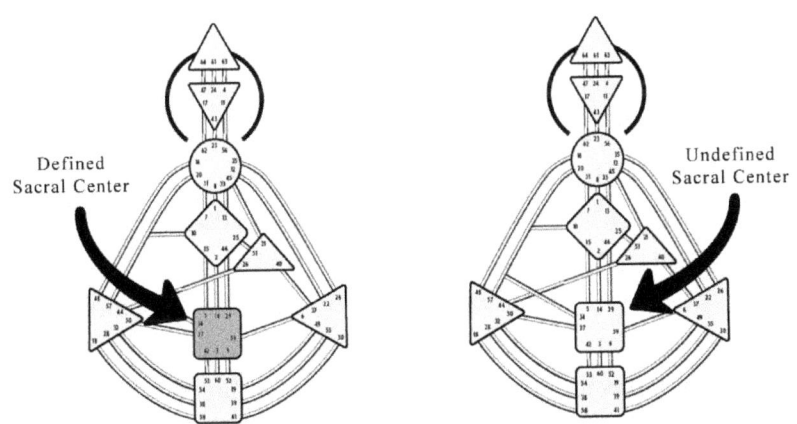

The Sacral Center specifically is where life-force energy is generated—the energy to literally build an idea, taking it from theory to form. It's tied to our ability to do, create, and engage with the physical world. Whether this center is defined or undefined in your Human Design chart determines how you're designed to engage with energy and work—there's no design that's better or worse, just...*different*.

SACRAL ENERGY TYPES: THE BUILDERS

If you're a Master Builder or Accelerated Builder, you have a defined Sacral Center, which means you're part of the 70 percent of the population designed to have a steady supply of energy for doing. But here's the kicker: Even Sacral Types aren't designed to be *on* all the time.

Sacral energy thrives in a cycle of work and satisfaction, not endless grind mode. Yes, you have the natural ability to engage with work more consistently than non-Sacral Types, but that doesn't mean you're a machine. Builders still experience ebb and flow—it just looks different. You need rest. You need to listen to your Sacral instinct (your gut), saying yes as often as possible to things that light you up, resisting overcommitting to the things you or others think you *should* do. Misaligned Sacral energy feels heavy, resentful, and like pushing a boulder uphill. Clean Sacral energy, on the other hand, is magnetic and energizing—not just for you but for everyone around you.

And here's why that matters: Sacral energy doesn't just power the Builders—it fuels the entire collective. Some Leadership Types don't have a defined Sacral Center, which means they don't generate consistent "doing energy" of their own. Instead, they absorb the energy around them, often sourcing it from the Builders in their environment. When a Builder is lit up by what they're doing—truly aligned and saying yes to the work that excites them—their energy naturally radiates like clean-burning fuel. It's magnetic, motivating, and nourishing for everyone nearby. But when that energy is tangled up in obligation, resentment, or burnout, it becomes more like sludge—heavy and unhelpful. This is why Builder alignment isn't just a personal win—it's a gift to the whole ecosystem. Aligned

Builders create a ripple effect of vitality, inspiration, and energetic flow that benefits every Type around them.

Non-Sacral Types: The Burst-and-Rest Crew

Then there are the Innovating Catalysts, Possibilitarian Guides, and Reflective Evaluators—the non-Sacral types who collectively make up about 30 percent of the population. Without a defined Sacral Center, you don't have consistent access to that steady energy for doing. And that's *not* a flaw—it's a unique feature. You're designed to operate in bursts of efficient energy, followed by periods of rest and recalibration.

Your gift lies in your ability to innovate, guide, and evaluate, bringing wisdom and perspective to the collective. But living in a Sacral-dominated culture can be challenging. The hustle mentality wasn't built for you (not that it was really built for anyone), but trying to keep up with it can leave you chronically depleted, overwhelmed, and feeling less than. Here's the reframe: Your ebb-and-flow rhythm isn't a liability. It's an asset. It allows you to work smarter, not harder, and to bring depth and clarity that others might miss in the frenzy of constant activity.

Note about cocreative magic: non-Sacral Types also have the ability to tap into the energy of Sacral Types when they're working together. It's like one of those wireless chargers: just being in proximity to a Sacral Type doing what they love can give you a boost of energy to help you ride the wave and get things done. This is why it's so important for Sacral Types to keep their energy clean and aligned—it's clean fuel for the non-Sacrals of the world!

The Collaboration: Why We Need Each Other

Here's the beauty of this system: neither Sacral nor non-Sacral Types are designed to function in isolation. Together, they create a dynamic, symbiotic ecosystem where each Type brings something essential to the table.

Sacral Types (Builders and Master Builders) contribute the sustainable energy that moves ideas into form. They respond to opportunities—sometimes from their own inner sparks, sometimes from the world around them—and carry the capacity to build, refine, and sustain what is ready to be made real. Their consistency and devotion create momentum and stability.

Non-Sacral Types bring vital clarity, perspective, and course correction. Innovating Catalysts initiate and spark new directions. Possibilitarian Guides offer insight and guidance, seeing where energy can be applied most efficiently. Reflective Evaluators mirror the truth of the collective, offering valuable feedback on what's working and where adjustments may be needed.

When we honor this natural diversity of energy, the whole system thrives. Sacral Types learn to trust their internal guidance, discerning how and where to invest their energy for the greatest return. Non-Sacral Types embrace their rhythm of bursts and rest, contributing their brilliance when the timing is right, and resting without guilt when recovery is needed. Each role is essential; each contributes to the harmony and sustainability of the whole.

THE BIGGER PICTURE: MOVING BEYOND BURNOUT

Burnout happens when we live out of alignment with our design. Sacral Types burn out when they say yes to everything, draining their energy on things that don't light them up. Non-Sacral Types burn out when they try to live like Sacral Types, forcing themselves into a constant doing mode that goes against their natural rhythm.

Understanding your energy design is the first step to moving beyond burnout. It's permission to stop comparing yourself to others and start honoring your unique flow. Whether you're a steady hum or a brilliant burst, your energy is valid, valuable, and necessary for the collective to thrive.

As we explore each type in detail, remember this:

> Your energy is enough. Your rhythm is right. And when you live in alignment with it, you unlock not only your potential but the potential of everyone around you.

THE MECHANICS OF ENERGY AND ALIGNMENT

At its core, Human Design is about energy. Remember the whole quantum physics conversation we had earlier? Well, we're back to it again.

Each Type operates with a unique energy field—or aura—that interacts with the world in a specific way. Your aura is an invisible but palpable force that signals to others who you are and how you naturally contribute. These auras aren't static; they're dynamic, responding to alignment and misalignment in real time.

When you're aligned with your Type, your aura functions smoothly, attracting the right people, opportunities, and experiences with ease. Remember, this isn't some fluffy manifestation talk—it's grounded in quantum physics, which shows us that energy resonates at specific frequencies. When your internal energy is coherent, your external reality responds in kind. But when you're misaligned, your energy becomes dissonant; therefore, you repel what's meant for you and attract struggle instead.

Each Type in Human Design has a unique path to alignment, known as its Strategy—a road map for living in harmony with your authentic self. Each Type's Strategy is a bit like the bumpers on a bowling lane—following Strategy helps you stay in your lane and keeps you from falling too far into the ditches of life. This isn't just a concept; it's the science of Human Design in action. It's the mechanics of how your aura interacts with the vast field of infinite possibilities. Strategies aren't arbitrary rules; they're deeply practical tools rooted in the science of resonance. By following your Strategy, you send out a clear, coherent energetic signal, inviting life to respond with synchronicities, ease, alignment, and flow.

But embodying your Type does more than just organize the chaos around you—it's also a guide to getting into your body, the sacred space where your inner voice of alignment lives. This is the voice that bridges insight and embodied truth, translating intellectual understanding into lived experience. When you align with your Strategy, you're not just navigating life more smoothly; you're learning to trust the quiet wisdom of your body, the unfiltered whispers that guide you toward what's truly meant for you. It's not about forcing outcomes; it's about creating resonance—within yourself and with the world around you. And resonance feels so much better than forcing life.

THE WISDOM OF EMOTIONAL SIGNATURES

We live in a culture that glorifies logic and intellectualization, often at the expense of emotional intelligence. From a young age, we're taught to suppress, override, or rationalize our emotions rather than listen to them—or God forbid, feel and express them! *Gasp!* We're encouraged to be reasonable, to push forward even when something *feels* off, and to dismiss emotions as obstacles rather than the powerful messengers they are. But part of aligning with your design means becoming wise about your emotional world—especially the unique emotional signatures that act as your built-in guidance system.

Your emotions are actually key players in this dance of alignment. Each Type has a distinct emotional signature that clues us into your alignment and misalignment. These emotional indicators are like an emotional GPS, guiding you toward your authentic path and alerting you when you may have strayed.

When aligned, you'll feel emotions like satisfaction, success, peace, or surprise—indicators that you're living in harmony with your design. When misaligned, emotions like frustration, bitterness, anger, or disappointment arise as red flags. These feelings aren't failures or flaws; they're natural human emotions, *and* they can be powerful guides, inviting you to pause, reflect, and recalibrate.

But here's the nuance: Sometimes the discomfort you feel isn't a sign of misalignment—it's simply the tension of being in process. Waiting for the right opportunity to respond, or for the clarity to arrive, can feel frustrating or even stagnant. This is a natural part of working with energy rather than forcing outcomes. Learning to discern between misalignment and the discomfort of waiting is part of the wisdom you'll gain as you come to understand your Type more deeply.

Navigating Burnout and Building Resilience

In a world that glorifies hustle and endless output, burnout is a common trap for every Type—but the causes and solutions are unique to each. Misalignment often leads to overgiving, overcommitting, or overcompensating in ways that drain your life force. By understanding your Type's specific pitfalls, we hope that you can avoid some of these traps and instead cultivate resilience through practices that restore and realign your energy.

For each Type, we'll explore the challenges that lead to burnout, as well as the practices and tools that support your well-being and keep you aligned. These aren't one-size-fits-all solutions. They're strategies that honor the wisdom, gifts, and challenges of your unique design.

What You'll Learn About Each Type

As we step into the exploration of the five Leadership Types, we'll look at each through the lens of:

- **Purpose and role:** What is this Type's unique contribution to the collective ecosystem?

- **Aura mechanics:** How does this Type's energy field interact with others and the quantum field?
- **Alignment strategy:** What practical approach keeps this Type in flow?
- **Emotional signatures:** What emotions signal alignment or misalignment?
- **Challenges and traps:** What common pitfalls lead to burnout or disempowerment?
- **Alignment practices:** What tools and habits support this Type's well-being and authenticity?
- **Powerful reflections:** What reflections support this Type in gaining insight and awareness?

We'll keep reminding you that this journey isn't just about intellectual understanding or flashy insight—it's about embodiment. As you come to know your Type and its role in the ecosystem, you'll discover how to actually *live* in resonance with your authentic design, creating a life that feels good and contributing to a collective where everyone is more likely to thrive.

Let's dive in.

Chapter 3
Innovating Catalyst

The Role of the Innovating Catalyst in Our Cocreative Ecosystem

Imagine the first spark that sets a wildfire ablaze—not reckless or destructive, but purposeful, intentional, igniting new growth where stagnation has taken root. That's the energy of the Innovating Catalyst. Composing only 9 percent of the population, Innovating Catalysts are rare forces of transformation. They're the ones who step into the unknown, not with fear, but with conviction. Their gift is initiating groundbreaking ideas, bold processes, and fresh energy that moves the world forward.

Innovating Catalysts are the fire starters of the cocreative ecosystem, bringing clarity and movement to places, projects, and ideas that have grown stale. Their role isn't to maintain or sustain; it's to disrupt, to shake loose the old patterns so new possibilities can emerge. Their energy sets the stage for others to build upon, creating a ripple effect of evolution and growth.

But here's the thing—this kind of trailblazing work requires a unique energy field. The aura of the Innovating Catalyst is said to be naturally closed and repelling, an intentional design that protects their autonomy and independence. It creates the space they need to move decisively and without interference, carving out room for their visionary ideas to take shape. While this aura can feel polarizing at times, it serves an essential purpose, ensuring Innovating Catalysts can lead boldly, without being drowned out by the noise of external expectations.

It's important to note that while their aura is naturally repelling, this does *not* mean Innovating Catalysts are repelling as people. Personality and aura are distinct. Their personality may be warm, engaging, and loving, even as their aura maintains boundaries to safeguard their creative flow. This distinction allows them to spark new ideas, challenge the status quo, and move forward with clarity. The balance of an independent aura and an openhearted personality is part of what can make Innovating Catalysts so uniquely effective in their roles.

THE MECHANICS OF THE INNOVATING CATALYST AURA

Let's talk a bit more about the Innovating Catalyst's aura because it's… well, different. While other auras are open, magnetic, or absorbing, theirs is intentionally closed and repelling. It acts as a shield, keeping external influences at bay so they can operate autonomously. This doesn't mean they're closed off emotionally or unavailable—it means their energy is designed to protect the forward movement of their creative energy.

This energetic boundary is what allows Innovating Catalysts to initiate transformative change without getting bogged down by the opinions or resistance of others. It's also why they can sometimes feel misunderstood or even intimidating. Their aura is focused, clear, and direct—it doesn't ask permission. And that's the potent creative magic of it.

But here's the catch: While their aura naturally clears the way for bold, independent action, it also comes with a responsibility. Innovating Catalysts must inform others of their intentions to avoid conflict and misunderstandings. Without this key step, their actions can come across as abrupt or alienating, creating unnecessary interpersonal friction. Informing isn't about asking for approval or permission; it's about building trust and fostering collaboration. It's the bridge between their inner creative impulses and the external world.

ALIGNMENT STRATEGY: INFORM AND ACT DECISIVELY

If Innovating Catalysts were to tattoo their alignment strategy on their forearms, it would say: *Inform first. Then act.*

This process starts with a gut-level, nonverbal, and purely instinctual urge, a creative impulse that signals it's time to move forward. When this happens, Innovating Catalysts thrive by taking bold, independent action—ideally after they've informed those around them. Informing creates transparency. It reduces resistance. It ensures their movements are understood rather than misinterpreted, and since they tend to move so quickly, it also allows others to offer support, if needed, to carry the creative vision to completion.

For an Innovating Catalyst, a type that's literally designed to move quickly, informing can feel counterintuitive. Why take the time to explain when the vision is already clear in their mind? Why risk inviting input that might slow them down? The answer is simple:

> Informing isn't about slowing down—it's about making the path smoother and clearing the way.

When they inform, they create space for others to adjust, support, or at least not obstruct their creative ideas.

Taking this pause to inform can be challenging, especially when their creative energy feels like a tidal wave demanding immediate action. But skipping this step often leads to misunderstandings, pushback, or unnecessary obstacles. Informing isn't a hindrance; it's a tool for empowerment, ensuring their vision lands in the world with clarity and positive impact.

Once they've informed, Innovating Catalysts are unstoppable. Their ability to act decisively and confidently is what sets them apart. They don't wait for permission. They lead. And when they do so in alignment, they inspire others to step into new, out-of-the-box possibilities with courage and creativity.

Emotional Signatures of Alignment and Misalignment

Alignment: The Emotional Signature of Peace

When an Innovating Catalyst is in alignment, you can feel it. They radiate a calm, steady peace—not the stillness of doing nothing, but the grounded clarity of someone living their purpose. This peace arises when they honor their autonomy, trust their creative process, and communicate openly with those around them. It's the natural result of a life lived in alignment, where their energy flows freely and their contributions feel meaningful.

Peace doesn't mean Innovating Catalysts avoid challenges or conflict. It means they move through life with intention, unencumbered by unnecessary constraints or external expectations. They feel most alive when they're free to innovate, chart their own course, and create from a place of inner clarity. Peace is their North Star, the signal that they're channeling their creative impulses and energy with a sense of freedom and without obstruction and resistance from others.

Misalignment: The Emotional Signature of Anger

When Innovating Catalysts veer off course, anger shows up. It may not be the kind of anger that lashes out—it's the deep, internal frustration of energy that's blocked or misdirected. This anger often arises when they suppress their creative urges, fail to inform others, or try to conform to external expectations that clash with their authenticity.

Anger is a powerful signal, pointing to the places where they've compromised their autonomy or allowed external forces to derail their vision. It's a reminder to pause, reflect, and recalibrate. Anger says: *Something isn't right here. Let's fix it.*

Rather than viewing anger as a failure, Innovating Catalysts can use it as a compass. It's not there to punish them; it's there to guide them back to alignment.

Peace and anger aren't just feelings—they're feedback. For Innovating Catalysts, these emotional signatures serve as a built-in guidance system, offering essential tools for navigating their energy and decisions.

Peace whispers, *Keep going. You're aligned and on the right path.*

Anger on the other hand signals, *Pause. Something isn't working, and it's time to take a breath, get curious, and reevaluate.*

The nuance (because to be human is to dance with nuance): Anger can show up in two ways—as an internal experience or an external reflection. Internally, Innovating Catalysts may feel it bubbling up from within—perhaps because they've allowed their freedom to be compromised or ignored their need to inform others about their plans. Externally, anger may seem to come from those around them, creating the impression that others are upset or resistant to their actions. This external anger is often a mirror, reflecting what happens when Innovating Catalysts move forward without first informing. For example, they might decide to make a move without informing key collaborators, leaving others feeling blindsided or left out, which can create tension or conflict.

By tuning into these emotional cues—whether they arise within themselves or are reflected by others—Innovating Catalysts can refine their choices, honor their need for freedom, and direct their energy toward what truly matters. When they trust their inner authority and practice clear, intentional communication, they not only reduce anger but also unlock their full potential as visionaries and leaders, creating a ripple of peace that extends far beyond themselves.

Challenges and Risks of Burnout

Let's be real, being a trailblazer isn't easy. Innovating Catalysts face unique challenges that can lead to burnout if they're not careful.

These include the following:

- **Suppressed Creativity:** Holding back ideas out of fear of judgment or rejection.
- **Energetic Overextension:** Trying to match the sustained energy of other Types instead of honoring their own rhythm.
- **Rebellion and Resistance:** Reacting to feeling restricted or unsupported in ways that sabotage relationships or progress. (This can look like tendencies to be a little slippery or sneaky so that they don't get slowed down or challenged.)
- **Neglecting to Inform:** Skipping the critical step of communication, which creates unnecessary friction and isolation.

To thrive, Innovating Catalysts must balance their independence with practices that support their well-being and alignment.

Nurturing Alignment: Practices for Innovating Catalysts

Thriving as an Innovating Catalyst means embracing unique rhythm and gifts. Key strategies include the following:

- **Honoring Rest Cycles:** Recognizing the natural ebbs and flows of energy as a non-Sacral type prevents burnout and supports sustainable creativity.

- **Cultivating Self-Trust:** Listening to inner urges and acting with confidence.
- **Creating Supportive Environments:** Surrounding themselves with people who value their independence and innovation more than their productivity.
- **Embracing Emotional Awareness:** Using anger as a tool for self-reflection and recalibration.
- **Informing Proactively:** Clear communication reduces resistance and builds trust, paving the way for smoother collaboration.

Innovating Catalysts' Contribution to the Ecosystem

Innovating Catalysts are the spark that ignites powerful new ideas and forward movement. They bring bold ideas, fresh energy, and courageous action to the collective, inspiring others to dream bigger and move forward with confidence.

When they honor their design, they become beacons of possibility, reminding us all that true progress starts with daring to lead from a place of purpose and integrity. Through their vision and action, they create ripples of change that uplift not just themselves, but everyone around them.

Innovating Catalysts are living proof that when we trust our inner authority and embrace our unique gifts, we can create a world that's not only different but better.

Chapter 4
The Master Builder

The Role of the Master Builder in Our Cocreative Ecosystem

Master Builders are the heartbeat of creation, the pragmatic architects who bring dreams to life. Making up roughly 36 percent of the population, they are the steady, grounded energy that turns vision into reality. While others may brainstorm or spark change, Master Builders are the ones who ask, "Okay, but how are we actually going to make this happen?" And then—methodically, purposefully—they roll up their sleeves and get to work.

Their gift is inspired action, rooted in an intuitive understanding of what's truly needed in the moment. They bridge the gap between ideas and execution, embodying a rare blend of precision and purpose. Master Builders are just that—those who are here to master the art of building ideas by infusing creative visions with integrity, sustainability, and grounded momentum.

In the grand ecosystem of collaboration, Master Builders are the ones who anchor us. They remind us that meaningful progress doesn't come from rushing or forcing—it comes from steady, aligned effort. Their role is both simple and profound: to create. Not for the sake of busyness, but for the deep satisfaction of contributing something lasting and valuable to the world.

The Mechanics of the Master Builder Aura

The Master Builder's aura is like a warm invitation—magnetic and welcoming. People and opportunities are naturally drawn to them—not because they're chasing, but because their energy says, "I'm here, ready to respond." This openness creates a field of connection and collaboration, but it's not chaotic or indiscriminate. Their aura acts as a discerning filter, carefully sorting what's worth their energy and what isn't.

Here's the key: Master Builders aren't here to initiate. Their energy isn't designed to charge forward unprovoked. Instead, it thrives on response, literally responding to life. Something external—a request, a need, an interaction, an invitation—sparks a primal response in their Sacral Center (their gut), which literally *responds* with a primal and visceral yes or no—often sounding like *mmm hmm* or *uh-uh*. This intuitive, embodied Sacral response guides them toward aligned action so that they know where to invest their energy and attention.

This waiting-to-respond process isn't passive; it's deeply dynamic. Their Sacral wisdom ensures they invest their energy only in what resonates, creating a ripple effect of purposeful productivity. And when they honor this process, their aura becomes a finely tuned beacon, attracting the right people, projects, and possibilities into their orbit.

Alignment Strategy: Responding from Sacral Wisdom

For Master Builders, the secret to thriving lies in one simple—but often challenging—skill: *waiting* for the right thing to respond to.

Their sacral response is their embodied compass, a nonverbal, unfiltered reaction that tells them whether an opportunity authentically aligns with their energy. It's a full-body yes or no, felt as expansion or contraction, lightness or resistance, a guttural *uh-huh* or *uh-uh*. When they honor this response, everything flows. When they ignore it, frustration sets in, and burnout follows.

But here's where it gets tricky: Master Builders live in a world that idolizes hustle, logic, and instant decisions. Waiting for their Sacral clarity can feel countercultural. They've been taught to push, to initiate, to make things happen. And so, they often override their gut instincts in favor of external validation or societal expectations.

This is where the real work begins—not in the doing, but in the unlearning.

> Master Builders must relearn how to trust their bodies over their minds, how to embrace the natural rhythm of response over the artificial pressure to perform, and how to *say no*.

Waiting for the right opportunity isn't always convenient. It means saying no to things that look good on paper but don't *feel* right. It means disappointing others who want them to bring their dream into form. It means sitting in the discomfort of having energy but nowhere to direct it yet. But the rewards? They're everything.

When Master Builders align with their Sacral wisdom, they conserve their energy for what truly matters. Their decisions become clear; their actions, intentional. They build with precision and purpose, creating lives that are deeply satisfying, inspiring, and joyful—not just for themselves, but for everyone around them.

Emotional Signatures of Alignment and Misalignment

Alignment: The Emotional Signature of Satisfaction

For a Master Builder, satisfaction is the gold standard. It's the feeling of a job well done, of energy well spent, of being in the exact right place at the exact right time.

Aligned Master Builders radiate vitality. Their work isn't just productive—it's meaningful. They thrive when they're creating something that resonates with their Sacral response, whether it's a tangible project, a thriving relationship, or a moment of connection. Satisfaction feels like the steady hum of a motor running at full efficiency: smooth, grounded, and deeply rewarding.

This emotional signature is their green light, their confirmation that they're living in alignment. It's not about external accolades, feeding the insatiable beast that is the conditioned ego, or checking things off a to-do list—it's about the quiet joy of knowing their energy is being used exactly as it's meant to be.

Misalignment: The Emotional Signature of Frustration

Frustration is the red flag in the Master Builder's world. It often shows up when they push themselves to initiate instead of waiting to respond, when they make a habit of saying yes to obligations and shoulds that drain their energy, or when they try to force outcomes or timelines that aren't aligned with their design.

The Nuance of Frustration: A Master Builder's Guide to Energy Mastery

Let's get one thing straight: Master Builders are *not* here to throw their precious, potent Sacral energy at anything and everything.

Their gift isn't just in having energy—it's in *mastering* it. They are designed to cultivate clarity, discernment, and deep expertise in what truly lights them up so that when the right opportunity arrives, they can meet it with a fully resourced, joyful, all-in *yes*. But if they don't learn how to navigate frustration—one of their most important emotional indicators—they'll find themselves drained, disillusioned, and wondering why their abundant energy isn't translating into the success, fulfillment, and impact they desire.

Master Builders are energetic powerhouses, but they're not meant to be in constant motion. Their strategy is to *wait to respond*, which means there will be times when their energy is *ready*, but the right opportunity hasn't landed yet. And that? That can feel *deeply* frustrating and cringey.

But here's the nuance: Frustration isn't always a sign of misalignment—it's often a natural byproduct of the waiting process. Imagine a racehorse at the starting gate, muscles coiled, ready to *go*—but the bell hasn't rung yet. That restless, edgy, almost electric tension? That's what it can feel like to be a Master Builder between aligned opportunities. It's not a signal that something is wrong; it's a sign that their energy is gathering, refining, preparing. They're cultivating mastery, building resilience, and getting primed for the big show.

Frustration as a Guide: Misalignment Versus Sacred Preparation

The key is understanding *which* type of frustration is showing up:

Misalignment frustration happens when a Master Builder pours energy into the wrong things—saying yes out of obligation, logic, or fear-based shoulds instead of following the pull of their Sacral wisdom. It's the burnout of chronically overgiving, overcommitting, and trying to make things work that were never truly aligned in the first place.

Waiting frustration is different. It's the restless, itchy feeling that arises when they're in a holding pattern, waiting for the next right thing to respond to. This isn't something to fix or override—it's something to *work with*. It's an invitation to trust their Sacral intelligence, their gut instincts, and engage with the world in ways that keep them energized, inspired, and primed for when the real deal opportunity shows up.

How to Stay Resourced While Waiting

When frustration arises, the worst thing a Master Builder can do is throw their energy at just *anything* in order to relieve the tension. The most powerful thing they can do? Tend to the things that light them up—without trying to force an outcome.

While waiting for that dream collaborator, the book deal, or the green light on a passion project, their "work" might look like:

- Diving into a hobby that excites them (even if it has nothing to do with work)
- Spending time with friends who energize them
- Prioritizing rest and pleasure as legitimate productivity
- Following small yeses that don't seem practical but feel right in their gut

Why? Because every aligned yes—no matter how small—charges up their Sacral Center like a battery and refines their aura to call in the right things. So when the right, purposeful opportunity finally arrives, they won't be unclear, exhausted, resentful, or spread too thin. They'll be fully fueled and ready to say *yes* with their whole being.

The ultimate skill for a Master Builder is learning to sit with frustration without rushing to relieve it. When they stop fearing frustration and start *listening* to it, they unlock its deeper wisdom.

- *Is this frustration telling me I'm in the wrong place, pouring my energy into the wrong thing?*
- *Or is this frustration simply part of the waiting—an invitation to trust the timing and tend to my energy while the right thing lines up?*

Whether it's an urgent red flag or simply the growing pains of waiting, frustration is a powerful guide. When Master Builders learn to stay curious, discern the message, and trust their Sacral wisdom above all else, they step into the full potential of their design—creating, building, and bringing into reality *only* what are truly aligned, sustainable, prosperous opportunities.

THE WISDOM OF EMOTIONAL SIGNATURES

Satisfaction and frustration aren't just emotional states—they're GPS signals. Satisfaction says, "You're on the right path. Keep going." Frustration says, "Pause. Get curious. Something may need to shift."

By tuning into these emotional signatures, Master Builders can navigate life with clarity and purpose. They learn to trust their energy, to say yes to what lights them up and no to what doesn't. And in doing so, they create lives that are as fulfilling as they are impactful.

CHALLENGES AND RISKS OF BURNOUT

Master Builders are powerhouses, but even powerhouses have limits. Their biggest risks include the following:

- **Overcommitting:** Saying yes out of obligation rather than alignment
- **Chasing Validation:** Prioritizing external approval and being productive over internal alignment
- **Boundary Struggles:** Taking on too much, too often
- **Forcing Outcomes:** Ignoring their Sacral rhythm in favor of pushing through

To avoid burnout, they must honor their energy and trust the process of waiting for aligned opportunities.

Nurturing Alignment: Practices for Master Builders

Thriving as a Master Builder isn't about doing more—it's about doing what's right. Helpful practices include the following:

- **Reframing Waiting:** Seeing waiting as a form of active discernment, not inaction
- **Listening to the Sacral:** Trusting their gut over external expectations
- **Saying No:** Protecting their energy by declining misaligned commitments
- **Creating Spaciousness:** Building in rest and reflection to recharge
- **Infusing Pleasure:** Prioritizing joy and creativity to fuel their vitality

Master Builders' Contribution to the Ecosystem

Master Builders are the ones who keep everyone grounded. Their ability to generate and sustain energy through aligned action creates a ripple effect of progress, inspiration, and practical impact.

When they trust their Sacral wisdom and lean into their natural rhythms, Master Builders transform ideas into reality, paving the way for collective growth and innovation. They show us the beauty of steady, intentional effort, proving that the most meaningful, sustainable creations are born from alignment, not force.

In honoring their role, Master Builders remind us of the power of responding authentically to life.

> Through their leadership, they inspire us to build lives, communities, and systems that are rooted in integrity, vitality, and sustainable success.

Chapter 5
The Accelerated Builder

The Role of the Accelerated Builder in Our Cocreative Ecosystem

Imagine a bubbling fountain of energy, ideas, and momentum—that's the essence of an Accelerated Builder. Making up about 32 percent of the population, this one-of-a-kind hybrid Leadership Type blends the grounded mastery of the Master Builder with the innovative spark of the Innovating Catalyst—all while still fundamentally remaining a Builder Type at its core. While their energy contains elements of innovation, velocity, and trailblazing, their primary role in the ecosystem is still bringing ideas into form—just with greater speed, efficiency, and momentum than any other Type.

Unlike most Types who function best when focusing on one thing at a time, Accelerated Builders are the only Type designed to multitask effectively, thriving in dynamism, engagement, and flow. Their comfort zone is movement—responding, pivoting, refining, and staying in momentum. Their energy is quick, energizing, and impossible to ignore, bridging creativity, efficiency, and practicality to build smarter, not harder.

Accelerated Builders aren't just here to build—they're here to streamline, refine, and discover the most effective shortcuts between inspiration and execution. If there's a way to make something happen in half the time or effort, they'll discover it, test it, and teach the rest of us how to work more efficiently. Their gift is momentum—turning ideas into action at lightning speed.

At their best, Accelerated Builders balance speed with intention, ensuring their dynamic energy remains aligned with their deeper purpose. Their mastery isn't just in what they build, but in how they build it—with efficiency, adaptability, and an unshakable trust in the flow of alignment. As the fast-track Builders of the collective, they remind us that big things don't have to take forever—they just need the right kind of energy behind them.

THE MECHANICS OF THE ACCELERATED BUILDER AURA

The aura of an Accelerated Builder carries a distinctive pulse—it's magnetic, enveloping, and infused with momentum but also capable of shifting closed when necessary. Unlike their Master Builder counterparts, whose auras remain consistently open and drawing things in, the Accelerated Builder's hybrid aura is both an energetic beacon and a powerful filter.

At their best, this dual nature allows them to magnetize opportunities while simultaneously keeping out anything that could slow them down, disrupt their flow, or box them in. Their energy is potent, but not chaotic. It's channeled with precision, efficiency, and an instinct for what's worth their time. There's an unmistakable hum of movement around them—a frequency that signals their capacity to bring ideas to life at lightning speed.

Like all Builders, their Sacral Center remains their compass, providing clarity about what truly deserves their energy. When they encounter the right opportunity, their response is immediate and visceral—a Sacral *yes* that surges through them like a full body green light. But unlike Master Builders, who thrive on steady, sustained engagement, Accelerated Builders are designed for bursts of intense creative flow, followed by redirection, refinement, and pivots when something no longer holds their Sacral energy.

This is where their dynamic aura's protective, closed-off quality comes into play. If an opportunity, person, or environment threatens their freedom, disrupts their creative flow, or tries to box them into a rigid structure, their aura instinctively tries to shut it out. This is a key distinction—they are both grounded and dynamic, blending the gifts of the Master Builder's endurance with the Innovating Catalyst's drive for efficiency, speed, and self-directed momentum.

At their most aligned, Accelerated Builders move through life like a finely tuned race car—fast, able to pivot on a dime and expertly maneuver around obstacles. They thrive when they trust their Sacral responses to guide them—pulling in the right experiences, filtering out distractions, and moving with dynamic precision toward what energizes, inspires, and lights them up.

Alignment Strategy: Respond, Inform, Act

The Accelerated Builder's magic lies in balancing speed with alignment, but the key to sustainably channeling their dynamic energy is mastering the strategy of responding, informing, and *then* taking clear, decisive action—in that order.

Like Master Builders, their process begins with waiting to respond. Their Sacral response—a gut-level yes-or-no reaction—acts as their internal GPS, guiding them toward what is authentically aligned and away from what isn't. But unlike Master Builders, who are designed to immerse deeply in the process, master their craft, and build over time, Accelerated Builders thrive in motion, are designed to start and stop things at the speed of alignment, and often feel extra restless when waiting.

> Learning to pause and feel that Sacral yes or no before acting is one of their most significant challenges… but the one that can most positively transform their life.

Next, before jumping in at full speed, which they were probably ready to do yesterday, Accelerated Builders must *inform*—a strategy they share with Innovating Catalysts. Informing isn't about being polite or asking for permission; it's about creating smoother collaboration, preventing resistance, and clearing the path for their creative momentum. If they don't inform, they're likely to hit unexpected roadblocks, face unnecessary pushback, or invest energy in navigating annoying misunderstandings. Their energy moves so fast that others may struggle to keep up—but a moment of quick communication can create flow.

Once they have responded and informed, then comes the part that feels most natural: taking action with speed and efficiency. Unlike other Types who may hesitate or deliberate, Accelerated Builders are designed to move swiftly, pivot when needed, and find the fastest, smartest route forward. Their brilliance lies not just in action, but in optimizing processes, testing shortcuts, and teaching the collective what works and what doesn't.

The Discipline of Waiting (Even When It Feels Wrong)

For an Accelerated Builder, waiting to respond can feel immensely frustrating. They thrive on momentum, movement, and dynamism, so pausing—even briefly—before acting can feel wildly unnatural. Thanks to our culture that glorifies speed and hyper-productivity, this is made even more challenging. But here's the thing: As much resistance as they may initially feel, this pause *is* their power. Without it, they risk pouring energy into misaligned opportunities, overcommitting, or burning out by saying yes for the wrong reasons (logic, fear, or succumbing to external expectations).

An Accelerated Builder who learns the art of waiting, trusts their response, and informs before acting will feel energized, efficient, and lit up. One who rushes forward without waiting for alignment will feel scattered, drained, and prone to burnout. The difference isn't in the pace—it's in the clarity of the starting point.

Embracing the Learning Process

Because Accelerated Builders are here to take, try, and test the best pathways to efficiency, missing steps along the way is part of their design. Unlike a culture that prizes getting it right the first time, Accelerated Builders are designed to learn through action—refining their process by doing, adjusting, and innovating. Their missteps aren't failures, they're feedback. They are designed to be the masters of "failing forward" toward clarity and efficiency. Practicing self-compassion when they miss a step or have to course-correct is just as crucial as learning to trust their response.

When they master the discipline of responding, informing, and *then* acting, Accelerated Builders become unstoppable. Their blend of discernment and decisive action allows them to sustain their energy, avoid burnout, and bring rapid innovation into the world in a way that feels expansive, exhilarating, and deeply aligned.

Emotional Signatures of Alignment and Misalignment

The Dynamic Balance of Satisfaction, Peace, Frustration, and Anger

The Accelerated Builder is a dynamic force—quick, adaptable, and highly efficient. But even with all that speed, alignment isn't just about getting more things done—it's about moving in harmony with their natural flow. Their emotional signatures hold a hybrid quality, blending the Master Builder's deep sense of satisfaction with the Innovating Catalyst's signature of peace. These two emotions act as green flags, signaling that they're aligned and using their powerful energy wisely. On the other hand, frustration and anger often show up as powerful indicators inviting them to reflect and recalibrate.

ALIGNMENT: THE EMOTIONAL SIGNATURES OF SATISFACTION AND PEACE

For Accelerated Builders, satisfaction is a sign that they've used their energy in a way that feels good and fulfilling—that they've created something of value and have done so aligned with a sense of authentic inspiration and purpose. It's the feeling of seeing tangible results from their efforts and of knowing they've spent their time and energy wisely.

But peace is just as important. Unlike Master Builders, who are built for sustained effort, Accelerated Builders are designed for efficiency over endurance. Peace isn't about stillness—it's about feeling clear, unobstructed, and free to move without unnecessary resistance. When they inform before they act, they remove friction from the equation, clearing the way for their dynamic energy to move unimpeded.

Peace is what indicates that they're flowing with life, allowing things to happen with ease instead of struggle. It's the deep exhale that says what follows:

- *I'm moving fast, but I'm not rushing.*
- *I'm creating, but I'm not forcing.*
- *I'm leading, and I'm pausing to inform.*

When an Accelerated Builder feels both satisfaction and peace, they know they're moving in alignment with their natural energy—responding to what's correct, informing those impacted, and taking decisive action without friction or burnout.

Misalignment: The Emotional Signatures of Frustration and Anger

When they're out of alignment, frustration and anger are the Accelerated Builder's red flags. These emotions are not failures or personality flaws—they are feedback mechanisms, guiding them toward a pause for reflection.

Frustration often arises when they:

- say yes to opportunities that don't light up their Sacral Center but seem logical or practical
- override their instincts, forcing progress instead of responding to what's naturally unfolding
- hold onto projects, commitments, or relationships past their expiration date, draining their energy instead of redirecting it toward what truly excites and inspires them

Anger, on the other hand, is often a sign that their creative momentum is being blocked or interfered with. It tends to show up when:

- they feel micromanaged or restricted, unable to execute freely
- they move too fast without informing, leading to pushback that halts their progress
- they're forced to follow rigid structures, outdated processes, or unnecessary bureaucracy, making efficiency feel impossible and stifling their ability to create impact at their natural pace

The Wisdom of Emotional Signatures: Flow Versus Force

Satisfaction and peace confirm that an Accelerated Builder is on track, using their energy in a way that is both productive and easeful. Frustration or anger, however, signal a need to pause, recalibrate, and either inform or wait for the right opportunity to respond.

The key lesson for Accelerated Builders is understanding the difference between frustration that signals misalignment and frustration that signals readiness. One is a warning to course-correct; the other is an invitation to trust the timing and gather energy for what's coming next.

When Accelerated Builders master the art of responding first, informing next, and only then taking action, they move through life without unnecessary resistance. Their emotional signatures become reliable guides, helping them navigate life with greater clarity, momentum, and alignment—allowing them to thrive as the creative, dynamic, and efficient forces of progress they were designed to be.

CHALLENGES AND RISKS OF BURNOUT

Accelerated Builders are powerhouses, but even powerhouses have limits. Their fast-paced energy makes them particularly vulnerable to burnout. Common challenges may include any of the following:

- **Overextending Themselves:** Saying yes to too many projects or tasks, just because they can.
- **Overlooking the Pause:** Moving so quickly that they overlook important details or forget to pause long enough to reflect on what worked (and what didn't) and to hear their inner alignment.
- **Ignoring Their Sacral Response:** Letting societal pressure or external expectations override their unfiltered inner guidance.
- **Forcing Outcomes:** Trying to push things forward without waiting to respond, ensuring alignment.

To thrive, Accelerated Builders must balance their dynamic energy with the often-counterintuitive practice of pausing, waiting, and recalibrating.

Nurturing Alignment: Practices for Accelerated Builders

Thriving as an Accelerated Builder isn't about doing *everything*, it's about doing the *right* things.

Essential practices for these Types:

- **Pausing to Respond:** Creating space to check in with their Sacral wisdom before saying yes, committing, or charging forward.
- **Reframing Waiting:** Viewing waiting as an active process of discernment, not an annoying or passive delay.
- **Prioritizing Joy:** Focusing on what genuinely lights them up and energizes them.
- **Streamlining Commitments:** Saying yes to fewer but more aligned opportunities.
- **Letting Passion Be Enough:** Just because they *can* turn an interest into a side hustle doesn't mean they *should*. Allowing themselves to pursue hobbies and passions *for the joy of it*—without the pressure to monetize—nourishes their energy and creativity in ways that are just as valuable as financial success.

Accelerated Builders' Contribution to the Ecosystem

Accelerated Builders are the movers and shakers of the co-creative ecosystem. Their ability to combine speed with precision ensures that ideas don't just get off the ground—they soar.

When they trust their Sacral response and honor their unique rhythms, they create a ripple effect of momentum and progress. They show us what's possible when creativity meets pragmatism, when action is guided by alignment, and when individuality is celebrated within the collective.

In embracing their role, Accelerated Builders remind us all of the power of saying yes to what truly matters—and the magic that happens when we move through life with both intention and momentum.

Chapter 6
The Possibilitarian Guide

The Role of the Possibilitarian Guide in Our Cocreative Ecosystem

Possibilitarian Guides are like the lighthouses in the stormy seas of life—steady, focused, and guiding the way home. Representing roughly 20-22 percent of the global population, these individuals hold a unique and essential role in the cocreative ecosystem. They aren't here to generate energy or sustain long-term momentum but instead are here to guide projects, people, and ideas forward with precision and insight, ensuring that everyone and everything finds its proper alignment.

Possibilitarian Guides are the visionaries who see and sense what others can't. They have an uncanny ability to sense inefficiencies, untapped potential, and the possibilities hiding just beneath the surface. Their purpose is to offer transformative guidance, aligning people and systems with their highest potential and amplifying collective growth.

Their aura—penetrating, focused, and absorptive—is a finely tuned instrument that naturally attunes to the energy of people and environments. Like a living sensor, they feel and absorb the energy of others, which helps them navigate the complexities of human dynamics, ensuring that individuals, teams, and projects move toward harmony and impact. But their gift is magnified only when it's invited. When Possibilitarian Guides are recognized and asked to share their insights, their guidance has the power to unlock untold possibilities.

The Mechanics of the Possibilitarian Guide's Aura

Let's talk a bit more about that aura for a moment, because it's very unique. While some are expansive and welcoming, the Possibilitarian Guide's aura is more like a laser beam—focused and deeply penetrating. It homes in on the energy of others, offering unparalleled clarity about what's working, what isn't, and what needs to change.

This penetrating quality is both their superpower and their Achilles' heel. Without an invitation, their aura can feel intense and invasive—like someone shining a spotlight on places we'd rather not examine. But when their guidance is sought out and their insights are welcomed, their aura becomes a powerful tool for transformation, cutting through confusion and paving the way for truly aligned action and expansion.

This unique design means that Possibilitarian Guides are most effective when they wait for recognition and an invitation. Without these, their wisdom can feel invasive and offensive, leaving them frustrated and those around them resistant. But when recognized and invited to share their unique perspective and guidance, their insights are like keys that unlock doors to next level clarity, efficiency, and success.

Alignment Strategy: Waiting for the Invitation

For Possibilitarian Guides, waiting for the invitation can feel like an irritating test of patience rather than a strategy. But hear this:

It's not about passivity—it's about power. Their aura creates a highly intimate energetic connection with others (whether they realize it or not), often seeing deeply into their essence, including their strengths, blocks, and blind spots. Because of this level of depth, their guidance works best when it is fully welcomed.

> Waiting for the invitation isn't just polite—it's what filters out the wrong people and opportunities and paves the way for the right ones so that their guidance is most impactful and valued as the precious commodity it is.

Here's how this plays out:

- **Honoring the Aura's Intimacy:** Their aura isn't casual—it's inherently, deeply personal. It connects energetically with others in a way that reveals truth, even truths that people might not be ready to face. Waiting for an invitation ensures their insights are received with openness and trust rather than resistance.
- **Filtering for Alignment:** Not every person or project deserves their energy. Waiting for recognition helps them discern who genuinely values their guidance and who doesn't. It saves them from the frustration and heartbreak of offering wisdom to those who aren't ready to receive it.
- **Building Trust Through Recognition:** When someone invites their insight, they're saying, "I see you. I value you. I'm ready for what you have to share." That recognition creates the fertile ground for their guidance to take root and flourish.

Emotional Signatures of Alignment and Misalignment

Alignment: The Emotional Signature of Success

For Possibilitarian Guides, success isn't just about hitting goals or achieving milestones. It's a deeply fulfilling sense of purpose that radiates through their interactions and contributions. Success feels like being truly seen and valued for your unique gifts, regardless of external metrics.

When you're aligned, you're invited into spaces where your insights are celebrated and your guidance creates meaningful transformation. Success feels like resting in the assurance that your role isn't to hustle or push things forward, but to guide with wisdom and precision. It's the joy of knowing that your intangible contributions and unique wisdom are positively impacting others and opening new possibilities for the collective (group, team, project, etc.).

Fun fact: A Possibilitarian Guide who is authentically resourced (rested up), recognized for who they are, and responding to an aligned invitation can look (and feel) like an Accelerated Builder. This isn't a sustainable state, as they are fundamentally a non-Sacral Type, but for this Leadership Type, the right recognition and opportunity to guide is quite literally their fuel for creation. It gives them energy; it charges them up. From this place, they are able to create and guide powerfully and efficiently as the creative forces for transformation that they are.

Misalignment: The Emotional Signature of Bitterness

Bitterness is the Possibilitarian Guide's clear signal of misalignment. It creeps in when they try to force their guidance into spaces where it hasn't been invited, when they overexert themselves in an attempt to prove their worth through doing, or when they invest their energy in people, projects, or environments that don't truly see or value their gifts.

Bitterness often arises when they pour their time and energy into spaces that do not recognize or appreciate their unique way of seeing the world. When their insights are dismissed, when they aren't acknowledged for their natural gifts, or when they give their energy to dynamics that drain rather than nourish them, their system protests. Their wisdom is meant to be valued, and bitterness is a clear indicator that it's time to step back and recalibrate.

This emotional signature is also likely to surface when they ignore their need for rest, trying to keep up with the fast-paced, output-driven world of the Builder types. They are not here to grind, hustle, or prove themselves through constant doing—they are here to guide, illuminate, and refine. When they push themselves into endless action, their energy becomes depleted, their wisdom loses its potency, and their body sends distress signals in the form of deep exhaustion and resentment.

And here's a key truth: Possibilitarian Guides absorb the energy of those around them—which means they need time away, even from the people they love. When they don't regularly retreat into their own energy field—through rest, stillness, alone time, or even lying down for short periods—they carry the weight of the world's energy without realizing it. Over time, this leads to deep exhaustion and emotional fog, making it harder to discern what's theirs and what they've unconsciously absorbed.

But bitterness isn't a failure—it's a built-in recalibration system. It's not punishing them; it's redirecting them back to their true nature: waiting for recognition, honoring their energy, valuing their gifts, and trusting that the right invitations will come when they align with their worth. When they embrace this, bitterness transforms into deep satisfaction and the peace of being seen, valued, and aligned.

THE WISDOM OF EMOTIONAL SIGNATURES

Success and bitterness aren't just feelings—they're feedback loops. Success affirms that Possibilitarian Guides are living in alignment with their design, operating in spaces where their gifts are honored and amplified. Bitterness, on the other hand, is a red flag. It's a call to reflect on where they've strayed from their truth.

By tuning into these emotional currents, they can refine their discernment, conserve their energy, and focus their attention on the relationships and opportunities that truly align with their gifts. When they honor their emotional signatures, they create a ripple effect of transformation that is felt deeply by those they are here to serve.

CHALLENGES AND RISKS OF BURNOUT

Possibilitarian Guides live in a world that often values doing over being. This can lead to some unique challenges:

- **Overextending Themselves:** Taking on roles or responsibilities that don't align with their energy.
- **Chasing Validation:** Trying to prove their worth through unsolicited guidance or overwork.
- **Boundary Struggles:** Saying yes to everyone and everything, leaving no room for rest or reflection.
- **Comparison to Builders:** Measuring themselves against Leadership Types that are naturally wired to do sustainably can lead to feelings of inadequacy

To thrive, they must embrace their unique rhythm, value their intangible, yet essential gifts, and trust in the power of waiting for aligned opportunities.

Nurturing Alignment: Practices for Possibilitarian Guides

Thriving as a Possibilitarian Guide requires intentional practices that honor their energy and amplify their gifts. Here are a few to consider:

- **Prioritize Rest:** They recharge by stepping back, reflecting, and allowing inspiration to flow naturally. Time alone in their own energy is essential for clarity and renewal.
- **Trust Timing:** The right invitations will come at the right time. Releasing the pressure to initiate allows them to step into their role with ease and impact.
- **Create Supportive Environments:** Surrounding themselves with people and spaces that value their guidance ensures their wisdom is received and appreciated.
- **Honor Boundaries:** Protecting their energy by saying no to misaligned opportunities prevents depletion and fosters alignment.
- **Celebrate Their Gifts:** Embracing the value of their unique perspective and trusting in the impact of their insights strengthens their confidence and purpose.

Possibilitarian Guides' Contribution to the Ecosystem

Possibilitarian Guides are the seers and wise guides of the co-creative ecosystem. They steer individuals and systems toward alignment and efficiency, ensuring that energy flows where it's most needed.

When they honor their design, they inspire trust, collaboration, and transformation. Their insights illuminate untapped potential and create pathways for growth and harmony. They remind others of the beauty of intentionality and the power of cocreating with purpose and precision.

> By embracing their role as Possibilitarian Guides, they become beacons of clarity and wisdom. They empower others to step into their highest potential, and in doing so, they help build a more aligned and sustainable future for all.

Chapter 7
The Reflective Evaluator

The Role of the Reflective Evaluator in Our Cocreative Ecosystem

Imagine a mirror that doesn't just reflect your image but your soul, your energy, your truth. That's the Reflective Evaluator. Representing only 1 percent of the population, they are the rarest and most neutral guides of all. Their superpower lies not in doing or producing but in their ability to simply *be*—to absorb the world around them with stunning openness and reflect its unvarnished reality back to us.

Reflective Evaluators are the wisdom keepers of the cocreative ecosystem. They see everything: what's working, what's broken, what's yearning for growth. Their role isn't to direct or control but to illuminate. Their mere presence offers clarity, fostering alignment in teams, families, and communities. Their gift is essential and their neutrality is a balm in a world often clouded by ego and agendas.

With no defined Centers in their Human Design, Reflective Evaluators are pure openness. This makes them sensitive, adaptive, and profoundly wise. But it also means that they are very affected by their environment. Thriving requires them to carefully curate their environments and relationships, ensuring they remain in spaces that energize rather than deplete. When they're in the right place, their brilliance shines. When they're not, their clarity becomes clouded.

The Mechanics of the Reflective Evaluator Aura

The Reflective Evaluator's aura is unique—like a prism that refracts the light around it into its purest colors. It is sampling and reflective, taking in the energy of people and environments without holding onto it. This means that Reflective Evaluators don't carry their own fixed energy. Instead, they reflect the dynamics around them, acting as a living barometer and mirror of the health and alignment of the systems they're part of.

This adaptability is both their power and their challenge. Their openness allows them to see and feel everything—every crack in the foundation, every untapped potential. But it also leaves them deeply sensitive to the chaos of misaligned environments. Their neutrality requires careful boundaries; otherwise, they risk absorbing energies that are not their own.

Reflective Evaluators thrive when they are in spaces that are growth-oriented, dynamic, and nourishing. In the right environments, their openness becomes a superpower, offering clarity and perspective that no other type can match. In chaotic or toxic environments, however, their gifts are dulled, and their energy becomes scattered.

Alignment Strategy: Waiting for Clarity and Right Environments

If Reflective Evaluators are the wisdom keepers of the ecosystem, their wisdom is only as clear as the space they occupy.

> Their alignment strategy centers on two nonnegotiables: giving themselves time to process and ensuring they're in the right environments.

---

1. **Allowing Time for Clarity:** Reflective Evaluators don't operate on impulse or urgency. They need time—often a full lunar cycle (approximately twenty-nine and a half days)—to feel into decisions. This isn't procrastination; it's depth. By allowing themselves this time, they can see all sides of a situation and gain the clarity needed to make aligned choices.

   In a culture obsessed with speed, this rhythm can feel countercultural. There's pressure to know now, to act before clarity arrives. But for Reflective Evaluators, rushing leads to frustration and confusion. Their power lies in honoring their slower, more deliberate process.

2. **Thriving in Aligned Environments:** The environment is everything for Reflective Evaluators. They absorb and amplify the energy of their surroundings, so being in the right space is nonnegotiable. They thrive in environments that are uplifting and growth-oriented, where their insights are valued and their neutrality respected.

   If a space feels stagnant, toxic, or out of alignment, their clarity becomes compromised. Recognizing when it's time to leave a misaligned environment—and having the courage to do so—is critical to their well-being.

3. **Practicing Sound Boarding:** Reflective Evaluators often find clarity by hearing their thoughts and feelings reflected back to them through trusted confidants. This process isn't about seeking advice; it's about creating a space for their reflections to take shape. Trusted relationships that provide this kind of resonance, space holding, and listening are invaluable.

Emotional Signatures of Alignment and Misalignment

Alignment: The Emotional Signature of Surprise

For Reflective Evaluators, alignment feels like surprise—the kind that sparks wonder and invites them deeper into the mystery of life. When they release rigid expectations and allow life to unfold organically, they open themselves to moments of unexpected clarity, insight, and delight.

Aligned Reflective Evaluators experience the world as a series of magical revelations, where their ability to mirror and reflect reveals hidden beauty, deeper truths, and new possibilities. Their unique gift is seeing without agenda—offering reflection without judgment, pressure, or force. Rather than clinging to a predetermined outcome, they remain fluid, reflecting and adapting as needed to maintain their own well-being and energetic alignment.

This sense of surprise is a clear signal that they're living in harmony with their design. It means they are in environments that feel nourishing, honoring their need for spaciousness and flexibility and allowing clarity to emerge in its own time. When they embrace this, they empower others simply by being present—offering reflections that illuminate truth, expand awareness, and gently guide those around them toward greater well-being and growth.

Misalignment: The Emotional Signature of Disappointment

When misaligned, Reflective Evaluators experience disappointment—the disheartening sensation that signals they have veered off course. Unlike the lightness and wonder of surprise, disappointment feels like a weight, a sense that something isn't quite right. This often arises when they stay too long in environments that are chaotic, misaligned, or energetically draining, or when they ignore their need to shift, adapt, or disengage from what no longer serves them.

Disappointment can also creep in when Reflective Evaluators succumb to external pressures—trying to force clarity, rush decisions, or conform to societal expectations that don't honor their natural rhythm. When they push against their own nature—believing they should stick it out, be more decisive, or hold things together for others—disappointment sets in as a clear indicator that they have overridden their innate wisdom.

But disappointment isn't failure—it's feedback. It's an invitation to step back, reassess, and reorient toward what feels nourishing. It's a call to trust their natural process, release attachment to how things "should" be, and allow life to unfold in its own timing. When they listen to this cue, they can shift back into alignment—returning to the spaciousness, clarity, and openness that allows them to experience life's surprises with ease and wonder once again.

The Wisdom of Their Emotional Signatures

Surprise and disappointment act as an internal compass for Reflective Evaluators, guiding them toward alignment and signaling when they've strayed off course. Surprise—the kind that feels like a delightful revelation—affirms that they are living in harmony with their design, engaging with life in a way that is fluid, open, and free from rigid expectations. It's a sign that they are in the right environments, allowing clarity to emerge naturally rather than forcing outcomes.

Disappointment, on the other hand, serves as a warning signal. It arises when they override their need for adaptability, remain in misaligned environments, or attempt to conform to external pressures that don't honor their true nature. When disappointment surfaces, it's not a sign of failure—it's an invitation to pause, recalibrate, and shift back into alignment.

By tuning into these emotional signatures, Reflective Evaluators refine their choices, protect their energy, and embrace the natural ebb and flow of their experience. When they honor their unique rhythm and trust the wisdom of their emotions, they reclaim their power to live as clear, unbiased mirrors—offering the world their profound gift of reflection with authenticity, neutrality, and grace.

Challenges and Risks of Burnout

Reflective Evaluators are uniquely sensitive, and their openness can leave them vulnerable to burnout if not carefully managed. Their natural ability to mirror and reflect is an incredible gift, but in a world that prioritizes speed, action, and constant productivity, they may feel pressured to prove their worth through doing rather than being. When they fall into this trap, they risk disconnecting from their true role as wise observers, leading to exhaustion, frustration, and a deep sense of misalignment.

Common risks include the following:

- **Energetic Overwhelm:** Absorbing chaotic or negative energy from misaligned environments, leaving them drained and disconnected.

- **Identity Confusion:** Succumbing to societal pressure to conform, perform, or tact when their wisdom lies in witnessing and reflecting. This can erode self-trust and create inner conflict.

- **Overinvolvement:** Feeling like they must actively fix, guide, or control situations instead of simply reflecting what is, leading to frustration and depletion.

- **Isolation:** Feeling unseen, undervalued, or dismissed can cause them to withdraw, losing their sense of purpose and the joy that comes from sharing their insights in aligned spaces.

For Reflective Evaluators, burnout often comes from over-identifying with the energies around them rather than maintaining their role as a neutral observer. When they honor their own rhythm, prioritize environments that feel clear and supportive, and trust that their reflection is more than enough, they can preserve their energy and fully embody their wisdom.

Nurturing Alignment: Practices for Reflective Evaluators

To thrive, Reflective Evaluators must embrace practices that honor their unique design. These include the following:

- **Prioritizing Environments:** Choose spaces and relationships that feel energizing and aligned. Let go of those that don't.
- **Embracing Patience:** Trust the rhythm of the lunar cycle for major decisions. Clarity takes time.
- **Practicing Sound Boarding:** Seek trusted confidants who can reflect your insights back to you.
- **Setting Boundaries:** Protect your energy by saying no to misaligned opportunities.
- **Celebrating Surprise:** Savor moments of delight and curiosity as signs that you're aligned.

Reflective Evaluators' Contribution to the Ecosystem

Reflective Evaluators are the quiet powerhouses of the co-creative ecosystem. Their ability to mirror the truth of a situation with clarity and neutrality helps others see themselves more clearly. They create pathways for alignment, growth, and harmony, ensuring that energy flows efficiently and effectively.

When Reflective Evaluators honor their design, they inspire curiosity, openness, and possibility in those around them. They remind us of the power of reflection and the magic of creating environments that support authenticity and growth.

Their leadership is a testament to what happens when we honor our true nature and cocreate with intention and clarity.

> Through their presence and insights, Reflective Evaluators teach us the beauty of pausing, observing, and allowing life to unfold in its most aligned and magical form.

Chapter 8
Storytime: The Messy and Magical Path of Living Our Design

At this point, it can be easy to get in our heads about facts and definitions, i.e., I am this Type, you are that Type. (Be honest, you probably looked up the chart of your entire family once you looked up your own!) But it would do a *deep* disservice to Human Design to talk about it only as a mental construct. Human Design is a *lived* experience. As with all archetypal systems, we are *all* of the Types, and we have a unique relationship with our particular story. We are meant to be in a living, breathing, dynamic relationship with our chart. It is here to help us understand ourselves first, and then who we are in relationship to those around us, and even how we are designed to serve the whole of humanity. It is truly a blueprint of our calling, our strengths, our weaknesses, what we are here to learn more about, where we are naturally gifted, and what it takes for us to remember who we truly are (a spiritual being having a human experience) again and again.

So with that understanding, we want to give examples throughout the book of our own lived experiences. That means that sometimes, we will be switching to the first person so that we can tell our stories. We will do that by saying something like "Laura here," or "Hey, it's Meghan," to help you identify where we are switching on you. This makes it easier for us to talk directly to you about our lives. If you are curious why we decided to do it this way, try telling your best friend about your weekend in the third person.... It doesn't go very well, but it will make you laugh. With that said, let's give it a try.

Hey, Laura here...

Meghan and I have a running joke about how I tend to energetically back myself into growth opportunities—like I miss that something big is happening until I'm already knee-deep in it. That's exactly how I stumbled into the world of energy medicine.

It all started when my kiddo was diagnosed with dyslexia and ADD. In my search for support, we came across a practitioner doing a modality called Brain Integration. From the jump, I was wildly curious about what he was doing... and, I'll be honest, a little skeptical. I didn't know anything about the energy body (yes, that's a thing) or how we could work with it to heal. I just wanted someone to help my brilliant kid stop calling themselves stupid—which had already started by second grade—and I was a *hard* no for that shit.

So week after week, we went to sessions with Wes (our amazing practitioner), and I watched, fascinated, as he did his thing. And then the results started to show up. Not just in big ways—like reading more easily or retaining information better—but in the small, everyday stuff too. Like picking up their wet towel after a bath (which had *never* happened before, no matter how many times I asked). I was *in*!

I started researching the modality and how to train in it. Then I went back to Wes and asked if he'd be okay with my pursuing it myself. I didn't want to step on his toes, but the work felt so important—so needed. He was not only okay with it, he encouraged me to pursue it!

Now, I need to set the stage a bit here: I knew *nothing* about energy work. Brain Integration uses muscle testing and applied kinesiology, so to me, it felt like some sort of chiropractic bodywork. I didn't realize I was entering the realm of energy healing. Back then, energy work felt a little, woo. I didn't *not* believe in it, but I definitely side-eyed it.

So off I went to my first training. And on day one, our teacher started talking about *working with energy*, and I was like, "Wait…, what??" I looked around the room and everyone else was nodding like this was totally normal. Internally, I was screaming, *"I did not sign up for some woo-ass shit! WTF!"* Externally, I smiled and nodded politely—because I'm a Libra sun *and* rising, which basically means I'm a professional people-pleaser. I wasn't about to make a scene.

So, I settled in and did my best to stay open. What helped was that I *knew* this worked—I'd seen it firsthand with my kiddo. And I'm pretty good at going along for the ride when something feels aligned.

This is what I mean about backing my way into things—I was already fully registered and sitting in Colorado at a two-week training before I realized: *Oh, I just signed up for a career in energy work.*

But looking back, it was *totally* a Sacral response. Classic to my Master Builder design. Up until that point, I'd been an art jeweler—and I *loved* it. I mean, I truly loved it. But I'd burned myself out by growing too fast, without the right systems or support (more on that another time).

After one particularly brutal show where I'd shelled out a ton of money and barely sold anything, I came home, defeated. I went out for a beer with two of my closest friends, and one of them asked, "Laura, didn't you start making jewelry for fun? Do you still love it?" That landed like a jarring lightning bolt. It *wasn't* fun anymore. The next day, I emailed all my accounts and said I was taking an indefinite sabbatical. I had no clue when—or if—I'd return.

I spent the next six months curled up on the couch, pondering my purpose. And it was during that time that we started Brain Integration sessions for my kiddo.

There are a few important things I want to highlight here. First, if I had known back then how I'm *designed* to respond, I might not have pushed so hard with my jewelry business. I could have followed my Sacral yeses and noes more clearly. I would have known which shows were a good fit and which weren't, rather than trying to do *it all*.

But here's the magic: If I hadn't quit, I wouldn't have been available to hear the call of my next chapter. So, I believe it all happened in the exact timing it was meant to.

And also? There's such richness here in understanding what "response" really means. It's not just about how we start things. It's also about how we *end* them.

I had been thinking about quitting for a while. The frustration of misalignment was growing. But instead of jumping into a new idea (which, let's be clear, was my natural tendency), I sat in the discomfort of not knowing. I waited until life gave me something to respond to—my friends, gently asking if this still felt good. I felt the no viscerally. And *that* was my moment to respond.

But honestly? I didn't try to figure out the next step either.

Well, that's not entirely true. I knew I needed to rest—deeply—so I gave myself a few months to recover. And in that time, something began to stir. I got curious (which happens to be a quality of the PROSPER framework that we'll explore later). I'd scroll through job listings, wondering what might be next, but this little voice kept whispering, *Sure, Laura… Trader Joe's could be fun, but you're here for something else.*

I wasn't just looking for a job—I was searching for my *purpose*. Not a title or role, but that deep sense of *who* I am and how I'm meant to serve something bigger than myself.

Let me be clear: Sometimes, in the space between what is and what's becoming, we need a job that pays the bills. Sometimes that job is exactly right, in its simplicity and stability, and we stay. Purpose doesn't always equal career. Sometimes a job is just a job and as long as it is adding to the quality of your life and not taking away from it long-term, it can be a beautiful thing to not stress about money.

But for me? I knew they were entangled. I couldn't ignore the pull. I had to keep seeking.

And yes—I honor the privilege I had in being able to take that time. My husband supported me while I healed and regrouped. Not everyone has that. And still, I believe we *all* have access to little pockets of pause, ways to listen for what's next—even if only for a breath. But that's a conversation for another day.

I didn't *know* any of this at the time. This is all the wisdom of hindsight, the kind that arrives slowly, after the storm passes.

What that season gave me was space. Space to heal. To be curious. To let Divine Timing do its thing. Not because I was hustling to figure it all out—but because I let myself *be*.

And then came the opportunity to train and work with Wes. The decision felt so aligned that, shortly after my training ended, Wes told me he was moving to Florida—and offered to sell me his business. He would mentor me until he left. It was miraculous, really. I literally walked into a whole-ass purpose-driven business!

I'm not saying it wasn't hard. But there was an ease to it, born from alignment. I didn't have to dream it up and force it into existence. The path revealed itself, one step at a time. *That's* the lived experience of a Master Builder—if we can get out of our own way.

And now, zooming out, I want to bring this into the broader Human Design ecosystem.

My husband—let's call him Pat (because that's his name)—is an Innovating Catalyst. A Manifestor by design. He's here to follow his own internal rhythm, to move with his creative impulses. And in *this* story, it was Pat who found Wes in the first place. One day, he just felt pulled to hop online and research holistic approaches to dyslexia. He found Wes, shared it with me, and the rest unfolded. (It's worth noting that Pat was always way more into "woo" than I was.)

He set up that first appointment. That was it. From there, I took over—going to the sessions, getting curious, responding. He didn't *try* to catalyze anything for me. He was just being himself. But his flow sparked a whole new path for me—one that continues to expand, personally and professionally.

Meghan and I often call the Innovating Catalyst energy the "pinball release." If you've ever played pinball (and if you haven't, I'm sorry… also, that reveals our age… also, please go find one!), you know that nothing happens until someone pulls the lever. The ball releases. That's the Innovating Catalyst. They don't have to play the game, but they create the spark of momentum the rest of us get to respond to.

And one of the friends I had drinks with after the jewelry show? A Possibilitarian Guide. She saw my frustration and gently guided me into a new possibility. She also asked me the powerful question that allowed me to respond to quitting.

Because of the brilliance of the ecosystem, and how it all played out for me, I'm more aligned than I've ever been—with my purpose, with who I'm here to *be*, and with what I'm here to *do*. I have these incredible people in my life to thank for that. Not because of what they did for me—although they *did* a lot—but because they were simply *be*ing themselves. That gave me something to respond to.

This is what we mean when we say Human Design isn't just another personality test. It's not just about understanding your traits. It's about how you're *meant to move through the world*. It's about your *being*—and how you live that out in the little moments and the life-changing ones.

Okay, Meghan here with a bit more storytime from a Possibilitarian Guide perspective:

I didn't grow up seeing healthy models of my Leadership Type. I was surrounded by Builder Types—those powerful beings who could do, do, do without needing the same deep rest, pauses, and spaciousness that I craved. Their energy was tangible, productive, and praised. Mine felt different—sensitive, subtle, and often invisible. My willpower helped me keep up, sure—but at the cost of overriding my body and silencing the quiet inner voice that always whispered, *This just doesn't feel right.*

Looking back, I can see how deeply I internalized the message that being different meant being *less than* and that I had to do more, prove more, push harder to earn the gold stars of approval I so desperately wanted. And in many ways, I did. On the outside, I was high achieving. But on the inside, in addition to working hard to suppress and hide my sensitivity and emotions, the cost of trying to keep up was real—migraines, fatigue, anxiety, and skin issues. The body has its own wise ways of trying to get our attention and guide us back into alignment.

But I was stubbornly committed to fitting in and was used to suffering and hustling for my value, so I kept going. It took years to unlearn the story that I was somehow broken or failing at life simply because I wasn't designed like everyone else. And yet... the signs of my authentic design were there all along.

In fourth grade, an impromptu advice line started forming daily on the playground—literally. I know it sounds odd but stick with me. One friend must have asked for some sort of emotional or relational guidance, and suddenly I became the unofficial counselor stationed at the parallel bars during recess, offering perspective that apparently made an impact. I didn't initiate this; I never asked to lead. But other kids recognized something in me. They came to me and invited me to share. And that kind of intuitive recognition would follow me throughout life—from babysitters and teachers to peers and adults who'd share their challenges with me, instinctively knowing I could hold space and offer guidance.

Still, I spent a long time trying to be someone I wasn't and chasing success in ways that didn't fit. Early in my career as a child and family psychotherapist, I left agency work because intuitively I knew that my body couldn't withstand the ongoing, unrelenting trauma load and crisis energy swirling around the high-needs population I served. I was skilled at doing the work, but knew that staying would burn me out, as I could feel that the late-night unexpected crisis calls were already frying my nervous system. So, I made the decision to go into private practice far earlier than I'd planned—after getting an invitation (Possibilitarian Guide style) from a friend to join his practice. This invitation came just months after I found out I was pregnant, and strangely, I wasn't nearly as stressed as I expected—in spite of having to navigate a pretty steep learning curve with insurance filing, marketing, and other entrepreneurial things. Pregnancy hormones had a magical way of taking the edge off of the familiar low-grade anxiety I was used to navigating, but I also think the move was deeply aligned, which made it feel easier. And eventually I found my rhythm of part-time therapy and full-time momming, which felt good.

But years later—after becoming a mom, navigating the end of my first marriage (to a Master Builder), and feeling the very real need to provide for myself and my child—the pressure increased. Real, practical survival fear has a way of taking us pretty quickly back to our most familiar patterns, so, I started to hustle, worry, and *do* a lot more. I poured myself into building my practice and *trying* to be more successful—writing newsletters, attending networking events, creating groups and classes and energetically trying to prove my value to myself and others, hoping to "make things happen." I regularly compared myself to others who seemed to be able to do it all and magnetize success with ease, while I was stuck grinding, overgiving, training to be a professional worrier, and secretly resenting how hard it felt. Yet, in spite of all of my work, I kept getting just enough clients and income to make it. I was exhausted and increasingly bitter.

I didn't show the classic Possibilitarian Guide bitterness on the outside—but I carried it in my energy. And that fatigue mixed with bitter, overproving energy? It repels aligned invitations. Which in hindsight, I'm very clear only made things harder. I was consistently attracting barely enough work because the truth was that I could only energetically handle that much opportunity. I was using most of my precious energy to worry and fill my time doing any busy entrepreneurial task that made me feel more worthy of success. And the headache of it all was that it just kept pushing the success I wanted further away. *Ugh.* My work with the clients I did have was magically fulfilling, yet I still felt like such a failure.

But life has creative ways of showing us what we need to see, and a powerful contrast became obvious when I opened myself up to dating. Unlike my relationship with my business, I didn't feel desperate or agenda-driven in this area of life. I loved being single but was entertaining the idea of inviting someone in to enhance my already fabulous social life. So, I went into it open, grounded, clear about my value, and wildly unattached. I had fun. I received more invitations than I anticipated—which was surprising considering I spent all of the years leading up to my first marriage feeling like a total wallflower! But this—it felt easy. That difference—between my thirsty energy in work and my effortless energy in dating—was significant. And I couldn't unsee it.

Fast-forward to more recently. My second marriage, again with a Builder Type, had been under stress for a long time. It started off great, but our paths began to diverge. We had done the work—gone to therapy, taken the workshops, read all sorts of books, and had countless hard conversations. But in the end, it became clear: His Sacral yes had faded, and I no longer felt recognized for who I was. Our minds wanted it to work, but our deeper knowing knew that the marriage we committed to was over. Not because either of us were bad or broken, but because our alignment, and the soul contract to grow each other, had run its course.

Fun fact: It has been through understanding deeper aspects of my Human Design that I have learned that a significant part of my purpose is to embody healthy, new paradigm relationships, to surrender and let things go when it's time, and to be a role model for really embodying what it means to heal our "relationship stuff." This insight totally shifted how I felt about being someone who has now navigated two divorces. None of it was a failure but an essential part of my purpose-full becoming and guidance I now get to offer others. My design offered a powerful reframe.

Okay, back to the story…

During these years of intense marital work, my professional work had slowed down. I realize now that my primary energetic job had been trying to hold my marriage together, and life knew that I didn't have an abundance of energy for much else. During the years of trying to make it work, and hold it together, I found myself getting sick more often, feeling deeply tired (which I later found out was acute Lyme disease), and I navigated various physical discomforts (spinal misalignments, muscle tension, etc.). These were all very physiological signs of my burnout… the burnout my mind didn't want to acknowledge. Given that my Possibilitarian Guide energy needs to be deeply resourced to attract the right invitations, it all makes sense. I didn't actually *have* the energy for the clients, work, and opportunity that my mind said I should be calling in. So, after years of pushing and holding, I paused. I let go. And I focused on recovering.

I took time to heal from the grief—and from the literal natural disaster that had flooded our entire community. Yes, it all happened in the same week that Hurricane Helene devastated Western North Carolina. Life doesn't mess around when it wants your attention—or wants you to master the art of letting go.

I stopped trying to force things—because I simply couldn't—and I surrendered in a way I never had before—a full swan dive into what I lovingly call "the God hammock." I focused on what was mine to do. I recommitted to the daily practice of only offering my energy where it was truly recognized and invited. I got extra "boundaried" about my need for rest and honoring my sensitivity. And I stopped *doing* just to fill the space or avoid discomfort.

And then—*only then*—the steadier flow of invitations started to arrive.

Some of my favorite clients reached out, asking to do deeper work. A massage therapist and chiropractor offered to trade their services for Human Design insights (exactly what my recovering body needed). A beautifully aligned workshop facilitation invitation for Laura and me came in through a friend. My inbox began to fill with aligned opportunities—personal and professional—that I hadn't gone searching for. The right invitations just started to arrive… without grasping, pushing, or trying to force things.

These weren't coincidences. They were the fruit of aligned energy. They were the natural result of living into the more empowered expression of my design.

And what's even more interesting is that none of those invitations came from other Possibilitarian Guides. They came from across the Leadership Type ecosystem we explore in this book. Because *that's* how this works: We each have a role to play. When we embody our unique magic, we attract the right collaborations—and *everyone* gets what they most need.

And that's pretty magically abundant.

Section 2: Introduction to "The Grind"

You've now reached the second phase of our journey together. You've been introduced to the unique Leadership Types and how they create a diverse ecosystem of gifts and energy to support collective thriving. You've hopefully reflected on your own Type and where you're aligned with it and where you've perhaps been taught to "perform" as a different Type. Now it's time to look at the cultural stories that get in the way of our being who we really are, leveraging our unique wisdom, and gifts. And seeing these stories more clearly helps us to *choose* different perspectives - ones that help us move beyond burnout, overwhelm, and normalized *meh*.

As humans, we absorb a *lot* from our environment. We learn what to believe. We learn how to define things like success, intelligence, goodness, and responsibility. And we inherit judgments about all sorts of things from pleasure and play to the stigma often associated with being different. The environment where we grow up and live has a powerful way of shaping our unconscious expectations, beliefs, and perspectives—and more often than not, we have *no* idea that it's even happening, which leads us to unknowingly accepting it all as truth without any questioning.

These unconscious stories and beliefs are often in
direct opposition to the quality of life and
relationships we say we want.

Weeeeeell, we are both professional question askers. We love to ask, "But, why?" And at our core, we are heart-centered rebels who are willing to challenge the way things are in order to explore the truth and possibility that lives beyond our default perspectives. These stories—or *conditioning* as we refer to it—are often hiding in plain sight. When we learn to spot these influences and see them for what they are (mostly made-up stories), we gain choice. And we've learned that living from a place of conscious choice instead of unconscious shoulds opens up all sorts of new potentials. Potentials that feel like flow, ease, fulfillment, and... magic.

So, if you're ready to join us on the path of questioning and maybe even a little heart-centered rebellion, then let's look at some of the main stories that keep us separated from our inherent wisdom, from our well-being, and from each other.

Note: Before we dive in, we also want to name something important. We are two cisgendered white women moving through these cultural stories with a significant amount of unearned privilege. While these narratives have absolutely shaped and impacted us, we also recognize that the ways they show up—and the harm they've caused—are not equally distributed. We are not positioning ourselves as experts on every lived experience, and we're not here to speak on behalf of those whose identities, bodies, or histories have been more systemically targeted and marginalized by these patterns. What we are committed to is doing our own ongoing work to recognize and question our blind spots, to listen and learn from voices beyond our own, and to challenge the parts of these stories that have kept any of us—especially those with less access to safety and power—from fully thriving. We share this chapter with humility, not as a final word, but as an invitation into deeper awareness and collective liberation.

UGH, THE GRIND

We know that learning to identify the conditioning that is limiting us can feel overwhelming, so we've created a framework to help you spot it more easily. Plus, who doesn't love an acronym?! Each letter of GRIND represents a story that, if you're living in an industrialized capitalistic country, you have inevitably been exposed to (unless you're living in a monastery, making a life exploring the vast wilderness, or are completely unplugged and off the grid).

The GRIND represents the conglomeration of stories that fuel disconnection from ourselves and each other.

The GRIND represents the beliefs we inherit about hustling for our value, having to do it all on our own, and suffering as a source of pride.

The GRIND teaches us to settle, betraying our own needs in order to perform and please others.

And *all* of that leads to guess what??? B-U-R-N-O-U-T! (Along with overwhelm, underwhelm, and a life that feels heavy or like it's just chronically missing something.)

So, let's cozy up, get brave, and look our learned limitations right in the eye.

CHAPTER 9
G—GREED: MONEY, CAPITALISM, AND VALUE, OH, MY!

"Don't get so busy making a living that you forget to make a life."
—Dolly Parton

The first stop on this leg of our journey together requires that we have a little chat about capitalism. The Oxford dictionary defines capitalism as an economic and political system in which a country's trade and industry are controlled by private owners for profit. Capitalism, therefore, defines success as profit, not necessarily well-being. In capitalist societies, money is rarely just about money. It is deeply entangled with self-worth, security, power, and survival.

From the Industrial Revolution to the present, money has not only been positioned as a symbol of individual success but has also become associated with moral character. Depending on the environment we grow up in, we inherit money stories—about having a lot of money as a bad thing and feeling morally superior by suffering, striving, and doing without *or* about financial hardship being an indicator of failure, all contributing to learning to associate one's value with how many zeros make up their bottom line. Regardless of the money story you inherited from your upbringing, the dominant cultural story you're swimming in, especially if you're reading this book that was purchased on the internet or in a store, is that of capitalism.

Present day capitalism thrives on a scarcity mindset, perpetuating the belief that resources (money, opportunities, power) are finite and must be earned through relentless hard work and competition. Capitalism teaches us that more is always better because there could never possibly be enough. *You* could never possibly be enough. (See how it translates?) And given that we've spent decades supporting individuals in all sorts of healing and personal growth work, we also know that one of the major core wounds that fuels pain is feeling like one is inherently not enough. Capitalism is fueled on this core tenderness of not enough-ness.

Scarcity mindset, and the resulting belief that there's never enough, and therefore *we're* never enough, reinforces the hustle culture we see so normalized and celebrated—long days, late nights, and prideful workaholism that de-prioritizes leisure, connection, and well-being. We get gold stars for spreading ourselves thin, being tired from working so hard, and suffering to get that raise, close that deal, and push toward that promotion.

Scarcity mindset is essentially a concocted story—meaning, there *are* actually enough resources in the world to feed, house, and clothe everyone, *but* (and this is a big ol' *but*), there are very real limitations in *access* to resources. If you are not a white, cisgendered, heterosexual male from a formally educated middle to upper class family… well, there are very real reasons why you've felt like you had to work harder, hustle more, and really prove your worth to make it.

You have.

If you haven't heard the phrase "systems of oppression" before, you can think of it in terms of the *isms*—racism, sexism, classism, ableism, and colonialism (along with any other framework that is inherently exclusive based on some aspect of one's identity). Capitalism on its own is actually somewhat neutral, believe it or not. It's just a system of exchange. However, the key here is that present day capitalism is shaped by the *systems and values* of our culture, and sadly our dominant cultural values are rooted in *systems* of *oppression*, which makes it... oppressive. Cultural values like hierarchy (climbing ladders), competition (winning and being the best), prideful independence (doing it all on our own), and pressure to conform to be safe and successful (cultural homogenization) are all values that feed and support the isms far more than they support any sort of collective thriving.

Capitalism as we know it reinforces a culture in which the wealth gap continues to widen, leaving many struggling to survive while the wealthy accumulate and horde resources unchecked. The sneakiest part of it all is that in this framework, the structural inequities are often "invisibilized," and individuals are held personally responsible for their economic circumstances without acknowledgment of the very real systemic obstacles they face (the whole bootstrap mentality that's been normalized feeds this shame-inducing set of expectations). And, if we haven't made it clear already in this chapter, all of us do *not* have the same ability to bootstrap our way to success in this ism-flavored culture.

In this system that equates financial accumulation with one's inherent goodness and value, those who do not "succeed" within this framework are often judged as lazy, undeserving, or somehow morally lacking. And these judgments are often internalized. We unconsciously create our own personal voice of judgment to remind us how insufficient we are, how we'd be better if we just worked harder, and how we might dodge the pain of failure if we just suffer a bit longer. *Ugh.* And as if those external influences weren't enough, we often learn very early to blame and shame ourselves at expert levels, making it feel impossible to escape the pressure to abandon our true needs in search of the "moreness" that we fantasize about making us feel complete.

In addition to the conditioning we inherit from family and the dominant culture, we also absorb it from the media—things like social media, television, movies, and advertisements. Many of us have a deeply enmeshed relationship with the screens of our world. We carry little baby computers in our pockets, we see thousands of people every time we open Instagram or Facebook, and with so much of life being virtual these days, we're exposed to the most carefully curated versions of people. (I mean we don't even know if Jordan on that Zoom meeting is wearing pants!)

Consumerism, fueled by capitalism, naturally promotes these strategically curated images of "successful living." Social media platforms amplify these ideals, encouraging comparison and inadequacy as individuals measure themselves against aspirational lifestyles that are often unattainable. The constant exposure to luxury and wealth in TV shows and movies reinforces feelings of scarcity and unworthiness, making it difficult for individuals to trust their inherent value or access a sense of financial sufficiency.

Understanding the cultural and systemic roots of money stuff is essential for deconditioning these narratives. By recognizing how capitalist conditioning has shaped your beliefs about money, you can begin to disentangle your self-worth from your financial status.

> Thriving, rather than merely surviving, requires dismantling the scarcity mindset, thought by thought and belief by belief, challenging cultural conditioning, and embracing a more expansive and humanized vision of prosperity, one that is rooted in alignment and inherent value.

Chapter Reflections: Deconditioning Greed, Scarcity, and Capitalism's Hustle Narrative

How does the idea of "never enough" show up in your life?
- Is it about money, time, energy, opportunities, love, success, or something else?
- Do you ever feel like no matter what you do, it's not quite enough?

If capitalism wasn't shaping your decisions, how would your life look different?
- Would you work the same job? Live the same lifestyle? Spend your time differently?
- Would you give yourself more space to rest, play, or create without expectation?

Have you ever glorified overwork or equated exhaustion with success?
- Have you worn burnout like a badge of honor?
- Do you feel guilty when you rest, relax, or step away from productivity?

Do you believe that financial success is a direct reflection of someone's worth or effort?
- How does that belief impact how you see yourself and others?
- Have you ever judged yourself (or someone else) for their financial situation?

What does true prosperity mean to you?
- If you were to define prosperity in a way that felt expansive, nourishing, and fully aligned—what would it include?
- How does that version of prosperity differ from what capitalism has conditioned you to believe?

Chapter Reflections for Each Leadership Type

Innovating Catalyst (Manifestors by Design)
- Reflect on how your natural drive to initiate and create has been influenced by societal pressure to go big or go home. Where have you felt the need to prove your value by overachieving or overdoing?
- Ask yourself: What does *enough* feel like in my body? How can I define success on my terms without the need for external validation or excessive accumulation?
- Practice informing others about boundaries you set to protect your energy and creativity from the hustle culture's constant demands.

Master Builders (Generators by Design)
- Consider where your energy has been used to chase external definitions of success, rather than to pursue what truly lights you up. Where have you felt trapped in doing for doing's sake?
- Ask yourself: How does satisfaction feel when it's free from monetary or societal expectations? What would my life look like if I only said yes to the work and activities that excite me?
- Practice checking in with your Sacral response when making decisions about your goals. Let your gut yes guide you toward aligned sufficiency rather than endless striving.

Accelerated Builders (Manifesting Generators by Design)
- Reflect on the ways you might have absorbed the more-is-better conditioning. Where have you taken on too much, confusing productivity with worthiness?

- Ask yourself: How can I embrace my multi-passionate nature without feeling the need to monetize every skill or passion? What does true abundance feel like in my diverse pursuits?
- Practice slowing down to ensure that each yes aligns with your authentic excitement and not just a reaction to societal pressure to do it all.

Possibilitarian Guides (Projectors by Design)
- Examine where you may have internalized the belief that your worth comes from how hard you work or how much money you produce. How have you felt the pressure to keep up with the hustle culture?
- Ask yourself: How can I shift my focus from doing to being? What does it look like to trust that my unique guidance and insights are inherently valuable, even if they don't result in immediate financial gain?
- Practice resting and waiting for the right invitations, knowing that slowing down is a powerful rebellion against scarcity mindset and a step toward sustainable prosperity.

Reflective Evaluators (Reflectors by Design)
- Reflect on how the environments and communities you frequent have shaped your beliefs about money, success, and value. Are you absorbing scarcity and hustle energy from those around you?
- Ask yourself: What environments allow me to feel abundant, secure, and expansive? How can I intentionally step away from spaces that reinforce scarcity or comparison?
- Practice regular emotional and energetic detoxes to release any conditioned beliefs about money and worth that don't belong to you.

CHAPTER 10
R—RIGIDITY: THE LIMITS OF THE LINEAR LIFE

"Blessed are the flexible, for they shall not be bent out of shape."
—*Anonymous*

It's time to discuss the aspirational fantasy of the "linear life"—this neat and tidy expectation we've been sold about what success is supposed to look like and how we're meant to move toward it. You know the one: Graduate from school, get a job, work hard, climb the ladder, retire gracefully, and live happily ever after. But let's be real: This story, baked into Western culture and reinforced through everything from workplace policies to social media feeds, is not just outdated—it's often a suffocating trap!

Here's the deal:

The linear life narrative defines success as predictable, incremental progress. It insists that sticking to the plan is virtuous and that deviation—whether that's quitting, pivoting, or even pausing to rest and recalibrate—is failure.

This rigid set of expectations limits creativity, fuels burnout, and stifles the kind of aligned, authentic living that actually leads to thriving. And just like capitalism fuels our cultural wounds around money and scarcity, the myth of the linear life encourages us to betray ourselves—our well-being, our joy, our passion—to stay the damn course no matter what.

Does somebody smell something burning? Oh, yeah, it's another one of the major sources of burnout!!

But where did it come from, you ask?

To understand how this cultural myth became so deeply ingrained and calcified as truth, we need to rewind to the Industrial Revolution. Back in the late 18th and early 19th centuries, society shifted from a more fluid, agrarian way of life to a factory-driven economy where productivity reigned supreme. People weren't just farmers or artisans anymore—they were laborers, clocking in and out, adhering to rigid schedules, and repeating the same tasks over and over. Predictability and consistency were rewarded, but innovation and individuality? Not so much.

This industrial mindset didn't just reshape how we worked—it reshaped how we lived. The idea of the career ladder emerged as a way to measure progress and success. Work hard, climb the rungs, and you'll achieve security, respect, and a sense of worth. But here's the thing: This narrative isn't actually about your well-being. It's about ensuring you stay productive and profitable—to the system, not necessarily to yourself.

By the post-WWII era, this linear path was further cemented as the gold standard for success. Economic recovery efforts glorified stability: steady jobs, long-term commitments, and homeownership. Corporate America turned the career ladder into a cultural ideal, and stepping off this path—whether through quitting, pivoting, or taking a sabbatical—became synonymous with irresponsibility or failure. Add to that the Protestant work ethic, which tied moral virtue to relentless effort, and you've got a recipe for generations of people hustling themselves into exhaustion, all in the name of "success."

The linear life may look like a straightforward climb, but underneath it is a tangled web of unspoken rules and beliefs that keep us trapped in hustle and shame. Let's unpack a few.

Success = Progress

The linear life narrative tells us that success means moving forward—always. If you're not advancing in your career, earning more money, or hitting the next milestone, you're failing. Simple as that. If you aren't productive and climbing, well… you're failing. This ignores the reality that growth is often cyclical, nonlinear, and deeply personal. Oh, and it doesn't take into consideration that you have a whole life outside of your career that might require your attention from time to time.

Quitting = Failure

Winners never quit, right? Wrong. The cultural shame around quitting convinces us to stay on paths that are misaligned, exhausting, or outright harmful because we fear being labeled as weak or incapable.

Suffering Is Virtuous

Hustle culture glorifies overwork and burnout as badges of honor. We're taught to equate our worth with how much we can endure, spreading ourselves thin in the name of productivity and progress.

One-Size-Fits-All

The ladder doesn't just ignore individuality—it actively resists it. The narrative assumes everyone should follow the same path, leaving no room for creativity, play, diversity, or exploration.

Here's the good-bad news:

> Life is *not* a straight line. It *is* something to be explored, *not* rigidly controlled.

We know this because we tried the linear life, we attempted to control our success, and we found that life had other plans…, *and* we're grateful that life won out and was more stubborn than our willful egos, because we sure wouldn't be writing this book if we had stayed on the professional paths that we started decades ago. When we rigidly set our expectations for ourselves and others based on this conditioning, we lose out on the richness of what it means to be an ever-evolving, growing, creative human. We miss out on the magical, inspiring adventure of life when we try to force it.

Rigidity limits creativity. And we are inherently creative beings, not cogs in a machine!

The linear life prioritizes predictability over possibility. It tells us to stick to the script, even when the script doesn't feel right. Creativity thrives in experimentation, risk, and play—things our rigid conditioning actively discourages.

By glorifying relentless progress, the linear life also sets an impossible standard. It pushes us to keep climbing, no matter the cost. The result? A culture where burnout is the norm and well-being takes a backseat.

The linear life promises security: Follow the rules, and everything will work out. But life is inherently unpredictable. Clinging to the illusion of a "safe" path can leave us unprepared to navigate uncertainty.

The linear life may promise predictability, progress, and security, but it comes at the cost of creativity, authenticity, and well-being. By breaking free from the rigidity of this narrative, we open ourselves up to the freedom of fluidity. We become supple with life—like the vine that naturally knows to grow over the fallen log. We stop fighting everything, including ourselves, and we find our way forward.

Life isn't meant to be a straight climb—it's an ever-evolving, beautifully messy adventure.

Chapter Reflections: Breaking Free from the Limits of the Linear Life

Success = Progress

Where in your life do you equate steady upward progress with your worth, and how would redefining success in a way that prioritizes well-being, creativity, flexibility, and authenticity change the way you move through the world?

Quitting = Failure

Think of a time when you stayed in a situation (a job, a relationship, a path) because quitting felt like failure—what did that choice cost you, and what would it look like to give yourself permission to walk away when something is no longer aligned?

Suffering Is Virtuous

Where in your life have you been rewarded—whether with praise, validation, or success—for pushing through exhaustion, ignoring your authentic needs, or sacrificing your well-being in the name of achievement? What would it look like to pursue success without using suffering as the currency to earn it?

One-Size-Fits-All

Where in your life have you forced yourself to follow the plan because it was expected of you, and if you had been free to choose without that pressure, what path might you have taken instead?

The Freedom of Fluidity

If you fully embraced the truth that life is an evolving adventure rather than a straight climb, what would you allow yourself to explore, pivot, or change… without guilt?

Reflections for Each Human Design Type: Breaking Free from Rigidity and the Linear Life Narrative

Innovating Catalysts (Manifestors by Design)

- Reflect on where you've felt pressured to follow a prescribed plan or stick to societal expectations of success. How has this rigidity stifled your ability to initiate and innovate freely?
- Ask yourself: What does true freedom look like for me, and how can I give myself permission to deviate from the plan when inspiration strikes?
- Practice embracing your role as a trailblazer by initiating bold, unconventional moves that align with your energy—even if they challenge traditional expectations.

Master Builders (Generators by Design)

- Consider how the narrative of constant progress has influenced your work and life. Where have you felt trapped in the cycle of doing, even when it no longer feels satisfying or aligned?
- Ask yourself: What does it feel like to trust the natural ebb and flow of my energy instead of pushing toward an imagined finish line?
- Practice listening to your sacral response as your guide to when to persist, when to rest, and when to pivot, trusting that fulfillment comes from alignment, not linear achievement.

Accelerated Builders (Manifesting Generators by Design)

- Reflect on how the one-size-fits-all ladder has limited your ability to explore your diverse passions and interests. Where have you felt pressured to choose one path and stick to it?

- Ask yourself: How can I honor my unique, multifaceted nature by creating a dynamic, nonlinear approach to my life and success?
- Practice giving yourself permission to pivot and play with multiple directions, knowing that your energy thrives on flexibility and adaptability.

Possibilitarian Guides (Projectors by Design)
- Examine how the linear life narrative has conditioned you to measure your worth by steady productivity or progress. Where have you felt the need to overextend yourself to fit into this framework?
- Ask yourself: What does success feel like when it's based on my insights, unique guidance, and authentic well-being rather than climbing a predefined ladder or achieving external metrics?
- Practice honoring your need for rest, reflection, and waiting for the right invitations, trusting that your success comes from living your unique design, not from forcing forward motion.

Reflective Evaluators (Reflectors by Design)
- Reflect on how the environments and people around you have shaped your beliefs about what success should look like. Are you absorbing rigidity and hustle from others?
- Ask yourself: What would it feel like to live in alignment with the natural cycles of life and my own evolving clarity, rather than chasing linear progress and the need to know now?
- Practice creating spaciousness to explore and adapt, allowing your path to unfold organically rather than adhering to external timelines or expectations.

By aligning with the wisdom of your Human Design Leadership Type, you can dismantle the rigidity of the linear life and embrace the freedom of fluidity. Life isn't meant to be controlled or forced—

it's meant to be cocreated. As you navigate this chapter, give yourself permission to grow over the fallen logs of life, trusting that your unique journey is more fulfilling than any beige societal script could ever promise.

Chapter 11
I—Isolation: Competition, Hierarchy, and the Individualization of Success

> *"Alone, we can do so little; together, we can do so much."*
> —Helen Keller

Let's start this chapter with a little check in:

How many gold stars have you earned from doing it all yourself?

How many affirming pats on the back have you gotten from winning or doing better than someone else?

How much pressure and expectation do you put on yourself daily to figure things out on your own or just do everything yourself?

The thing is, we all get some version of conditioning around prideful independence, hierarchy, and competition. We live in a culture that focuses on being the best and on climbing ladders of status, money, or reputation so that we'll be valued, successful, and respected.

Western culture has long celebrated competition and hierarchy as *the* path toward progress and success. This story—rooted in capitalist ideologies and the core values of systems of oppression (nod to the isms again)—tells us that power, value, and opportunity are concentrated in the hands of the privileged few at the top, and the only way to prove our worth and join their fancy exclusive club is to climb harder, outpace, and outperform. The bottom line is that this narrative isolates us. It builds walls of disconnection and mistrust, convincing us that we're alone in our journey toward success. It discourages us from recognizing the interconnectedness—the fundamental *interdependence*—that is essential to true thriving, not just as individuals but as communities, organizations, and humanity at large.

The American Dream narrative compounds this isolation, glorifying the lone hero who pulls themselves up by their bootstraps, climbs societal ladders, and reaches the top through sheer, individual grit. Success is framed as an individual achievement, not a communal effort.

> This cultural myth dismisses, and even judges, collaboration and support, leaving people to navigate life alone, disconnected from the strength of collective wisdom, and the very real human abundance found when a diversity of strengths, gifts, and perspectives are celebrated and shared.

The pressure to win at life is relentless—and loud. In a culture driven by competition and external validation, many people trade the quality of their health, relationships, and true passions for the next gold star or affirming pat on the back. But here's the thing: If you ask most people what truly brings them happiness and fulfillment, their answers don't center around another promotion or checking off yet another goal. Instead, they long for richer connections, more time with the people they love, and a life filled with fun, laughter, ease, and adventure.

We're conditioned to believe that happiness is just on the other side of achievement, but how often do we reach that milestone only to feel… underwhelmed? Depleted? Maybe even lonelier than before? This is the cycle of pressurized, externalized seeking—a hallmark of dopamine culture, which we'll explore in more depth later. It's a cultural narrative and neurological system that promises reward but actually can deplete our capacity to feel genuine pleasure and fulfillment over time. What's worse, it drains our authentic motivation and the vitality we need to pursue what really matters: meaning, connection, and joy. We deserve better than chasing a happiness that's always just out of reach. True fulfillment starts by turning inward, asking what we value most, and redefining success on our own terms.

So, if we're all swimming in that "story soup" of isolating and competitive hustle, it's no wonder most of us kinda suck at asking for help. It's no wonder many of us hop on the hustle hamster wheel and struggle to find a way off. It makes sense that anxiety, depression, and burnout are so widespread.

And here's a bit of science to confirm it all.

> This fiercely individualistic approach is fundamentally at odds with how our brains and nervous systems are wired.

As humans, we are biologically and neurologically designed for connection. Our ventral vagus nerve, a key player in the parasympathetic nervous system, activates feelings of safety, trust, and connection when we collaborate and cocreate. On the other hand, feelings of isolation—whether through competition or perceived disconnection—activate the fight-or-flight response, keeping us stuck in a state of hypervigilance, mistrust, and scarcity. And one of the most painful experiences to our nervous systems is the feeling of being deeply alone while being around people. Loneliness is different from actually being alone, and this conditioning often creates a confusing sense of loneliness, isolation, and emptyness that exists no matter how many people are around. This constant state of nervous system dysregulation can lead to burnout, anxiety, depression, and an often unrelenting sense of not enough. The unfortunate irony? The very systems we've built to "succeed" are the ones most likely to compromise our capacity to truly thrive.

Let's look to nature for some wisdom. Gentle reminder: We *are* nature, you know. The whole idea that we are separate from nature is just another conditioned story that's actually not true, but we'll unpack that one another day.

The thing is, nature doesn't adhere to a rigidly individualistic model of success. Ecosystems survive (and thrive!) because of collaboration and cocreation. Here are just a few examples of how the unique roles, shared gifts, and inherent abundance of the natural world supports collective well-being.

- The Mycelial Network

    Beneath the forest floor, fungal mycelial networks connect the roots of trees and plants, enabling them to share nutrients, water, and information. Older, more established trees will send nutrients to younger, struggling saplings, and plants under attack by pests can send chemical signals through the network to warn their neighbors. This interconnected system supports the health and resilience of the entire forest ecosystem.

- Pollination Partnerships

    Bees, butterflies, bats, and other pollinators collaborate with plants by transferring pollen as they collect nectar. This exchange supports the reproduction of flowering plants, which in turn provide food, shelter, and oxygen benefiting countless other species, including humans.

- Ant Colonies

    Ants work collectively to build nests, gather food, and defend their colonies. They communicate through pheromones, creating efficient systems where each ant's role contributes to the survival and thriving of the whole colony. One ant can't do a ton, but the colony can move mountains!

These natural systems demonstrate that thriving is not a solo act; it's an intuitive dance of mutual support, shared resources, and collective resilience.

Reflections: Identifying Personal Conditioning Around Isolation and Fierce Independence

The Lone Wolf Mentality

Where in your life have you equated doing things alone with strength, success, or self-worth? What might shift if you saw receiving support as a sign of strength and wisdom rather than weakness?

Competition Versus Collaboration

How has competition shaped your view of success? Where have you measured your worth by how well you outperform others? What possibilities might open up if you prioritized cocreation and shared success instead?

The Gold Stars of Overfunctioning

Where have you resisted asking for help because you felt like you *should* be able to handle it all yourself? How much of your exhaustion, stress, or overwhelm might be relieved by asking for help or allowing yourself to be supported?

The Disconnection Loop

Have you ever felt deeply *alone*—even while surrounded by people? What conditioned beliefs about self-sufficiency, hierarchy, or proving your worth might be keeping you from feeling connected and supported?

Redefining Success Through Connection

What would success look like if it wasn't about status, productivity, or being the best—but about the depth of your relationships, the joy of mutual support, and the richness of shared experience? How would you measure success differently?

REFLECTIONS FOR EACH LEADERSHIP TYPE: EMBRACING YOUR UNIQUE ROLE IN THE ECOSYSTEM

This journey into collaboration, cocreation, and interdependence invites each of us to honor our unique contribution to the collective. The myth of competition and hierarchy often makes us feel like we must be all of the Types, juggling roles we're not designed for in a relentless pursuit of worth and success—which inevitably leads to overwhelm and burnout. But the true magic of thriving ecosystems, both in nature and in Human Design, lies in trusting that every role is valuable and essential.

TYPE-SPECIFIC REFLECTIONS: ISOLATION, COMPETITION, AND FIERCE INDEPENDENCE

INNOVATING CATALYST (MANIFESTOR)

Reflection

Have you ever felt like you had to *protect* your independence by pushing forward alone? Have past experiences of resistance or misunderstanding made you hesitant to *invite others in* before taking action?

Invitation

Your energy is here to *initiate*, but that doesn't mean you have to go it alone. What might shift if you allowed yourself to *inform* the right people before making bold moves? Who are the trusted allies who could amplify your impact?

Practice

Before your next big decision or action, pause and identify someone you trust who might offer valuable insight or support. Inform them about what you're working on—not because you *need* their permission, but because shared vision can strengthen momentum.

Master Builder (Generator)

Reflection

Have you ever taken on work or responsibilities *alone* because you felt like asking for help would slow you down? Have you resisted collaboration because you feared it might dilute your efficiency or mastery?

Invitation

True mastery isn't about proving you can do everything yourself—it's about investing your energy in what *truly* lights you up while allowing others to support the process. How might embracing collaboration actually *enhance* your satisfaction rather than diminish it?

Practice

Next time you feel the impulse to push through alone, pause and check in with your Sacral response. Instead of defaulting to "I'll just do it myself," ask yourself: *Is this really mine to do?* If not, practice delegating or inviting someone to cocreate.

Accelerated Builder (Manifesting Generator)

Reflection

Do you find yourself moving so quickly that you avoid slowing down to ask for support? Have you ever turned down collaboration because it felt like it would get in the way of your efficiency?

Invitation

Your gift isn't just speed—it's adaptability and innovation. Imagine what might be possible if you allowed others to help refine and streamline your vision rather than always being the one to figure it all out. Where in your life could a collaborative shortcut actually serve you?

Practice

The next time you feel resistance to asking for help, pause and inform the people around you of what you're working on. Notice how sharing your process invites new insights, efficiencies, or unexpected support.

Possibilitarian Guide (Projector)

Reflection

Have you ever felt isolated because you *see* so much but don't always feel invited to share your insights? Have you withdrawn when your wisdom wasn't recognized, rather than seeking spaces where your guidance is truly valued?

Invitation

Your wisdom is meant to be *received*, not forced. What if success wasn't about proving yourself through doing, but about finding environments where your perspective is *deeply valued?* What relationships or communities already recognize your gifts?

Practice

Instead of trying to push guidance where it isn't welcomed, practice scanning your environment: *Where am I already seen and valued?* Invest your energy in *those* spaces and notice how much more fulfilling your contributions feel.

REFLECTIVE EVALUATOR (REFLECTOR)

Reflection

Do you ever feel like you're on the outside looking in, watching others chase success through competition and hustle while wondering if you're meant to follow the same path? Have you ever resisted asking for support because you felt like you *should* figure things out on your own?

Invitation

Your ability to reflect the world around you is a gift—but that doesn't mean you have to navigate life alone. What if your success wasn't about keeping up with the pace of the world, but about finding the right environments and relationships that *truly* support and nourish you?

Practice

Observe where you feel the most *seen and supported*—who truly values your insights without expectation? Lean into those spaces and give yourself permission to let go of environments or relationships that leave you feeling drained, unseen, or disconnected.

***

The myth of individualism and hierarchy has conditioned us to believe that we must be everything to succeed. But just as ecosystems thrive through the diverse contributions of trees, fungi, bees, and coral, our collective flourishes when each of us embraces our unique design.

Your Type is your gift, not a limitation. Trusting your role allows others to trust theirs, creating a ripple of collaboration, synergy, and interdependence. The health of the whole begins with each individual living fully into their design.

By leaning into your Type's unique strengths, you embody the wisdom of the ecosystem: that true progress—individually and collectively—arises not from competition or hierarchy but from celebrating the essential, cocreative role each of us is uniquely designed to play in the collective.

Chapter 12
N—Neglect: The Martyrdom of Success: Betraying Our Needs to Belong and Be Valued

*"When you say yes to others, make sure you
are not saying no to yourself."*
—Paulo Coelho

Somewhere along the way, many of us learned that to succeed, belong, or be worthy, we had to set our own needs aside. This conditioning has been so normalized, so baked into our culture, that we rarely stop to question it. Instead, we applaud self-sacrifice as a badge of honor and call it dedication, strength, or grit. But what's the cost of living a life where our authentic needs are consistently overridden, suppressed, and neglected?

The story of chronic betrayal of our authentic needs and well-being is deeply embedded in cultural conditioning, and nowhere is this more apparent than in the myth of "earning rest." For centuries, Western religious traditions glorified the martyr, elevating those who sacrificed their needs in service of others. While selflessness has its virtues, this narrative has been twisted into an expectation that worthiness is proven through suffering and relentless self-denial. The Industrial Revolution cemented this belief, shifting the societal gold standard to productivity above all else. People became valued not for their inherent humanity but for their ability to produce, work, and hustle—rest and well-being were reframed as indulgences reserved for the elite.

This mindset gave rise to the concept of retirement—the ultimate finish line where rest is finally "earned" after a lifetime of grinding. It perpetuated the idea that relief, ease, and well-being are luxuries, accessible only to those who endure decades of sacrifice. This elusive goal created a culture where suffering became a badge of honor and the only acceptable path to rest was through achieving enough to join the so-called elite. The myth of pulling yourself up by your bootstraps further compounded this story, suggesting that success is a solitary slog achieved through sheer willpower. Acknowledging personal needs became stigmatized as weakness, and seeking help was seen as an admission of failure. The result? A deeply entrenched belief that rest must be earned through suffering—a belief that keeps so many trapped in cycles of burnout and disconnection from their true selves.

For women, this conditioning is deeply rooted in both cultural expectations and biological realities, which can compound the confusion around healthy boundaries. Patriarchal gender roles have long socialized women to prioritize the needs of children, partners, and employers over their own, with cultural messages often labeling them "selfish" or "bitchy" if they dare to set boundaries or claim space for themselves. This conditioning is complicated by the biological truth that women are wired to nurture and protect, a survival mechanism ensuring the care of helpless babies and children. While this caregiving instinct is essential for human survival, patriarchal systems have exploited it, framing self-sacrifice as the ultimate measure of worthiness.

> Together, these cultural and biological influences have created a society that views neglecting one's own needs as not only normal but necessary for success, belonging, and purpose.

Our nervous systems are designed to alert us when our needs—physical, emotional, relational, or spiritual—are unmet. Chronic self-neglect pushes the nervous system into a state of dysregulation, resulting in experiences of:

- **Fight/Flight:** When we push through exhaustion, ignore our emotional pain, drink more coffee or wine, or overextend ourselves in pursuit of external validation, we stay in a heightened state of fight or flight. This can lead to anxiety, burnout, and a normalized sense of hypervigilance.
- **Freeze/Collapse:** Over time, the inability to meet our needs can lead to hopelessness, depression, and emotional numbness. We start to believe that advocating for our well-being is futile. The collapse response may also happen after months or years of living in the fight/flight and essentially exhausting the nervous system of any oomph.
- **Disconnection:** Chronic self-neglect also severs our overall connection to our bodies and intuition. When we ignore our needs, we lose touch with the natural and intuitive signals that guide us toward what's healthy and aligned. We struggle to hear the honest voices of our yeses and noes, and clarity about what we actually want and need can feel elusive.

The nervous system *wants* to feel safe, cared for, and resourced. But neglect creates a constant state of survival mode, leaving us depleted, reactive, and unable to show up authentically for ourselves, in our lives or in relationships.

When we chronically neglect our needs, the harm extends beyond ourselves and deeply impacts our relationships. Ignoring our needs while overgiving to others often breeds unspoken resentment; we feel undervalued or unseen, yet we've unintentionally trained those around us to expect our self-sacrifice. Suppressing our needs to fit in or gain approval also leads to inauthenticity, causing us to show up as a version of ourselves that isn't fully genuine. This prevents us from building trusting, reciprocal connections. Flimsy boundaries further complicate relationships, fostering codependency where we feel overly responsible for others and struggle to cultivate mutual respect. At the same time, neglecting our needs sends the message that we have no boundaries at all, creating imbalanced dynamics where our energy is depleted while others remain oblivious to our struggles. Together, these patterns erode the foundation of healthy, fulfilling relationships.

We cannot thrive—either as individuals or as a collective—when we neglect our needs.

> Thriving begins with reclaiming the truth that our well-being is not a barrier to success or belonging; it is the foundation of both.

Healthy boundaries, often misunderstood as selfish, are acts of self-respect and care. They allow us to show up authentically and sustainably, preserving our energy and alignment. Our needs are not inconveniences but internal guideposts, pointing us toward balance, fulfillment, and the life that aligns with our values. Thriving ecosystems remind us that interdependence is a strength, not a weakness. Mutual support and collaboration, rather than individual sacrifice, create the conditions for genuine flourishing.

Neglecting your needs does not lead to success, belonging, or purpose. Instead, it leads to burnout, disconnection, and a hollow sense of striving. The antidote to neglect isn't self-indulgence—it's self-honoring. By learning to set boundaries, meet your needs, and trust that you are inherently worthy without self-sacrifice, you not only thrive personally but also contribute to the thriving of the collective. When each of us reclaims our authenticity and well-being, we pave the way for a world where success is not built on self-betrayal but on mutual flourishing and aligned abundance.

The myth of self-sacrifice has conditioned us all to believe that neglecting our needs is virtuous, but the truth is that thriving begins with self-honoring. When we align with our Human Design Type and trust our authentic needs, we not only heal ourselves but also create a normalizing ripple effect of well-being and authenticity in our relationships and communities.

Reflections: The Martyrdom of Success

The Myth of Earning Rest

Where in your life have you learned or reinforced the belief that rest must be earned through exhaustion or suffering? How does this conditioning affect your experience of burnout, overwhelm, or exhaustion?

Self-Sacrifice Versus Self-Honoring

In what ways have you suppressed your needs in order to gain approval, belong, or be seen as successful? How often do your needs feel like an inconvenience rather than a sacred guide? What would need to change in your life or boundaries with others if you honored your needs as a fundamental part of your success and well-being?

Burnout as a Badge of Honor

When have you given yourself gold stars for pushing through exhaustion or overextending yourself to prove your dedication? Who in your life has celebrated your ability to push through? What would it look like to redefine success in a way that is unapologetically rooted in self-honoring, well-being, and ease?

The Cost of Self-Neglect on Relationships

How has neglecting your own needs impacted your relationships? When have you felt resentment, depletion, or frustration from overgiving? What new boundaries could support a more balanced, reciprocal dynamic in the relationships that are most central in your life?

Reclaiming Your Right to Thrive

If you fully trusted that your well-being was not a luxury but a necessity, how would you live differently? What daily practices would you implement to support your own thriving?

Reflections, Invitations, and Practices for Each Human Design Type

The journey of self-honoring requires unlearning the cultural and personal conditioning that tells us to neglect our needs in the name of success, belonging, or purpose. Each Human Design Type faces unique challenges in this deconditioning process, but all have the opportunity to reclaim boundaries, authentic needs, and their natural role in the ecosystem of thriving.

Innovating Catalysts (Manifestors by Design)

Reflection

Where have you felt pressure to constantly initiate, sustain momentum, or prove your impact rather than honoring your natural rhythm of rest and action? Have you neglected your need for solitude and spaciousness in order to be more available to others?

Invitation

Your power lies in initiating and sparking change—not in overextending yourself to sustain others. Trust that when you rest, recharge, and prioritize time alone, your creations are even more impactful.

Practice

Observe when you're pushing through fatigue instead of resting. Practice informing those around you of your energy needs and trust that creating space for yourself strengthens—not weakens— your leadership.

Master Builders (Generators by Design)

Reflection

Where have you overridden your gut response, saying yes to obligations or expectations rather than what truly lights you up? How has this led to frustration, depletion, or feeling taken for granted?

Invitation

Your energy is precious and powerful, but it isn't meant for everything. Trust that honoring your Sacral yes and saying no when needed supports both your well-being and the collective.

Practice

Before committing to a request or opportunity, pause and check in with your Sacral response. If it's not a full-bodied yes, practice trusting that your no is a service to yourself and those around you.

Accelerated Builders (Manifesting Generators by Design)

Reflection

Where have you ignored your need for dynamic variety and personal freedom in an attempt to fit into someone else's structure? Have you ever pushed yourself to stick with something long after it lost its inspiration?

Invitation

Your genius lies in your ability to pivot, refine, and move quickly. Trust that when you release what's misaligned, you create space for the projects and experiences that truly energize you.

Practice

Reflect on your commitments. What feels like an obligation rather than an opportunity? Practice giving yourself permission to let go of what no longer lights you up—without guilt.

POSSIBILITARIAN GUIDES (PROJECTORS BY DESIGN)

Reflection

Where have you overworked in an attempt to prove your worth, taking on responsibilities that drain you, rather than waiting for aligned invitations? How has this impacted your ability to rest and restore your energy?

Invitation

Your wisdom and insight are your greatest contributions—not how much you do. Trust that aligning with recognition and waiting for the right invitations allows you to guide powerfully and sustainably.

Practice

Schedule daily rest and "non-doing" time. Observe where you're offering advice, leadership, or support without being invited, and practice pausing until you feel truly recognized and valued.

REFLECTIVE EVALUATORS (REFLECTORS BY DESIGN)

Reflection

Where have you taken on the emotions, expectations, or needs of those around you, neglecting your own energetic well-being? Have you stayed in environments that felt draining or misaligned because you felt obligated to adapt?

Invitation

Your clarity emerges in the right spaces. Trust that your need for change, fluidity, and aligned environments isn't a weakness—it's an essential part of your design.

Practice

Take an inventory of your physical, social, and emotional environments. Do they support your well-being, or do they leave you feeling exhausted? Practice making small shifts—changing scenery, taking solo time, or stepping back from dynamics that don't serve you.

Chapter 13
D—Disconnection: Top-Heavy Living Versus Fully Embodied Leadership

"When we reconnect with our body, we reconnect with the earth, the cosmos, and the flow of life itself."
—Thich Nhat Hanh

Modern Western culture is deeply rooted in "neck-up living"—a way of being that worships intellect, logic, and measurable outcomes, often at the expense of emotional intelligence, intuition, and embodied wisdom. And as we're tying a bow on introducing the GRIND framework, it's essential to realize that conditioning lives in the mind, and truth, alignment, and wisdom live in the *body*.

The mind (that we've been taught to follow blindly and at all costs) is basically being used most of the time as a "conditioning library," regurgitating conditioned stories, fears, shoulds, and limiting expectations. In worshipping the mind's capacity and diminishing things like intuition, felt knowing, and body cues, we've become terrible at honoring our inner compass and fabulous at devoting ourselves to stories that make us chronically feel like shit.

This narrow definition of intelligence disconnects us from our true inner compass and keeps us chasing achievements while feeling hollow, overwhelmed, or burned out. Embodied Leadership flips the script, inviting us to blend the mind's brilliance with the body's wisdom, the heart's truth, and the spirit's quiet knowing. It's an integrated way to live and lead—one that's rooted in authenticity, alignment, and holistic success.

To understand how we got to this top-heavy way of life, let's time-travel all the way back to the Enlightenment era (1685-1815), where thinkers like Descartes famously declared, "I think, therefore I am," effectively splitting the mind from the body and putting rationality on a very fancy pedestal. This worldview laid the foundation for disembodied thinking, where emotions and physical instincts were demoted to supporting roles at best, and more often unapologetically judged, denied, or dismissed altogether.

Fast-forward to the Industrial Revolution, and the cultural messaging got even more disembodied. Efficiency, standardization, and mechanization became the cultural North Stars, reducing human beings to replaceable cogs in productivity machines. Creativity, emotional depth, and individuality were pushed aside in favor of cognitive output—planning, analyzing, calculating. Success became synonymous with intellectual mastery and the ability to override the messy and inconvenient wisdom of the body. Because let's face it, if people had been listening to their bodies, they would have heard them screaming for rest, joy, and nourishment of all sorts, and that simply wouldn't have been great for the relentless productivity standards of the time.

By the 20th century, science and corporate culture had doubled down on this intellectual obsession. Success was measured in cold, hard numbers: profits, productivity, spreadsheets, performance reviews. Emotional intelligence and intuition were dismissed as soft, unreliable, and unworthy of serious consideration. Leadership, decision-making, and progress were confined to the top floors of the metaphorical high-rise—leaving the body and heart sad and lonely in the basement.

This top-heavy way of being comes at a significant cost. When we're taught to prioritize logic and linear thinking over our authentic inner signals, we disconnect from the very wisdom that keeps us healthy and whole. In education, standardized tests reward intellect over creativity and embodied learning, conditioning us to ignore our instincts in favor of "right" answers. Workplaces emphasize metrics above emotional intelligence, collaboration, and well-being. Healthcare systems often treat symptoms in isolation, ignoring the proven interplay between mind, body, and spirit, thereby perpetuating a culture of disconnection. This disembodied approach fosters chronic stress, overwhelm, and a deep sense of misalignment.

> We're conditioned to override our intuition and bodily experiences in pursuit of external validation or logical solutions, leaving us out of sync with ourselves and the world around us.

For marginalized communities, the impact is even greater. Systems built on disembodied thinking often ignore unique lived experiences, reducing people's humanity to universally applied data points or policies. Cultural expectations grounded in logic and sterile metrics not only disconnect us from our own bodies and inner wisdom but also from the diverse experiences and creative potential of others. Living from the neck up traps us in cycles of overthinking, analysis paralysis, suppression of needs, and burnout. It isolates us, eroding trust and relationships through logical decision-making devoid of emotional connection.

The shift from top-heavy living to whole-self leading is a courageous act of reclamation—a journey of deconditioning from cultural narratives that glorify logic and intellect at the expense of embodiment. It's about reconnecting with the body, honoring emotions, and trusting intuition, weaving these aspects into a wise and empowering partnership with the mind and spirit. Fully embodied leadership harmonizes the mind's brilliance with the body's grounded wisdom, the heart's truth, and the spirit's quiet creativity, fostering authenticity, alignment, and a sense of wholeness.

This integrated approach doesn't reject the intellect but transcends left-hemispheric dominance to create a balanced synergy that prioritizes well-being and purpose. Frameworks like Human Design illuminate the body's innate ability to guide us toward aligned decisions and sustainable success.

> When we lead from the whole self, thriving replaces burnout, and success becomes a holistic process rooted in harmony with ourselves and the world around us.

In this model, leadership is not a linear grind but an ongoing practice of authenticity, integration, and embodied harmony. It is a pathway to resilience, creativity, and a life and leadership style that is as purposeful as it is sustainable. By listening to the body's signals, the heart's wisdom, and the spirit's knowing, we reclaim a way of living and leading that is deeply aligned with who we are and the world we want to create.

REFLECTIONS ON DISCONNECTION: RECLAIMING THE BODY'S WISDOM

The Prioritization of Logic Over Embodied Knowing

Where in your life (or from whom) did you learn to trust logic over intuition, intellect over instinct, or external validation over inner wisdom? What decisions have you made based on what made the most sense rather than what actually felt aligned?

The Cost of Overriding the Body's Cues

Think about a time when your body gave you clear signals—fatigue, discomfort, a gut feeling, or just the "icks"—but you pushed through because it "made sense." What happened as a result?

The Trap of Overthinking and Analysis Paralysis

In what ways do you find yourself stuck in cycles of over-analyzing, researching, or mentally strategizing instead of taking embodied, aligned action? How does this tendency keep you disconnected from your true alignment and authentic path toward well-being and fulfillment?

Reclaiming the Body as an Inner Compass

What daily practices or small shifts could help you reconnect with your body's signals and wisdom? What would it feel like to trust your gut, emotions, and inner knowing as much as (or more than) logic and external expectations?

Type-Specific Guidance: Connecting to Embodied Wisdom by Human Design Type

One of the most pervasive traps of disconnection is making decisions from the mind's attachments and conditioned expectations rather than the body's wisdom. Each Human Design Type has a unique way of accessing clarity—yet cultural conditioning often overrides these natural processes, pushing us to force, hustle, or analyze our way forward instead of listening to the body's cues. Reclaiming your embodied decision-making is an act of self-trust, alignment, and leadership.

Innovating Catalysts (Manifestors by Design)

You are designed to initiate and create movement, but when you push forward based on external pressure, fear, or urgency instead of embodied clarity, you risk burnout, resistance, and misaligned action. Your power comes from clear, informed initiation—not forcing or reacting.

Reflection Prompts

- When have I made decisions from urgency or expectation rather than true inspiration?
- How does my body feel when I'm about to initiate from alignment versus pressure?
- What practices help me slow down and recognize genuine creative urges rather than reactive ones?

Master Builders (Generators by Design)

Your Sacral response is your compass, guiding you toward what lights you up and away from what drains you. Yet, disconnection happens when you override your gut instinct out of obligation, practicality, or fear of disappointing others. Learning to trust your Sacral's clear yes or no is key to reclaiming your authentic path.

Reflection Prompts

- What does a full body yes feel like in my system? How does my body say no?
- Where in my life am I ignoring my gut instincts because I feel obligated or afraid to say no?
- How would my day-to-day decisions change if I truly trusted my Sacral response?

Accelerated Builders (Manifesting Generators by Design)

You are built for speed, variety, and dynamic energy, but when you rush into commitments without checking in, overwhelm and misalignment can follow. Your Sacral response and ability to pivot are your strengths—but only when you allow space to discern before diving in.

Reflection Prompts
- How does my body communicate when I'm taking on too much too quickly?
- Where in my life am I saying yes just because I can, rather than because I should?
- What would it feel like to slow down just enough to make aligned choices instead of reactive ones?

POSSIBILITARIAN GUIDES (PROJECTORS BY DESIGN)

Your wisdom comes from seeing deeply and guiding others, but pushing yourself to keep up with other energy Types leads to depletion and resentment. Rest, recognition, and waiting for the right invitations allow you to use your insight without overexertion. Your body is not designed for constant output, so honoring its signals is essential.

Reflection Prompts
- Where am I pushing myself to keep up instead of trusting my natural rhythm and need for rest?
- How does my body tell me when I need rest, stillness, or recalibration?
- In what ways do I ignore my need for recognition and try to prove my worth through doing instead of guiding?

REFLECTIVE EVALUATORS (REFLECTORS BY DESIGN)

You are deeply attuned to the energy around you, and misalignment happens when you make decisions too quickly or ignore your need for time, space, and the right environment. Your clarity comes through cycles and reflection not instant answers or forced direction.

Reflection Prompts

- How do different environments affect my sense of clarity, well-being, and intuition?
- Where have I made decisions too quickly, only to later realize they weren't aligned?
- How can I create more space and patience in my decision-making process, honoring my natural rhythms?

By reconnecting with your natural decision-making strategy—instead of trying to force logic, speed, or certainty—you reclaim your true alignment, energy, and leadership. Your body already knows the way forward. The question is this: Are you willing to listen?

Chapter 14
Storytime: Living Through the Grind

Do you feel a story coming on?

Of course you do—because how could we just burn through the concept of GRIND without talking about our lived experiences?! We also couldn't name a client that either of us has worked with (ever!) where GRIND wasn't part of the pain, struggle, and story.

Throughout these chapters, we've been looking at how culture has created the perfect storm for burnout, especially when so many of us wake up every day and go to a job we don't love—or even like—for the sake of keeping up the status quo and paying the bills. The story of burnout here is, unfortunately, way too common.

But burnout doesn't just live in the land of family, cultural, or corporate self-sacrifice. We also find it embedded in the entrepreneurial journey, wrapped in a blanket of if-you-build-it-they-will-come mentality. We are shown examples throughout our lives of people who had a dream or talent and stuck with it through blood, sweat, and tears to finally make it. And while these efforts are honorable and the rewards well deserved, there's a shadow side to this story we don't often shed light on: The sacrifices these people made, and the sacrifices that were made for them. Not to mention, it's just one more way we're conditioned to climb toward the elusive 1 percent.

Hey y'all, Laura here...

In the fall of 2014, I was so tired that some days I couldn't even drive my car.

And yet, when night came? Sleep and I would have a wrestling match. I'd lie there for hours—half asleep, half awake. My mind racing. My body wired. Add in a few hot flashes, the urge to pee every other hour, and a mother's instinct that stayed half-awake listening for her kids, and let's just say my nights were anything but restful. And even when I *did* sleep, I woke up feeling hungover—like my brain was wrapped in gauze. Exhausted. Foggy. Fragile. My body had been whispering for a while, but at that point, it was screaming.

I couldn't focus. My thoughts slipped through me like water. My emotions seemed to flatline or come out in waves of anger and irritability. I'd look at my kids—these beautiful little humans—and feel a strange distance, like I was there, but not really *there*. I just pushed through the day, trying to keep my shit together, but not really engaging either. I was anxious. Depressed. Numb. Easily triggered. I didn't want to do anything. I just wanted to disappear into TV shows and the occasional weekend drink with friends—anything to escape the ache of misalignment humming beneath the surface.

And still, I didn't stop.

That's what so many of us Builders do. We keep going. We *know* how to push. It's what we're conditioned to do: keep producing, keep proving, keep moving. Rest? That felt indulgent. Dangerous, even. Like I'd disappear completely if I stopped.

So, I pushed.

That was the first time I was diagnosed with adrenal fatigue.

I didn't even know what that was—but the symptoms read like my own private journal. Chronic exhaustion. Mood swings. Overwhelm at the smallest things. The maddening combination of being too tired to move and too wired to rest. My body had forgotten how to exhale. It had been in fight or flight for so long, it didn't remember anything else.

And the part that gutted me? I had *burned out* doing something I loved, living my passion. Wasn't I living that entrepreneurial dream? The one we are told will end our burnout when we just leave that job or career or boss or relationship that is draining us?

Jewelry-making had always been my joy. My studio was my sanctuary. I loved the artistry, the challenge, the spark of creation. I had built something real—something I was proud of. And I made some of the best friends of my life (to this day). But somewhere along the way, it stopped feeling like art and started feeling like survival.

I was working constantly. Not just in the studio, but in my home, my relationships, my mind. I'd leave a full day of soldering, filing, packing orders—and walk straight into parenting, cooking, laundry, homework, cleaning, the emotional labor of holding everyone together. I never stopped. I never even *paused*.

It wasn't just the external demands—it was the internal ones. That unspoken belief that I had to earn my place. That my value was measured in productivity and performance. That if I could just get ahead—just make enough, do enough, be enough—I could finally exhale.

I didn't know how to ask for help. I didn't trust it. I thought carrying everything on my own was noble. Necessary. And maybe the only way to feel in control.

But what it really was… was lonely.

I stopped listening to my body. I stopped tending to my joy. I stopped checking in with what I *actually* wanted. I just kept showing up. Smile on. Head down. Heart closed. And when the exhaustion came, it wasn't just physical—it was spiritual.

I was creating work that looked beautiful but felt hollow. Traveling to shows, hustling nonstop, making just enough to cover costs. I'd spend thousands on materials and booth fees, all for the *chance* that someone *might* buy a few pieces. When they did, they often questioned the price—like my worth, or the worth of my labor, was up for debate.

This is the shadow side of creative entrepreneurship. Working yourself to the bone to be told you're overcharging, while silently wondering how you'll pay the rent. I had positive press. I had customers. I had visibility. On the outside, I looked like I was thriving. On the inside, I was falling apart.

And then came that moment—the one I shared with you earlier. Just an ordinary evening on the surface. A few friends. A few drinks. Me, laughing through tears and trying to hide the exhaustion that had taken up permanent residence in my bones. But underneath it, something cracked open.

But I can tell you this:

Burnout isn't failure. It's a signal. A moment of truth. A sacred reckoning that says: *You are not meant to live disconnected from yourself.* And the path toward healing isn't always dramatic. Sometimes, it looks like giving yourself permission to rest. To cry. To say no. To stop hustling for your worth and start listening to your soul. That's what I began to do in the months that followed. And the path didn't appear all at once. It unfolded, moment by moment. One breadcrumb at a time.

It's only in hindsight that I can see how far I'd drifted from myself. The pushing. The proving. The performing. The quiet ache of trying to be everything for everyone while slowly disappearing inside my own life. When I stopped trying to do it all, be it all, prove it all… when I stopped abandoning myself for the sake of being enough… when I remembered that I was never meant to do it alone… *that's* when something new could begin.

And yet, even in the unraveling, grace was there.

That night with my friends—the moment when I let the truth slip out between sips and laughter—that was the turning point. Not because everything changed at once, but because *I* changed. I told the truth. I surrendered the hustle. I let go of the version of success that was slowly breaking me. And in doing so, I made space for something else to find me. Not immediately. Not all at once. But slowly, like sunlight creeping in through a crack in the curtains. Because this is how it works for us Builders. We work. We pour. We create. Until one day we realize we've been building something that no longer fits the shape of our soul.

And when we stop—even for a moment—we give life the chance to meet us in the stillness.

That's where remembering begins.

So if you're there now—bone-tired, questioning everything, trying to hold it all together—I see you. I've been you.

And I want you to know this: It's okay to stop.

It's okay to fall apart.

It's okay to listen for the whisper beneath the noise.

It may not feel like much at first.

But it will be enough.

Meghan Here with a Little Story About Living Through... and Moving Beyond the Grind

Before we dive in, I want to offer you something real. What follows isn't a perfectly packaged before-and-after story. It's more like a series of lily pad hops across the messy, magical pond of my lived experience with the GRIND—those deeply conditioned stories we all swim in that shape how we see success, worth, rest, and belonging. I'm sharing pieces of my own path not because it's universal, but because so often, we can see ourselves more clearly in the mirror of someone else's story. My hope is that as I name some of the ways I've navigated these cultural and internal pressures—and the ways I've begun to rise above them—you'll feel less alone in your own journey. And maybe, just maybe, you'll recognize some of your own courageous truth in the process.

Growing up, I didn't have models for the kind of leader I was authentically meant to be. I was raised in what I now recognize as a Master Builder culture—strong, determined, relentlessly doing. My single mother was a powerhouse (and still is at seventy-five!): literally a bodybuilder and marathon runner, who painted the exterior of our house every few years by herself, handled all the house and yardwork, worked long hours as a middle school counselor, and ran a peer mediation business on the side. She got shit done! And she was always moving. Doing. Producing. Creating. And not resting very much.

In that environment, the unspoken mantra was this: "What have you done lately?"

I was a deeply sensitive, creative child—emotionally attuned, intuitive, and constantly picking up on the undercurrents no one said out loud. But that sort of intelligence didn't earn gold stars. So I learned to perform in the ways that did. I overrode my needs. I read the room and adjusted accordingly. I crushed school—straight As, teacher's pet, praised for my old soul maturity. But beneath the polished exterior, I was internalizing a story that being different meant being less than and that conforming was the path to belonging. I crafted the story that the deep rest I craved, the nonlinear, intuitive way I felt called to live, the intangible ways I offered value… simply weren't enough.

G—Greed and the Grind

Scarcity was not just a cultural story—it was lived reality. Money was tight growing up. My mom made it all work with resourcefulness, tight budgets, and grit, but even still, we went three summers without air-conditioning during a major heat wave and drought. I remember sleeping on the living room floor next to a box fan and regularly escaping to the neighbor's house to cool off in their delicious coolness, aware even at a young age of the gap between what we had and what others did. My basic needs were always taken care of, and I was never hungry, but I also never remember feeling a comfortable sense of sufficiency when it came to money.

That sense of not enough seeped in early and stuck around. As an adult, I felt constant pressure to generate—more income, more impact, more visibility. I judged myself for not doing enough and not making enough. The cultural conditioning was loud: Your worth is measured by your output and your bank account. And because my energy wasn't built for constant doing, I lived with a low-grade (and at times high-grade) sense of failure. I didn't yet know that I wasn't designed to keep up—I was designed to lead differently and define my worth in other ways.

R—Rigidity and the Linear Life

My path has never been linear—though I tried to force it into a straight line more times than I care to count. I studied Spanish and Latin American Studies in college (two degrees in four years—helloooo overachiever!) I had idealistic dreams of advocacy work that, as it turns out, didn't pay enough to live on, especially since I graduated during a challenging economic era. I found jobs doing office management—a role I was used to from jobs I held during summers in college—then got an opportunity to teach middle school Spanish. Yay, an opportunity to use my degrees! I thought I'd found my path, only to discover I cared far more about the emotional well-being of my students than the rigid (and boring) textbook curriculum I was expected to teach. That awareness—of the mental health support the kids needed—led me to become a therapist.

Over the years, I built a thriving practice, got trained in applied neuroscience and somatics, got Reiki certified, and explored other alternative approaches to healing (which I didn't share publicly), pursued an intensive leadership training program with the Co-Active Training Institute (CTI), and—after struggling to keep the nontraditional, more woo approaches to healing separate indefinitely—I ultimately released my therapy license to fully embrace the holistic toolbox I had created. I made the decision to release those fancy therapist letters after my name to step fully into sharing my authentic gifts. I've now created a life and business that's rich in meaning and aligned with who I really am.

But for years, I judged myself for every pivot. Culture told me that quitting meant failure. That staying the course—no matter how misaligned—was noble. I've had to unlearn that deeply entrenched story over and over (#surrendersoulschool). Two divorces, career reinventions, and countless evolutions later, I now see those "detours" for what they really were: my soul's curriculum in gracefully and compassionately surrendering the known and claiming my evolving truth.

I—Isolation and the Individualization of Success

I come from a family where independence is the ultimate virtue. The message growing up was clear: Be strong. Don't need. Do it yourself. So, I did. I became the expert in being "fine." But after my first divorce, that mask started to slip. I simply couldn't hold it together all of the time. I was deeply overwhelmed, and my closest friends felt so safe that my body naturally dropped the "fine mask," and truth just seeped out... without my consciously choosing it. I remember one moment when a friend came over for a visit. Just seeing her walk down the driveway toward my house brought tears to my eyes. I couldn't hold them back, so she hugged me while I sobbed and then... she *thanked* me—for trusting her enough to let her support me in that tender moment.

Wait. What?! That blew my mind.

It was through these moments, and so many since, that I've learned the sacredness of letting others in. Of allowing myself to receive. And not just personally—but professionally, too. I've learned that my energy thrives in collaboration. I see magic and possibility most clearly in the relational field. I am not here to go it alone. I never was.

N—Neglect and the Martyrdom of Success

Like so many of us, I inherited the belief that being strong meant not needing things. And as a highly sensitive person, I learned early that expressing those needs made others uncomfortable. So I pushed through—relationships, work, even illness. It's a weird thing to be highly sensitive and simultaneously skilled at ignoring certain types of discomfort. I ignored my fatigue, bypassed my intuition, and shamed myself for not being able to do more. It was so automatic; I didn't even realize I had a choice.

But I began to notice how often my body would rebel. Migraines. Skin issues. Bone-deep fatigue that I pushed through. My nervous system was waving a giant red flag, begging me to listen. And over time, I did. It wasn't easy. Every request for help felt terrifying at first. But I practiced. I let friends reflect my worthiness back to me. I learned to breathe through the fear. And I slowly began to rewrite the belief that neglecting my needs was noble. I saw how taking care of myself wasn't just okay—it was essential to my being able to move through life whole and serve from a sustainable, solid place.

D—Disconnection and the Wisdom of the Body

Getting trained in somatics changed everything for me. Truly. I finally had a map for the quiet, intuitive signals I'd always felt but didn't know how to trust. I began to see the mind for what it is—a storage space for conditioned stories and identities. But the body? The body was the thing that would call BS on me every time. The good-bad news I realized was that the body doesn't lie. It speaks unapologetic, unfiltered truth, and is above all an advocate for our highest good.

And when I started following its guidance—really following it—I saw the transformation unfold. I made brave choices that made no logical sense but felt deeply right. I ended relationships. I left professional identities. I followed the breadcrumb trail of resonance into unknown territory. And every single time, I landed somewhere more aligned, more purposeful, more magical, more *me*.

This is what it means to rise above the GRIND. Not by rejecting the human experience of being conditioned by these stories, but by meeting it with compassion, curiosity, awareness, and truth. Our conditioning is not our fault—but choosing new stories is our opportunity.

I am not here to be productive. I am here to be wise. I am not here to climb someone else's ladder. I am here to forge a new path. I am not here to be strong by denying my needs. I am here to lead from a place of wholeness.

There's nothing linear about this life I've built. It's full of pivots, pauses, and sometimes dramatic leaps of faith. But it's real. It's honest. And it's uniquely mine.

And for anyone reading this—if you've felt the weight of the hustle culture, the shame of not being enough, the fear of slowing down or changing course—I hope you know this: You're not broken. You're responding to a system that was never built for your thriving. But there *is* another way. And you already carry the wisdom within that will show you where to begin to craft *your* most authentically resonant life.

Chapter 15
Okay, So You See the Grind More Clearly... Now What?

First of all, remember that you are not stuck forever. You are just caught in a story that no longer fits.

If you've made it this far, take a breath. Seriously—pause for a moment and inhale deeply. Let it out. Unclench your jaw. Drop your shoulders.

You've just journeyed through an exploration of who you are designed to be and the conditioned stories that have shaped how you see yourself, your worth, and have influenced your approaches to pursuing success. You've uncovered the ways your natural leadership gifts have been tangled in narratives that keep you hustling, proving, pushing, and sacrificing. You've examined the cultural stories that insist you must climb harder, earn more, and do more to be valuable, to succeed... and to survive.

And now, you're standing at the edge of something new.

Up until now, we've been pulling back the curtain to reveal the sneaky patterns that fuel burnout—how capitalism, linear thinking, isolation, self-neglect, and disconnection have shaped your choices, your nervous system, and your sense of possibility.

> But insight alone doesn't change your life. It creates the doorway, but you still have to walk through it.

Now, we begin the process of choosing to move beyond insight so that you can fully embody your story and reclaim your spark, your purpose, and a life built on a solid foundation of sustainable well-being.

You Were Never the Problem—The System Was

The fact that you have struggled, burned out, hit walls, or felt unfulfilled does not mean you are flawed or failing. It means you were given a playbook that was never meant to honor your full-spectrum humanity. You were handed someone else's blueprint of success, belonging, and well-being and told, "This is the way."

But what happens when the way forward isn't a straight line?

What happens when your authentic success doesn't look like grinding up a corporate ladder?

What happens when your nervous system rejects hustle culture and craves something slower, more purposeful, and more sustainable?

What happens when you finally listen to the part of you that's been whispering (or maybe screaming by this point) for something different?

Well, we hope that you begin to listen more. And that you dare to courageously craft a new, more nourishing, approach to life.

Section 3: The Bridge from Grind to Prosper

If the GRIND framework helped you recognize the stories you inherited that keep you stuck—about worth, success, safety, and identity—then the PROSPER framework offers foundational pillars to help you reclaim authorship of your life. It helps you build the bridge from external conditioning to internal authority. From living the familiar stories you absorbed… to living the stories you actually *choose*.

Where GRIND illuminated how the world around you has shaped your nervous system and sense of self, PROSPER offers a way to rewrite those patterns from the inside out. It's not just about naming what's holding you back—it's about learning to actually live into different stories.

Many of us spend a lot of energy focusing on what's *not* working, what we *don't* want, and where we haven't succeeded, but we realized that there's often not enough talk about what to move *toward*. Focusing on what's not working doesn't magically create something that does.

That's where PROSPER comes in.

PROSPER is the how. How to discover what you actually want, how to open to more possibility, and how to move toward a story that fits you better. It's a practical framework that helps you close the gap between what you want and what you actually do. It gives you the tools to meet resistance with compassion, to shift patterns that are keeping you stuck, and to align your body, brain, and energy with the future you *want* to create (not just the reality you're most familiar with).

PROSPER isn't an answer. It's a process.

It's a recalibration practice.

It's a road map of discovery guiding you toward *your* unique path to whole-life prosperity.

It's where leadership gets redefined, where purpose meets self-trust, and where you stop trying to force your life to fit into a conditioned mold—and instead create the capacity to build a life that actually fits you.

> Because here's the good-bad news: Getting unstuck and living your true purpose isn't just a cool concept, it's a new way of being.

And it starts by choosing the new way—again and again—in your body, your thoughts, and your daily choices. It's about weaving "the new way" throughout your life and teaching your whole self that it's actually safe to embrace it.

When you are living your design, you don't force or chase. You respond, initiate, pivot, guide, or reflect in a way that is authentic to you. You move in harmony with your energy, rather than overriding or fighting yourself every step of the way.

And here's something we want to be very clear about: This *isn't* about abandoning ambition. It's about redefining prosperity and success on *your* terms. It's about pursuing the most expansive version of yourself and crafting a life that inspires and nourishes you.

Often people talk about prosperity in terms of money, and that's certainly part of it, but in our world, true prosperity isn't just about financial abundance, it's the intersection of money, resources, purpose, *and* well-being. It's about having enough money, time, energy, support, and alignment to live and lead from a place of heart-centered purpose, connection, and health. It's about shifting from scarcity-driven survival to a reality where success is nourishing, sustainable, and enjoyable.

The Process of Really, Truly... and Finally Embodying *Your* Story

If you've spent years—or decades—being conditioned to override your body, ignore your instincts, and prove your worth through unrelenting effort, it makes sense that shifting into a more aligned way of living feels... a little terrifying.

Even when the GRIND is exhausting, it's familiar. And the nervous system loves the familiar.

That's why this next chapter of your journey isn't about simply deciding to *think* differently. It's about repatterning your nervous system, reconnecting with your body's truth, and embodying the version of you that isn't ruled by fear, pressure, or performance.

The PROSPER framework guides you through exactly that—a holistic leadership process rooted in science, somatics, Human Design, and truth.

In the next section, you'll be guided through a transformative process that helps you:

- reconnect with your purpose so that your life and leadership are rooted in something deeply meaningful to you
- rewire your nervous system for safety, so that alignment doesn't feel like a threat
- break free from reactivity to cultivate deeper self-trust, so that fear doesn't dictate your choices
- expand your capacity for success and abundance without constant self-sacrifice
- step into the full embodiment of your unique leadership and (capital P) Purpose, instead of trying to fit someone else's mold
- leverage your energy and resources more wisely, so that success is sustainable, not exhausting

This isn't about a quick fix or a mindset hack. It's about deep embodiment and integration of the insight you've gathered—an approach that rewires your body and brain so that alignment becomes your natural state, not just a cool idea.

Right now, you don't need to have it all figured out. You don't need a master plan or a perfect strategy.

All you need is willingness.

Willingness to pause.

Willingness to be curious.

Willingness to entertain the idea that a new way actually is possible.

And willingness to let this be a process—not a performance.

So, are you ready?

Let's begin the journey beyond the GRIND—so you can move into a chapter of life where you don't just survive…you PROSPER.

Chapter 16
The PROSPER Framework: Building Your Personalized Toolbox for Thriving

First and foremost, let's get something clear: You are not a walking checklist. You are not here to grind your way through life until your spark is extinguished. You are here to prosper. And when we say *prosper*, we don't just mean financial success or ticking off milestones on society's achievement chart. We mean thriving—feeling aligned, alive, and on purpose.

The PROSPER framework is your map to get there. This isn't about slapping a bandage on burnout or telling you to manifest your dream life without doing the deeper work. It's about understanding the intricate dance between your brain, body, and energy—your inner ecosystem—and aligning it with the larger, cocreative ecosystem of the world around you. It's about making conscious choices rooted in the truth of who you are so you can move beyond the stories that keep you stuck, unfulfilled, and disconnected.

In a culture that glorifies hustle, exhaustion, and the idea that suffering is the price of success, we take a different approach. To prosper is not just to accumulate wealth—it's to live in the intersection of resources and well-being. True prosperity isn't about grinding your way to financial security at the expense of your health, relationships, and joy. It's about aligning with your purpose in a way that generates both abundance and ease. When we define prosperity, we're talking about having the financial and energetic resources to sustain the life you're truly meant to live—one where success doesn't cost you your well-being.

> Because real prosperity isn't just about how much you *have*; it's about how aligned, nourished, and resourced you *feel*.

Many folks are chasing status, money, and achievements... but what they're really seeking is a sense of meaning, purpose, and well-being.

Purpose isn't a job title, a role, or a box you check. It isn't some elusive "answer" that you finally find. It's the core of your *being*—the unique essence you bring to the world. It's about who you're here to be, not just what you're here to do. Purpose is the thread that weaves together your gifts, experiences, and challenges, calling you forward (over and over again) to express your unique genius in service to the whole.

When you're aligned with your Purpose, life feels rich and resonant. Opportunities seem to find you—like magic. You stop trying to mold yourself into something you're not and start operating as the fullest expression of who you are. Purpose isn't static—it evolves as you do. It's a living, breathing force that invites you to keep growing, thriving, and contributing in ways that are deeply fulfilling and impactful.

THE BRAIN-BODY CONNECTION: THE FOUNDATION OF SUSTAINABLE WELL-BEING

To thrive, you can't just think your way there. Your brain and body are a team—a dynamic duo working together to shape your experience of the world. Modern science shows us that well-being isn't just about logic or willpower; it's about creating alignment in your entire system.

Your brain isn't a cold, calculating machine. It's an energy hub that translates the infinite field of possibilities into tangible experiences. But it doesn't work alone. Your heart generates a measurable electromagnetic field that influences your brain and body. Your gut—your "second brain"—processes intuition and emotional cues in ways your conscious mind can't even begin to articulate. Together, these systems create a feedback loop of thoughts, emotions, and sensations that shape how you feel, act, and connect.

And here's the kicker: This feedback loop doesn't just influence how you feel in the moment—it affects your DNA. Through the field of epigenetics, we know that your inner world—your beliefs, emotions, and perceptions—shapes the environment inside your body, influencing how your genes express themselves. In other words, the stories you tell yourself don't just live in your mind—they live in your cells.

That's why working with the brain-body connection is critical. It's not enough to analyze your patterns intellectually. You have to embody new ways of being—ways that honor your truth, align with your Purpose, and support your well-being.

Earlier in this book, we introduced you to the basics of quantum science and how it underpins Human Design. Let's revisit this for a moment, because as we step into the deeper work of alignment and purpose, this foundation becomes even more important.

Remember that at the quantum level, everything is energy. What appears solid—your body, your to-do list, your coffee mug—is, at its core, a swirling sea of vibrating molecules. And even those molecules, when you zoom in far enough, are made up of subatomic particles that are constantly moving, shifting, and interacting within a vast energetic field, the quantum field. This field, often called the field of infinite possibilities, holds every potential outcome before it becomes form.

In quantum science, this state of pure potential is known as *superposition*—where particles exist in multiple possible states simultaneously (kind of mind blowing, right?!). Reality doesn't fully "choose" a particular outcome until something causes that potential (those subatomic particles) to collapse into physical form. That "something" is often observation or attention—what we call *the observer effect*. This simply means that your focused awareness plays an active role in shaping which version of reality takes form. In every moment, countless possibilities exist—but your attention, intention, and energetic state act like tuning dials, pulling certain possibilities out of the energetic *what if* and into your day to day lived experience.

And it's not just that you're looking—it's *how* you're looking that matters. The beliefs you hold, the emotions you feel, and the subconscious meanings you've assigned to life all become part of that observation. Your nervous system, your thought patterns, and your internal narratives color the lens through which you interact with the quantum field. In other words, your personal reality is shaped not only by what you pay attention to, but by the meaning you give to what you see.

This is where archetypes enter the picture. Archetypes are deeply embedded patterns of meaning—universal storylines, roles, and symbols that live both personally and collectively within the human experience. They are like shared blueprints of possibility that your consciousness can access. Whether you resonate with labels like the Warrior, the Victim, the Healer, or the Martyr, these archetypes carry energetic signatures that influence how you interpret your experiences, how you see yourself, and ultimately, what potentials you invite into form.

Human Design itself is built upon a rich tapestry of archetypes—layers of energies, roles, and patterns that exist within the human experience. While the system contains many levels of depth, in this book, we are focusing on one of its most foundational archetypal layers: the Five Types. Each Type represents a distinct energetic way of moving through the world, making decisions, engaging with others, and generating success and fulfillment. These are not personality labels; they are archetypal patterns that reveal how your unique energy interacts with life itself.

You might think of your Type as your personal energetic signature within the field—a primary archetype that influences how you perceive, respond, and cocreate with the infinite possibilities available to you. As you work with your Type, you begin to see how your thoughts, emotions, and behaviors either bring you into alignment with this natural frequency or pull you out of coherence and into resistance. And with that awareness comes your power: the ability to shift your internal meaning-making, realign your energy, and open new doorways of possibility.

When you're aligned with your authentic design, your energy field becomes *coherent*. Coherence means that all parts of your being—your thoughts, emotions, nervous system, and energetic blueprint—are vibrating in harmony. Like a perfectly tuned instrument, you're sending out a strong, clear signal into the field. And in turn, that coherent signal naturally draws aligned opportunities, relationships, and experiences toward you. You're not forcing outcomes; you're magnetizing them... like magic!

When you're misaligned, the opposite happens. Your energy becomes scattered and fragmented. Competing beliefs, fears, and old conditioning create interference—like static on a radio dial—making it much harder for your energy to stabilize around what you desire. This creates resistance and dissonance, which often feels like burnout, frustration, or chronic struggle.

Quantum science teaches us that alignment isn't just a feel-good concept—it's an energetic reality. Your internal state becomes the organizing force that collapses infinite possibility into tangible outcomes. The more coherent you are, the easier it is to create, to receive, and to step fully into your purpose.

As we move into the PROSPER framework, you'll begin to see how alignment with your design—and learning to cultivate this coherence—becomes the foundation for real, sustainable transformation.

Embodiment: The Missing Link

The cultural story of *Disconnection*, which we explored in the GRIND framework, tells us to live from the neck up—focusing on logic, external validation, and intellectual mastery while ignoring the wisdom of the body. But here's the good-bad news:

> You can't think your way to fulfillment. You have to actually live it.

Embodiment is the process of aligning your actions, choices, and daily rhythms with your deeper truths and desires. It's about letting your body become a vehicle for Purpose, not just your mind. Without embodiment, Purpose remains an abstract concept—a nice idea that never quite makes it into the messy, beautiful reality of your life.

This is why the PROSPER Framework includes reflections, prompts, and practices designed to get you out of your head and into your body. You'll explore how your beliefs, emotions, and sensations shape your experience, and you'll practice aligning your energy with your intentions so that you can live your Purpose, not just dream about it.

By the time you've reached this chapter, you've already begun the process of questioning the cultural stories that keep you stuck, separate, and unhappy. Now, we turn inward to the personal stories—those patterns, tendencies and beliefs that shape your life and keep you tethered to old ways of being.

The PROSPER Framework invites you to rewrite these stories, not just with your mind but with your whole being. Through the lens of Human Design and the tools of reflection, embodiment, and aligned action, you'll learn to navigate life with a sense of sovereignty—a deep knowing that you are the author of your own experience.

Your Toolbox for Thriving

This framework isn't a one-size-fits-all solution. It's a map, a compass, and a guide for you to create your unique path to thriving. As you journey through PROSPER, you'll experience the following but in no particular order:

- **Reconnect with your Purpose** and understand how it shapes your life beyond roles or labels.
- **Work with your brain-body connection** to create sustainable well-being and alignment.
- **Tap into the quantum field of possibilities** to align your energy and attract what's meant for you.
- **Use embodiment practices** to ground your truth in action and live from a place of authenticity.
- **Reflect on your patterns** and rewrite the internal stories that keep you stuck.

This isn't about fixing yourself—because remember (we're going to keep saying this), you aren't a failure and were never broken. It's about remembering who you are, aligning with your innate design, and stepping into the life you were always meant to live. Plus, you've likely invested a *lot* of time doing things the old (exhausting) way. It's time to truly *prosper*.

CHAPTER 17
P—PURPOSE:
THE TRUTH OF WHO WE *BE*

BEFORE YOU DIVE IN

How do you define purpose? Is it a feeling, an achievement, or something else entirely?

You are here with a purpose. You were designed to seek it. From the depths of your brain to the core of your being, the impulse to explore, discover, and grow is hardwired into you. But seeking isn't just about chasing goals or finding the next shiny object. It's about aligning with something deeper—a sense of purpose that connects you to your true essence and the world around you. This chapter explores the science behind your seeking brain and how aligning it with purpose can heal burnout, bring clarity, and help you thrive.

THE SCIENCE OF SEEKING: WHY IT MATTERS

Your brain has a built-in system that propels you to seek. Known as *the seeking pathway*, this neurological circuit drives everything from basic survival instincts—like finding food and shelter—to higher pursuits, like searching for meaning and connection. It's powered by dopamine, a neurochemical that fuels curiosity, motivation, and anticipation.

At its best, this pathway helps you thrive. It encourages you to try new things, pursue your goals, and grow as a person. But when out of balance, it can lead to exhaustion, overwhelm, and a constant chase for external validation. To heal from burnout and create a life of purpose, it's essential to restore harmony in this system, balancing external desires with internal fulfillment.

EXTERNAL SEEKING: THE DOPAMINE DANCE

External seeking is primal and essential. It's what motivates you to go after the things you need to survive and thrive—food, shelter, companionship, and comfort. When you successfully achieve these things, your brain rewards you with a hit of dopamine, the chemical that makes you feel good and reinforces the behavior.

But in today's overstimulated world, external seeking can easily go haywire. Modern life offers an endless buffet of quick dopamine hits: scrolling social media, bingeing TV shows, eating processed foods, or chasing likes and praise. These activities trigger short bursts of pleasure but don't provide lasting satisfaction. Over time, your brain builds tolerance, needing more and more stimulation to achieve the same effect. The result? You're stuck on a hamster wheel, chasing fleeting highs while feeling increasingly depleted and disconnected.

INTERNAL SEEKING: THE SHIFT TO MEANING

The good news? You don't have to stay on that hamster wheel. The same seeking system that propels you outward can also guide you inward. When we redirect our energy from chasing surface-level validation to nurturing soul-level alignment, everything begins to shift.

Internal seeking is the quiet (but powerful) drive to find deeper meaning, deeper connection, and to return to our *higher self*. It invites us to ask the big, beautiful questions:

"Why am I here?"

"What does this all mean?"

"What is trying to move through me?"

And when we honor those questions, we find ourselves moving toward something far greater than success or achievement—we move toward connection with the (capital S) Self (your highest self), Source (God, the Universe, Love, whatever you call it), and with life itself.

When you engage in activities that align with your values and your deeper sense of purpose—like creating, learning, connecting, or giving back—your brain's reward system recalibrates. Dopamine no longer works alone. It joins forces with serotonin (for mood), oxytocin (for connection), and endorphins (for natural stress relief). Together, they create a more sustainable, nourishing form of fulfillment. The act of *seeking* itself becomes rewarding—not just the outcome.

You begin to live a life fueled by meaning, not just moments. Rather than chasing fleeting hits of pleasure or external approval, you're pulled toward experiences that feel true, alive, and deeply aligned. Purpose becomes your compass, it becomes your state of being, balancing external striving with inner growth. And in that shift, you don't just survive—you thrive.

How Purpose Shapes Your Brain and Body

Aligning with your purpose doesn't just feel good—it rewires your brain for long-term well-being. Here's how:

- **Enhances Neuroplasticity:** Purpose-driven activities engage your brain's Default Mode Network (DMN), which supports self-reflection and creativity. This network helps you to get curious and wonder about deeper meaning helping you to integrate experiences and create a meaningful narrative for your life.

- **Calms Stress Responses:** The prefrontal cortex, responsible for higher-level thinking and planning, takes the reins, reducing fear-based reactions from the amygdala. This makes you more resilient and better equipped to handle challenges.
- **Creates Flow States:** When you're immersed in purposeful activities, your brain enters a flow state—a harmonious blend of focus, effortlessness, and intrinsic reward.
- **Supports Physical Health:** Balanced neurochemicals reduce inflammation, improve immune function, and promote overall health. Purpose also lowers cortisol, the stress hormone, creating a calmer, more grounded state of being.

Purpose as the Path to Thriving

Purpose isn't a luxury; it's a necessity. It's what keeps your seeking system balanced, your brain and body aligned, and your energy flowing in sustainable ways. When you live with purpose, you move from chasing short-term gratification to cultivating long-term fulfillment. You stop *just* surviving and start thriving.

By aligning with your purpose, you tap into the full potential of your seeking system. You create a life that feels not only rewarding but deeply meaningful—a life where every step, every challenge, and every success reflects the truth of who you are. This is the foundation of the PROSPER framework and the path to living fully, authentically, and joyfully.

Personal Practice and Reflection: Understanding Your Seeking Patterns

You've been seeking your whole life. Seeking validation. Seeking meaning. Seeking success. Seeking love. Seeking enoughness. And as we've explored in this chapter, seeking dopamine.

But the question is—what are you actually seeking? And more importantly, are you aware of your current seeking patterns? And are they bringing you closer to success, purpose, and well-being or are they pulling you further away?

This section will help you identify where your energy is going, where you might be caught in loops of external seeking that leave you exhausted or unfulfilled, and where you have the opportunity to redirect your seeking toward what actually nourishes and sustains you.

This isn't about shaming yourself for old habits—it's about gaining clarity. It's completely normal—especially in the world we live in—to lose sight of our true purpose and to become addicted to seeking all sorts of stuff outside of ourselves. So please go ahead and forgive yourself for not seeing what you couldn't see, for losing sight of what you really needed, and for falling into the dopamine-flavored temptation that is all over the place. We all fall into some version of it. But here's the thing:

When you understand where your energy has been going, and you see that more clearly, you gain the power to reclaim it.

So now you have an opportunity to see where your energy is going. Take a deep breath, wrap yourself in compassion and take some time to identify the things on the following checklist that you invest your time and energy into regularly. And be honest with yourself... it's the only way to really get unstuck.

Checklist 1: Reflecting on Where You Invest Your Energy Seeking Outside of Yourself

Social Media and Digital Engagement

- ☐ Checking for likes, comments, or shares on posts.
- ☐ Scrolling through social media feeds (e.g., Instagram, TikTok, Facebook).
- ☐ Obsessing over follower count or engagement metrics.
- ☐ Constantly checking notifications or messages.
- ☐ Refreshing your email inbox unnecessarily.
- ☐ Watching viral videos or trending content for quick laughs or entertainment.
- ☐ Doomscrolling through negative news or events.
- ☐ Participating in online arguments or debates for a sense of importance.

Entertainment and Media

- ☐ Binge watching TV shows or movies to escape reality.
- ☐ Constantly playing video games for rewards or achievements.
- ☐ Streaming music, podcasts, or audiobooks to avoid silence or for constant stimulation.
- ☐ Overconsumption of online articles, blogs, or threads.
- ☐ Watching how-to videos or tutorials as a way of procrastination.

Work and Productivity

- ☐ Overchecking work emails or Slack messages for validation.

- ☐ Seeking praise or recognition from colleagues or supervisors.
- ☐ Overachieving or taking on extra work for external acknowledgment.
- ☐ Becoming addicted to completing tasks just to cross them off a to-do list.
- ☐ Pursuing certifications, awards, or titles for external validation.

Shopping and Consumption

- ☐ Online shopping as a way to feel good temporarily.
- ☐ Adding items to cart without needing them.
- ☐ Impulse buying during sales or promotions.
- ☐ Collecting luxury or trendy items for status or self-worth.
- ☐ Buying books, courses, or tools you may never use.

Food and Drink

- ☐ Eating comfort food or junk food for quick gratification.
- ☐ Drinking coffee, energy drinks, or alcohol for mood boosts.
- ☐ Overindulging in sugary snacks or treats.
- ☐ Dining out or ordering food for the excitement of new flavors.
- ☐ Using food as a reward or emotional coping mechanism.

Fitness and Appearance

- ☐ Obsessing over body image or physical appearance.
- ☐ Chasing fitness goals purely for validation or social approval.
- ☐ Overposting workout achievements or selfies.

- [ ] Seeking compliments for physical changes or outfits.
- [ ] Spending excessive time or money on beauty products or services.

Relationships and Social Validation

- [ ] Seeking constant approval or affirmation from friends or partners.
- [ ] Overanalyzing how others perceive you or your actions.
- [ ] Engaging in gossip for a sense of connection or excitement.
- [ ] Flirting for attention, even if not genuinely interested.
- [ ] Relying on others' opinions to guide personal decisions.

Financial and Material Goals

- [ ] Checking bank accounts or stock portfolios excessively.
- [ ] Comparing your financial status with others'.
- [ ] Fixating on earning more to feel secure or validated.
- [ ] Seeking status through material possessions (e.g., cars, gadgets, homes).

Recognition and Status

- [ ] Entering competitions or contests just to win recognition.
- [ ] Volunteering for tasks or projects to be seen as helpful.
- [ ] Chasing titles, accolades, or awards in personal or professional life.
- [ ] Bragging about achievements or milestones for validation.

Experiences and Escapism

- [ ] Constantly planning trips or events for excitement.

- ☐ Pursuing adrenaline activities (e.g., skydiving, extreme sports) for thrill-seeking.
- ☐ Seeking new hobbies or skills to feel accomplished or unique.
- ☐ Overindulging in spiritual or self-help workshops for breakthroughs.
- ☐ Using fantasy or daydreaming to escape real-life challenges.

Subtler Sources

- ☐ Overpracticing mindfulness or meditation to achieve a bliss state.
- ☐ Seeking constant emotional highs from motivational content.
- ☐ Creating drama or conflict to feel a sense of aliveness.
- ☐ Helping others excessively to feel needed or valued.
- ☐ Engaging in overintellectualization or philosophical debates to prove intelligence.
- ☐ Comparing your healing, growth, or success journey to others'.
- ☐ Chasing perfection or control in areas of life to avoid discomfort.
- ☐ Using humor or sarcasm to deflect vulnerability or seek attention.

Spirituality and Personal Growth

- ☐ Overrelying on tarot, astrology, or Human Design readings for answers.
- ☐ Seeking signs, synchronicities, or messages in everything.

- ☐ Constantly pursuing spiritual breakthroughs or enlightenment.
- ☐ Fixating on being seen as wise, evolved, or spiritual.
- ☐ Using healing tools (e.g., crystals, rituals) for external comfort.

Escapist or Addictive Behaviors

- ☐ Gambling or playing the lottery for the thrill.
- ☐ Using substances (e.g., nicotine, cannabis) for relaxation or stimulation.
- ☐ Overindulging in porn or casual sex for validation or escape.
- ☐ Addictive behaviors like nail-biting, fidgeting, or overcaffeinating for relief.
- ☐ Using humor, sarcasm, or overtalking as a distraction.

SHIFTING FOCUS: CHOOSING WHAT NOURISHES YOU

Reflections

Take a moment to go back and notice what you checked off from the list. And remember that none of these external seeking patterns are inherently bad or wrong, but anything done mindlessly, excessively or with grabby, addictive energy behind it probably isn't serving you and is likely adding to a sense of stress, disconnection from Self and Purpose, and burnout.

Where is most of your external seeking energy being invested? Identify the top three to five external seeking tendencies.

What happens in your body when you focus on these external markers? Do you feel energized, stressed, or disconnected?

What are you willing to minimize, decrease, or shift to reclaim some of your energy?

Letting go of old patterns—especially ones that have been wired into your brain through years of conditioning—doesn't happen by simply deciding to stop. You can't just remove a habit; you have to replace it. When we begin recognizing and releasing depleting forms of external seeking, we need new pathways to direct that energy—ones that actually nourish, replenish, and realign us.

This next checklist isn't about rigid self-improvement or doing better. It's about offering yourself new, sustainable ways to seek fulfillment, purpose, and balance. The goal isn't perfection—it's curiosity. What feels more expansive? What feels grounding? What feels like it brings you home to yourself rather than farther away?

Now, explore "the swap"—choose one of your old, depleting, seeking patterns from the last list and identify one from the following list that you're ready to replace it with. Maybe instead of doomscrolling, you choose a grounding breathwork practice. Instead of overcommitting to work for validation, you make space for a creative outlet that actually energizes you. Instead of chasing external approval, you actively practice focusing on celebrating how far you've come.

Note: This second checklist isn't a list of things that will always be a good choice for everyone, just like the activities checklist isn't always inherently bad. This is a practice of listening—like really listening—to your inner wisdom, your energy, and your body to figure out what fits for *you*.

So, as you explore this next list, reflect on which new habits feel like they would truly support, nourish, and sustain you. What small, intentional substitutions can you make today to begin rewiring your seeking system in a way that actually fuels your well-being?

> Remember, transformation doesn't happen in one giant leap—it happens one conscious, un-sexy choice at a time.

Checklist 2: A New Menu of Nourishing Practices

Mindful Awareness and Presence

- ☐ Practice mindful breathing exercises to connect with the present moment.
- ☐ Spend time observing nature—walks, sitting under a tree, or gardening.
- ☐ Journal to reflect on your thoughts, feelings, and patterns.
- ☐ Practice gratitude by listing three things you're thankful for each day.
- ☐ Engage in body scanning or progressive muscle relaxation to tune into physical sensations.
- ☐ Use guided meditations or sound healing to ground yourself.

Physical Nourishment

- ☐ Engage in joyful, noncompetitive movement like yoga, dancing, swimming, or tai chi.
- ☐ Take regular walks in natural settings to reduce stress and restore mental clarity.
- ☐ Prioritize restorative sleep with a consistent bedtime routine.
- ☐ Eat whole, nutrient-dense foods that nourish your body and support brain health.

- [ ] Incorporate strength or resistance training to build a sense of embodied power and confidence.

Emotional Regulation and Connection

- [ ] Practice naming your emotions and allowing them to be felt without judgment.
- [ ] Use self-soothing techniques like placing a hand on your heart or deep belly breathing.
- [ ] Connect with loved ones for meaningful, heart-centered conversations and quality time.
- [ ] Seek support through therapy, coaching, or group counseling to process emotions.
- [ ] Create art, write poetry, or engage in other creatively expressive practices.

Intentional Rest and Play

- [ ] Dedicate time each week to rest *without guilt* (e.g., napping, lounging, and intentional nonproductive time).
- [ ] Prioritize hobbies or activities that bring joy without external validation or competition.
- [ ] Play games or engage in activities that bring fun and laughter.
- [ ] Spend time with animals or pets for their grounding and calming presence.

Nervous System Regulation

- [ ] Practice vagus nerve activation techniques such as humming, chanting, or gargling water.
- [ ] Try cold water immersion (e.g., splashing your face with cold water or taking cold showers).

- ☐ Engage in rhythmic activities like drumming, walking, or rowing to stabilize your system.
- ☐ Use grounding exercises like holding a warm cup of tea, feeling textures, or walking barefoot.
- ☐ Practice heart-focused breathing to shift into a state of coherence and calm (more on this later in the book).

Spiritual and Inner Connection

- ☐ Set aside time for prayer, intention-setting, or connecting with your higher self or higher guidance.
- ☐ Practice intuitive journaling to connect with your inner guidance.
- ☐ Spend time in silence or stillness.
- ☐ Create rituals or ceremonies to honor transitions, emotions, or desires.
- ☐ Reflect on your life's purpose or core values.

Purposeful Living

- ☐ Infuse meaning and intention into daily tasks, no matter how small.
- ☐ Volunteer or engage in acts of kindness to foster a sense of contribution and connection.
- ☐ Create a vision board or list of intentions to inspire focused growth and joy.
- ☐ Celebrate small wins and milestones as a way of acknowledging your growth.

Creative Flow and Growth

- ☐ Dedicate time for flow state activities—those that make you joyfully lose track of time.

- ☐ Learn a new skill or dive into exploring a topic that excites your curiosity.
- ☐ Read books or watch documentaries that inspire or expand your perspective.
- ☐ Take up mindful crafts like knitting, woodworking, or gardening.
- ☐ Explore playful self-expression through improvisation or free-form dance.

Community and Connection

- ☐ Build a supportive community by spending time with interesting people who uplift and inspire you.
- ☐ Join local meetups or groups that align with your interests or values.
- ☐ Participate in group mindfulness or yoga sessions.
- ☐ Reach out to supportive friends or family regularly, even for simple check-ins.
- ☐ Create or join (healthy, non-hustle) accountability groups to foster shared growth and encouragement.

Healthy Relationship with Technology

- ☐ Set designated times and boundaries around checking email or engaging with social media.
- ☐ Use focus apps or timers to limit time spent on screens.
- ☐ Schedule phone-free time or digital detox days to recharge.
- ☐ Replace mindless scrolling with mindful activities like reading or journaling.
- ☐ Organize your digital spaces (e.g., declutter your inbox) to reduce overwhelm.

Energy and Time Management

- ☐ Schedule downtime in your calendar as nonnegotiable.
- ☐ Avoid overcommitting and practice saying no to protect your energy and authentic needs.

Supportive Self-Talk and Mindset

- ☐ Reframe challenges as opportunities for growth or learning.
- ☐ Develop affirmations or mantras to shift negative thought patterns, and post them as visual reminders.
- ☐ Practice detaching from outcomes, focusing on the process, enjoying the journey instead.
- ☐ Build a mindset of abundance, acknowledging what is working in your life and where you're already enough.
- ☐ Celebrate and actively honor your unique strengths and gifts.

Playful Exploration of Pleasure

- ☐ Savor small sensory experiences like a warm cup of tea, a favorite scent, or a sunset.
- ☐ Dance, sing, or move freely to connect with your body.
- ☐ Spend time laughing—whether through comedy, play, or connecting with friends.
- ☐ Practice really receiving (compliments, support, or care) with gratitude and openness.

Cultivating Sustainable Joy

- ☐ Set boundaries that protect your energy and honor your needs.

- ☐ Focus on what you can control and release attachment to what you cannot.
- ☐ Create rituals or routines that ground and center you daily.
- ☐ Track your emotions or habits to notice what truly supports your well-being.
- ☐ Practice letting go of perfectionism in favor of progress and balance.

Reflections

What on this list are you willing to prioritize moving forward? What's your new commitment?

What small, daily shift could help you invest in a greater sense of balance and inner harmony, rather than chasing what feels fleeting or externally defined?

Let's make some seeking swaps!

What isn't working or sustainable:	**What I choose instead:**
_____	_____
_____	_____
_____	_____
_____	_____
_____	_____
_____	_____
_____	_____

Chapter 18
R—Response-Ability:
Reclaiming Your Power to Choose

Before You Dive In

What's the first thing you think about or feel when you hear the word *responsibility*? Does it feel like a weight or an opportunity?

When you hear the word *responsibility*, your mind might immediately flood with a list of obligations—duties, expectations, and all the people and tasks that rely on you. No wonder it often feels heavy, like a weight to carry. But what if responsibility isn't about what's expected of you, but about how you choose to respond to the world?

"Response-ability" flips the script. It's not about shouldering burdens or meeting external expectations. It's about cultivating your ability to respond intentionally to life's challenges, triggers, and opportunities instead of automatically and mindlessly reacting. It's about stepping beyond knee-jerk reactivity and into the spacious freedom of aligned choice. This subtle but profound shift helps you reclaim your power—not to control what happens, but to choose how you meet it.

To move from automatic reaction to thoughtful response, we need to understand the mechanics of reactivity. Why do we sometimes lash out, freeze up, or fall into old patterns? The answer lies deep in the subconscious layers of your brain and nervous system—systems designed to keep you alive, but that often get stuck in overdrive.

Reactivity: When Your Brain Decides Before You Do

Think about a time you snapped at someone or froze in fear before you even realized what was happening. These moments aren't failures of willpower; they're the result of a brilliantly efficient survival system. Long ago, this system kept us alive in the face of saber-toothed tigers and other immediate threats. Today, the same system responds to emails, deadlines, and difficult conversations as if they were life-or-death situations.

Here's how it works:

1. Your brain is always scanning for danger. Subconsciously, it evaluates your surroundings for cues of safety or threat, a process known as neuroception.
2. When a potential threat is detected, your survival brain kicks in, triggering an automatic reaction before your conscious mind can catch up.
3. Chemicals like adrenaline, cortisol, and norepinephrine flood your system, priming you to fight, flee, or freeze.

This system is lightning fast and incredibly effective for immediate survival. But when it stays stuck in overdrive—responding to everyday stressors as if they were emergencies—it can wreak havoc on your health, relationships, and sense of well-being.

The Key Players Behind Reactivity

To understand how to shift out of reactivity, it helps to meet the parts of your brain running the show:

- The amygdala: Your bodyguard, always on alert for danger. It reacts first and "thinks" later, triggering fight, flight, or freeze responses before you're even aware of a threat.
- The hypothalamus: The command center that activates your autonomic nervous system. It revs up your heart rate, pumps out stress hormones, and puts your body on high alert.
- The basal ganglia: Habit headquarters. This part of your brain automates responses, making them fast and efficient—but also hard to change if they're rooted in stress.
- The thalamus: Your sensory switchboard. It decides what gets your attention and routes urgent signals straight to the amygdala.
- The prefrontal cortex: The logical thinker and planner. This part helps you assess, reflect, and choose—but it's often bypassed when you're in a reactive state.

Together, these systems create a rapid-response team designed to protect you. But without conscious intervention, they can trap you in reactive loops, making it hard to respond thoughtfully.

Your Nervous System: The Gearbox of Reactivity

Your autonomic nervous system (ANS) governs how your body responds to stress. It has three main states, as explained by Dr. Stephen Porges' Polyvagal Theory:

1. Ventral vagal state (safe and social): When you feel calm and secure, your nervous system supports connection, creativity, and problem-solving. This is your rest and digest mode.

2. Sympathetic state (fight or flight): When your brain perceives a threat, your body shifts into high alert—heart pounding, breathing quickening, ready to fight or flee.
3. Dorsal vagal state (freeze or shut down): If a threat feels overwhelming or inescapable, your system can shut down entirely, leaving you numb, disconnected, or immobilized.

You move through these states all day, often without realizing it. But when stress dominates, your system gets stuck in fight, flight, or freeze mode, leaving little room for calm, connection, or conscious choice.

Here's the good news:

Your brain is changeable. Through a process called neuroplasticity, you can rewire your neural patterns of reaction and create new, more empowering responses.

The first step is learning the power of the pause.

THE POWER OF THE PAUSE

Pausing may sound simple, but it's truly revolutionary. When you take a single deep breath before reacting, you interrupt your survival brain's automatic loop. That pause creates space for your prefrontal cortex to step in, helping you reflect and choose instead of reacting on autopilot.

- In the moment: A pause helps calm your nervous system, signaling safety to your brain and body.
- Over time: Regularly practicing pausing strengthens neural pathways for reflection and response, making it easier to stay grounded in challenging situations.

RESPONSE-ABILITY AS FREEDOM

Building response-ability doesn't mean you'll never react again. It means you'll have more choice in how you navigate stress, challenges, and uncertainty. Over time, you'll find it easier to pause, reflect, and choose actions aligned with your values and purpose.

This is what it means to lead yourself—stepping into your role as the conscious conductor of your life. Instead of being carried away by old patterns, you become the architect of your responses, shaping a life rooted in alignment, growth, and connection.

This is where true resilience lives—not in avoiding stress, but in meeting it with awareness, flexibility, and choice. Response-ability is your invitation to reclaim your power, one breath, one pause, and one thoughtful response at a time.

REFLECTIONS:
GAINING CLARITY AND CRAFTING YOUR PAUSE

1. In which areas of your life—work, relationships, or otherwise—do you feel the most reactive? Pinpoint those triggers so you can meet them with choice instead of reactivity.
2. When life cranks up the pressure, how do you respond? Are you a snapper, a ghoster, a freezer, a people-pleaser, or an overachiever? Identify your unique stress tendencies so you can stop them from running the show.
3. Think back to a time you reacted on autopilot—maybe you fired off a snarky email, gave the cold shoulder, or overcommitted yourself. What could've shifted if you'd paused, taken a deep breath, and chosen a different response?
4. Your body and emotions have a secret language for telling you when you're about to lose your cool. Is it a clenched jaw, a racing heart, or a wave of irritability? Reflect on the signals from past reactive moments so you can spot them next time.

5. Create a sticky note on your desk with a helpful reminder, post a mantra like "pause and breathe" on your car dashboard, or set a daily reminder to pop up on your phone to check in with yourself. Choose one simple tool to interrupt your default patterns of reactivity and give yourself the intention and space to respond with intention.

THE PRACTICE: TOOLS FOR MAKING RESPONSE-ABILITY REAL

The most powerful tool you have for shifting from reactivity to response-ability isn't flashy, complicated, or something you have to buy. It's your breath. It might not sound wildly exciting, but it's the thing that works—every single time. Your nervous system simply cannot maintain a high-stress physiological response when you're bringing in an excess of oxygen, extending your exhales, or stimulating the vagus nerve. The body and brain are wired to instinctively respond to breath as a primal signal of safety or danger, and when you breathe with intention, you send the message: *I'm okay. I have the ability to choose a response, not react.*

This means that no matter what's happening around you—whether it's a tense conversation, a sudden wave of overwhelm, or an old trigger trying to pull you into autopilot—you can *trick* your system into shifting gears. With the right kind of breathwork, you can override stress patterns, reclaim your ability to choose, and step into a state of clarity and grounded presence. And that? That's a power move.

The following practices are simple, science-backed ways to help your nervous system downshift, giving you the space to move from automatic reaction to intentional response. Try them, experiment, and notice how even one deep breath can change everything.

Your Response-Ability Quick and Easy Toolbox

Box Breathing (4-4-4-4)
- Inhale through your nose for four seconds.
- Hold for four seconds.
- Exhale through your mouth for four seconds.
- Hold for four seconds.
- Repeat for one to three minutes.
- **Why it works:** Engages the parasympathetic nervous system, creating an immediate calming effect.

Humming or Singing Your Favorite Song
- Take a deep breath in, then hum on the exhale.
- Extend the exhale as long as possible.
- Option: Sing a comforting song or a simple "mmm" sound.
- **Why it works:** The vibrations stimulate the vagus nerve, shifting the body into a calm, connected state.

Hand on Heart, Hand on Belly
- Place one hand on your heart and the other on your belly.
- Inhale deeply through your nose, feeling your belly expand.
- Exhale slowly through your mouth, letting your belly soften.
- Repeat until you feel more centered.
- **Why it works:** Signals safety to the nervous system through touch and breath.

Sighing It Out
- Inhale deeply through the nose.
- Exhale audibly with a big sigh, dropping your shoulders.
- Repeat three to five times.

- **Why it works:** Helps discharge built-up tension and reset the nervous system.

Five-Second Inhale, Ten-Second Exhale
- Inhale through your nose for five seconds.
- Exhale through your mouth for ten seconds.
- Repeat five to seven times.
- **Why it works:** A long exhale activates the parasympathetic nervous system, reducing anxiety.

Three-Deep-Breaths Reset
- Close your eyes.
- Take a deep inhale through your nose.
- Hold for a moment at the top.
- Exhale fully and slowly.
- Repeat two more times.
- **Why it works:** Quickly interrupts reactive patterns and grounds you in the present.

Chapter 19
O—Openness: The Courage to Expand

Before You Dive In

When life feels uncertain, do you find yourself leaning into control—trying to predict, plan, or fix—or do you allow curiosity to guide you?

Openness is more than just a mindset—it's a way of being that invites the world in. It's a willingness to engage with life as it unfolds, to trust in possibilities, and to remain curious even when the path ahead is uncertain. At its heart, openness is an act of receptivity, a choice to stand in the vastness of what could be instead of clinging to the safety of what is.

Yet, for many of us, openness feels risky. It means being vulnerable, letting go of control, and stepping into the unknown. Fear convinces us to close ourselves off, to armor against potential disappointment or rejection. But in doing so, we cut ourselves off from the very energy that fuels growth, connection, and creativity.

When we cultivate openness, we are connected—not just to ourselves but to others, to whatever bigger and inherently benevolent "something" you connect with, and to the infinite potential of life itself. This chapter is an exploration of what it means to live with an open heart and mind, why fear causes us to shut down, and how we can gently guide ourselves back into openness.

What Is Openness?

Openness is not the absence of fear but the willingness to feel it and stay receptive anyway. It's choosing curiosity over certainty, connection over walls of protection, and possibility over familiar limitations.

When we are open, we step into the role of cocreator. From this space, we see the world not as something to fear but as a playground of collaborative potential. Openness transforms the mundane into the magical, inviting us to engage with life fully and authentically.

Openness is also deeply tied to our connection with the energy of Source. Whether you call it God, the Universe, or Divine Intelligence, Source is the animating force behind all creation. It flows through the spaces within and around us, offering infinite creativity, support, and guidance. By tuning into this flow, we align ourselves with our higher purpose and tap into a wellspring of inspiration and possibility.

The Neuroscience of Openness

Openness is not just a mindset; it's a neurological state. When we are open, our brain's Default Mode Network (DMN) comes alive.

The DMN is like the brain's imagination engine. It activates during introspection, daydreaming, and creative thinking—those moments when the mind wanders freely, unbound by external demands. This network connects memory centers, synthesizes ideas, and generates new possibilities. It's the seat of curiosity, allowing us to ask "what if" and explore expansive possibilities without judgment.

But here's the catch: The DMN operates best when balanced. Too little activation, and we're stuck in reactive, habitual thinking. Too much, and we fall into overthinking, rumination, or worry.

> Openness requires a rhythm—an oscillation between doing and being, effort and rest, seeking and allowing.

This rhythm is where creativity thrives. It's why moments of insight often arise not when we're forcing a solution but when we're relaxed, letting our minds wander. As physicist Amit Goswami so aptly put it, life should be a dance to the chorus: "Do be do be do."

Think about it: How many aha moments of insight and creative inspiration have happened in the shower, while driving, or while otherwise letting your mind wander?

The DMN allows solutions to just sort of bubble up when we're relaxed and open, instead of trying to force the answer from a rigid stress state.

Fear and the Closure Reflex

So, if openness is our natural state, why do we close off? The simple answer is fear. The unknown triggers a primal response in the brain, activating survival mechanisms designed to protect us.

The amygdala, the brain's alarm system, plays a key role here. It scans for threats, real or imagined, and reacts in milliseconds. This is helpful when we're dodging danger but less so when we're trying to stay open to new experiences or ideas.

When fear takes over, we contract—emotionally, mentally, and even physically. We cling to the familiar, avoid risks, and shut ourselves off from opportunities for growth. Over time, this pattern can become automatic, leaving us stuck in cycles of reactivity and disconnection.

The Art of Reopening

Reclaiming openness isn't about banishing fear—it's about learning to dance with it. Fear isn't the villain here; it's like that awkward friend who blurts out uncomfortable truths. It shows up to highlight where you're stuck, where you need healing, and where your courage is waiting to break through. Here's how to gently ease yourself back into openness, one brave step at a time:

1. Hit Pause and Play Detective

When fear or resistance creeps in, don't shove it into a corner. Pause and ask yourself:

- Where do I feel this in my body?
- What's this feeling trying to tell me?

Treat it like a curious puzzle instead of a roadblock. Fear often carries clues about what you need to move forward. And, something we've seen and experienced time and time again in our own lives and with clients is that fear, while uncomfortable, is often actually a positive signal—a sign that you're right on the edge of your familiar comfort zone and are daring to move beyond it, expanding your desires, faith, and movement toward the life you really want.

2. Trade Certainty for Curiosity

Fear loves control—it wants a ten-point plan and all the answers *right now*. Curiosity, on the other hand, whispers, "What if there's another way? What if we tried something different?" When we lean into curiosity, we activate our natural sense of wonder, which engages the DMN, allowing us to stay open to new perspectives and unexpected possibilities.

- Ask yourself: *What else could this mean? What could I learn here?*

Curiosity cracks open the door fear is trying to slam shut.

3. Build Your Brave Zone

Openness doesn't mean diving into the deep end without a life vest. Start small.

- Prioritize time with people who make you feel safe and seen.
- Spend time in spaces with others who are being brave, taking leaps, and living in the direction of their dreams.

Intentional pockets of safety and courage create a foundation for bigger leaps of vulnerability. And literally, our brain is supported on both a conscious and unconscious level in being more flexible when we're around others who are living more open lives. That whole saying about us being the average of the five people we spend the most time with… it's true.

4. Plug Into Source

Whatever Source means to you—God, the Universe, your inner wisdom—cultivating that higher connection is key. Meditation, deep breaths, or even a walk in nature can help you tap into that flow of energy that reminds you: *I'm held. I'm safe. I'm here. I'm enough.*

From this grounded place, it's easier to let go of fear and lean into possibility. Even the simple practice of asking for support—even if it feels foreign at first—can be life-changing.

Example: While walking your dog and processing a conflict with your partner, you can simply breathe, open to the idea of support, and say something like, "I'm overwhelmed by this conflict, please help me see the solution and gain the perspective that will help us find understanding and peace."

Just imagining support beyond yourself begins to powerfully shift your brain out of an "I'm alone and overwhelmed in life" fear response to a more creative and open "There's a web of support far bigger than me that I can tap into when I need it" place.

5. GET YOUR CREATIVITY ON

Creativity is basically openness with a paintbrush, a pen, or a curious heart.

Whether it's doodling, journaling, trying a new recipe, dancing, or just daydreaming, let your imagination run wild.

Creativity makes space for possibility and helps you see the world—and yourself—in new ways.

Reopening is an art, not a race. It's about learning to navigate life with curiosity and courage, one step at a time.

> Openness as a practice is sending a clear message
> to life that fear doesn't get to call the shots here—
> *you* do.

At the quantum level, most of the universe isn't made of solid particles. It's made of space—99 percent of everything is nothingness. But this "nothingness" is far from empty. It's alive with energy, teeming with infinite potential.

The same is true within us. The spaces in our minds, hearts, and lives are not voids to be filled but fertile ground for creation. When we embrace the space between—between certainty and doubt, between what we know and what we don't—we open ourselves to the infinite possibilities that exist within us and around us.

OPENNESS AS A WAY OF BEING

Openness is not a destination but a practice. It's the choice to remain receptive in a world that often encourages us to close off. It's the courage to face fear, hold space for our emotions, and trust in the flow of life.

When we live with openness, we step into the role of cocreator. We align with Source energy (quantum potential), spark new possibilities, and expand into the fullness of who we are. Openness invites us to see the world—and ourselves—not as fixed, but as dynamic, infinite, and full of magical possibility.

Openness is the birthplace of creativity, connection, and purpose. It's where we begin to truly thrive. So take a breath, loosen your grip, and step into the spaciousness of what *could be*. The world is waiting for you to open.

Reflections: Cultivating (and Practicing) Openness in Your Life

Recognizing Your Closure Points

When do you find yourself shutting down to new ideas, opportunities, or perspectives? Is it when you feel uncertain, when emo-tions feel too big, or when past experiences have made you cautious? What situations, people, or thought patterns trigger contraction in your body and mind?

Your Personal Ingredients for Openness

Think about the times when you've felt most open, creative, and receptive to possibility. Who were you with? What were you doing? What practices or environments made that openness feel safe and natural? How can you intentionally invite more of those elements into your daily life?

Navigating Fear with Curiosity

Fear often convinces us to tighten our grip and seek control, yet openness requires us to soften into curiosity and expanded receptivity to life.

Where in your life is fear currently leading the way? What would shift if, instead of grasping for certainty, you asked, "What else could be possible here?"

Your Relationship with the Unknown

Openness requires trust—not just in yourself but in life's divine unfolding.

How do you currently relate to uncertainty? Do you see it as a threat or an invitation? How might re-storying the unknown as fertile ground for possibility change the way you move through life?

Choosing Openness as a Daily Practice

Openness isn't a one-time decision; it's a way of being that requires consistent practice.

What is one small, tangible way you can practice openness today? Whether it's saying yes to something unfamiliar, engaging in creative play, or simply noticing where you resist and softening into curiosity—how can you take a step toward expansion?

Chapter 20
S—Self-Worth:
Reclaiming Your Inherent Value

Before You Dive In

How have you been taught to measure your worth?

What if your worth didn't depend on what you do, achieve, or prove? What if it simply was—a quiet, unshakable truth that flowed through you, no matter the external circumstances? For many of us, this idea feels distant. We've been conditioned to tie our value to external metrics: gold stars, promotions, followers, and the ever-moving finish line of success.

But here's the truth: authentic self-worth isn't earned—it's remembered. It's not something you achieve, but something you reclaim. It's an inherent value that exists because you exist. And when you reconnect with this truth, you tap into a source of courage, creativity, and alignment that transforms how you live and lead.

And while your actual value is inherent, the daily experience and perception of self-worth can feel wobbly and wildly changeable. It moves with your thoughts, beliefs, and emotions. It's shaped by your inner dialogue and influenced by external conditioning. In a world that often seeks to devalue us—to sell us products, push us to produce, and compare ourselves to impossible standards—cultivating self-worth is an act of heart-centered rebellion.

As Dr. Karen Parker says, "You are valuable because you are a one-of-a-kind cosmic event." This truth is simple but profound. You are not your job title, your bank account, or your list of achievements. Your worth is actually not up for negotiation.

But the world doesn't always reflect this truth back to us. Instead, it teaches us to hustle for approval, to conform, bending ourselves into shapes that feel safe and acceptable, and to measure ourselves against others. Over time, these patterns erode our sense of self, leaving us disconnected from our inherent value.

The Shadows of Wobbly Self-Worth: Guilt and Shame

When we lose touch with our self-worth, guilt and shame often take the wheel. These emotions are deeply tied to our sense of value, but they play very different roles:

- **Guilt** focuses on behavior. It says, "I did something bad." At its best, guilt helps us reflect, realign with our values, and repair relationships. It's a compass for growth.
- **Shame**, however, focuses on the self. It whispers, "I *am* bad." It convinces us we are unworthy, flawed, and unlovable. Shame isolates us, hijacks our nervous system, and keeps us stuck in cycles of fear and disconnection.

Understanding these differences is critical. Guilt can guide us back to integrity; shame drags us into rigidity, protection, and hiding. And while guilt can serve as a healthy nudge to course-correct, shame is often weaponized—used by systems and industries to manipulate us into feeling inadequate so we'll conform, hustle, or consume.

But here's the truth:

> Worthiness is your birthright. When you embrace this truth—and practice it regularly in a world that teaches us otherwise—shame loses its power, guilt becomes a tool for growth rather than a trap, and your self-worth feels much more familiar and solid.

THE NEUROLOGY OF HEALTHY SELF-WORTH

Self-worth isn't just a feeling—it's a neurological state. When we operate from a place of inherent worth, our brain's reward and connection systems light up. Neurochemicals like oxytocin (the bonding hormone) and serotonin (the mood stabilizer) create feelings of belonging, compassion, and well-being.

But guilt and shame disrupt this system.

- **Guilt**, when balanced, activates the prefrontal cortex (our executive center that problem solves and accesses higher perspectives), encouraging self-reflection and growth. It helps us repair relationships and align with our values.
- **Shame**, however, activates the amygdala (our fear center), narrowing our focus and triggering fight-or-flight responses. It keeps us stuck in vigilance and self-doubt, disconnecting us from connection and creativity.

The antidote to shame is compassion. When we meet ourselves with kindness and curiosity—especially in moments of perceived failure—we deactivate the amygdala and reengage the parts of our brain that support healing, connection, innovation, and resilience.

RECLAIMING SELF-WORTH: A PATH TO FREEDOM

Reclaiming your self-worth isn't about puffing yourself up or convincing the world you're valuable. It's about dropping the exhausting act and remembering that you *already are*. It's about standing in your truth, unapologetically, and letting the rest fall into place. Here's how to get started.

Call Out the BS Stories

Take a hard look at the narratives running in your head about what makes you worthy and do some intentional filtering. Just because it's familiar, doesn't mean it's true.

- Who told you that hustling, proving, or achieving were prerequisites for earning value?
- Are those stories even true or are they just hand-me-downs from someone else's insecurities? Write them down. Then cross out the lies and rewrite the truth. (And yes, this is the truth: You're enough as you are.)

Talk to Yourself Like You Would a Friend

When you mess up, do you unleash the inner critic or the wise best friend?

Instead of beating yourself up with "I failed," try something like, "Okay, I'm learning. What's next?"

Kindness isn't weakness—it's the superpower that helps you grow without fear.

Stop "Should-ing" All Over Yourself

Every time you hear that little voice saying, "I should do this," hit pause and ask: *Says who?*

Are you acting out of alignment with what you truly want or out of fear of disappointing others? Shovel out those shoulds like the mental clutter they are. Make room for choices that light you up, not ones that drain you.

Set Boundaries Like a Boss

Boundaries aren't selfish—they're an embodied love letter to your self-worth.

- Where are you saying yes when you mean no?
- What would it feel like to protect your time, energy, and well-being without guilt?

Your honest yeses and noes are acts of rebellion against a world that loves to overstep.

Align with Your *Real* Purpose

Living in alignment with who you are—*not* who the world expects you to be—is the ultimate flex.

- Reconnect with what makes you *you*: your values, passions, and gifts.
- When you start living from that place, your worth becomes a beacon that guides your actions; no external validation required.

Reclaiming self-worth is about unlearning all the noise that says you're not enough and stepping into the truth that you've been enough all along. Now go live like it.

Embracing self-worth means daring to show up as your full, authentic self—flaws and all. It's about standing in your truth, even when it feels vulnerable, and trusting that who you are is enough.

And self-worth isn't just about you—it's about how you show up in the world. When you honor your value, you create ripples that inspire others to do the same. You become a beacon of possibility, showing that worth isn't earned or conditional—it's inherent.

In this way, self-worth becomes a collective force. When each of us reclaims our value, we contribute to a world where individuality, diversity, and authenticity are celebrated.

> Together, we create a culture that values people not
> for what they produce but for who they are.

So take a breath. Remember that you are a one-of-a-kind cosmic event. Stand in your truth, honor your worth, and let the world see the brilliance of who you are. You were never meant to prove your value—you were meant to live into it.

Self-Worth and Your Leadership Type: Reclaiming Your Value in Your Unique Way

Every Leadership Type we explored earlier in the book has a unique relationship with self-worth. While your worth is inherent, the way you experience it—how you struggle with it, reclaim it, and integrate it—can look different depending on your unique leadership type. So we invite you to take a moment to reflect on how self-worth shows up for you, through the lens of your Type.

Innovating Catalysts (Manifestors by Design)

You were born to trust your instincts and initiate boldly, but the world has likely told you to shrink, soften, or ask permission. Have you tied your worth to how others react to you? Reclaiming your self-worth means owning your power without guilt, knowing that your impact is valuable even if it's not always immediately understood.

Master Builders (Generators by Design)

You thrive when you are lit up by what you do, but has your worth become tangled up in productivity? Do you feel valuable only when you're helpful, needed, or working hard? Reclaiming your self-worth means realizing that your joy is enough—your value isn't just in what you produce, but in the energy you bring to the world.

Accelerated Builders (Manifesting Generators by Design)

Your fast-moving, multi-passionate nature is a gift, but has anyone ever made you feel like you're too much or all over the place? Have you judged your worth based on how efficiently you juggle everything? True self-worth for you means embracing your dynamic nature as an asset, not a flaw—you don't have to prove your value by doing more, faster.

Possibilitarian Guides (Projectors by Design)

You're here to guide, not grind, yet self-worth challenges may show up as feeling unseen, undervalued, or like you have to prove yourself by overworking. Have you felt pressure to act like an energy Type just to be "successful?" Your self-worth is strongest when you trust that recognition starts from within—your wisdom, perspective, and unique way of seeing the world are already enough.

Reflective Evaluators (Reflectors by Design)

As someone who mirrors the health of your environment, you may struggle with feeling undefined or uncertain about your own value. Have you ever questioned your worth because you don't fit into a traditional mold? Reclaiming self-worth means honoring your sensitivity as a gift, curating the spaces and people that nourish you, and trusting that your ability to reflect and sense the world around you is a rare and vital contribution.

Reflections:
Reclaiming Your Self-Worth

Let's get a bit more personal so that you can really—like *really*—rewrite your story of self-worth to embody your true value. It's time.

1. Pause and reflect on the stories you've absorbed about what makes someone worthy.

- What did your family, culture, or society teach you about value and success?
- How have those stories quietly shaped the way you measure your own worth?

Now ask yourself: Are those stories true, or are they someone else's baggage you've been carrying?

2. Let's get real about the shoulds running your life.

- What do you feel like you *should* be doing to prove you're enough? (at work, with family, with friends, etc.)
- Imagine that those shoulds were just lies dressed up as fancy life goals. What choices would you be able to make if you knew that the familiar shoulds simply weren't true?

3. When you screw up or fall short, how do you talk to yourself? Be honest—is it more like a mean boss or a supportive bestie?

- What would a kind, compassionate voice sound like in those moments? If it had a persona, what would it look/sound like? A compassionate grandparent? A fiercely empowering mentor? That trainer at the gym that makes you feel both stretched and strong?
- How would your life change if *that* voice was the one in charge?

4. Think about one area where you keep saying yes when your soul is screaming no.

- What would it feel like to honor your needs and set a boundary here?
- How might this small act of self-respect ripple into every corner of your life?

5. Close your eyes and imagine living each day rooted in the unshakable truth that you are *already enough*. You have already arrived.

- How would you show up differently in your relationships, your work, and your choices with nothing to prove?
- What could you let go of if you fully trusted that your worth isn't up for negotiation?

Here's the bottom line: You were never meant to hustle, prove, negotiate, or beg for your worth. It's yours—whole, untouchable, and infinite. Now, it's time to go live like you believe it.

Chapter 21
P—Pleasure and Play:
The Joyful Path to Presence and Resilience

Before You Dive In

When you hear the words *pleasure* and *play*, do you feel a sense of longing, resistance, or judgment? Take a moment to notice your reaction.

Let's start with a truth that needs reclaiming: Pleasure and play are not luxuries. They are essential. In a culture that equates worth with productivity, these elements of life are often dismissed as frivolous, indulgent, or worse, irresponsible. Yet they are the quiet antidotes to burnout, the secret keys to creative resilience, and the pathways to a life lived fully and joyfully.

But first, let's clear the air. The word *pleasure* often conjures up associations with sexuality, and while that's one important aspect, pleasure is much more expansive. Here, we're talking about the pleasure of presence—of being deeply rooted in your senses, attuned to the small joys of everyday life. It's the warmth of sunlight on your skin, the deliciousness of that first sip of coffee, the way laughter ripples through your body. Pleasure is about embodiment, connection, and the sensory experience of life.

As for play? It's not just for kids or for the lucky few with time to spare. Play is hardwired into us. It's how we learn, grow, and connect—not just in childhood, but throughout our lives. Together, pleasure and play invite us to step off the treadmill of endless striving and rediscover what it means to feel alive.

Pleasure is more than just feeling good. It's a gateway to presence. When we're overwhelmed, rushing, or stuck in our heads, we disconnect from our bodies and senses. We forget to savor life's small, nourishing moments. But pleasure—when consciously chosen—grounds us. It slows time, anchors us in the present, and gently reminds us: This moment is enough.

Pleasure has a profound impact on our well-being. Neuroscience tells us that pleasurable experiences trigger a cascade of feel-good chemicals—dopamine, serotonin, and oxytocin—that soothe our nervous systems and build resilience. Over time, these fleeting moments of delight can create lasting shifts in our emotional state.

This isn't about chasing constant euphoria or numbing discomfort with indulgence. Real pleasure, the kind that nourishes us, is subtle and sustainable. It's found in the rhythm of a favorite song, the smell of fresh coffee, or the softness of a worn sweatshirt. These small, sensory experiences recalibrate the nervous system, making us more adaptable and less reactive. They are a form of everyday magic, available to us when we choose to notice.

The Modern Problem with Pleasure

Our relationship with pleasure has been distorted by a culture obsessed with "more." We're taught to seek bigger thrills, louder experiences, and flashier rewards, often at the expense of quieter joys. This overstimulation hijacks our dopamine systems, leaving us constantly chasing the next, bigger dopamine hit. (Remember that checklist you explored earlier? It might be a good time to revisit it.) Meanwhile, authentic, grounded, truly nourishing pleasure often gets lost in the noise.

> Reclaiming pleasure means slowing down. It means untangling from the idea that savoring the simple pleasure of life must be earned. It's a quiet rebellion against the grind, a way to say: I already deserve to feel good, right here, right now.

PLAY: THE PATH BACK TO YOURSELF

If pleasure is about being present, play is about being curious. It's the spark that lights the fire of joy, the doorway to creativity, and the balm for a weary spirit. Yet somewhere along the way, many of us forget how to play. We trade joyful creativity for deadlines, silliness for efficiency, and curiosity for certainty. But play never stops being essential—it's as vital in adulthood as it is in childhood.

WHY PLAY IS SO POWERFUL

Play activates some of the most adaptive systems in our brain. It lights up the default mode network, where creativity and problem-solving thrive. It engages our social brain, building empathy and connection. It sharpens cognitive skills and teaches emotional regulation. Play isn't frivolous—it's a neurological necessity.

Through play, we experiment, imagine, and grow. It creates space for exploration without judgment, fostering resilience and adaptability. And when we're stuck, overwhelmed, or burned out, play can be the bridge back to ourselves—a way to rediscover our spark. Stuart Brown, a well-known play researcher, has identified seven core properties of play. And we bet exploring them will help even the most play-resistant of you to see it through a different lens. (Hint: It doesn't have to look like board games, improv, or cringey, forced fun. It can just be following a curious thread to see where it leads.)

1. **Apparently Purposeless**

   Play isn't about achieving, producing, or proving anything. It may look pointless from the outside, but that's the point. There's no practical value required, no productivity box to check. It's just for the joy of it. In a world that glorifies outcomes, play says, "You don't need a reason to have fun."

2. **Voluntary**

   True play isn't forced. The second something feels like an obligation, it stops being play. Its magic lives in choice—doing something because you *want* to, not because you *should*. This is freedom in action, and it's a direct rebellion against the pressure of people-pleasing and perfectionism.

3. **Inherently Attractive**

   Play feels good. It wakes up your senses, makes you laugh, and lights you up from the inside. Whether it's dancing in the kitchen, building a pillow fort, or making up ridiculous inside jokes, the experience itself is the reward. Play is a cure for boredom and a fast track to aliveness.

4. **Freedom from Time**

   Ever get so into something that you completely lose track of time? That's play. It frees you from the ticking clock of to-do lists and external demands. You drop into the now and experience time differently—spacious, expansive, and fully your own.

5. **Diminished Self-Consciousness**

   Play lets you drop the act. There's no need to look good or get it right. You're not worrying about what people think—you're too busy being in it. That's when we access flow. That peak moment where ego melts, joy expands, and you feel fully yourself.

6. **Improvisational Potential**

   Play doesn't stick to scripts. It's all about spontaneity and the magic of what if? You're free to experiment, make it up as you go, and follow the breadcrumbs of curiosity. This is how creativity is born—through messiness, missteps, and moments that surprise you.

7. **Continuation of Desire**

   Play makes you want to keep going. You tweak the rules, make up new versions, and find ways to extend the joy. When something feels this good, your brain wants more—not out of scarcity, but out of genuine pleasure. And from that place, new possibilities emerge.

These core properties remind us that play isn't a nice-to-have bonus for when you've got extra time—it's an essential lifeline to reconnect with your inner wisdom, divine spark, creativity, and resilience. Play engages your whole self—body, mind, and spirit—helping you practice being present, taking healthy risks, letting go of perfectionism, and improvising your way through life. It's a microcosm of living well: a space where you grow, adapt, connect, and, yes, laugh too loud for no reason at all. So go ahead, give yourself permission to play—it's not indulgence; it's essential.

Reclaiming Play in Adulthood

Reclaiming play often requires permission—the kind we rarely give ourselves. Permission to try something new, to be bad at it, and to laugh anyway. Permission to engage without a measurable outcome, to enjoy without justifying the time spent.

Play doesn't have to mean kickball or finger-painting (though it can). It can be a dance class, a spontaneous kitchen experiment, or simply letting yourself daydream. Play invites you to step out of the grind and into a state of flow where authentic pleasure and "unproductive joy" lead the way.

When we engage with play as defined by Brown's core properties, we remember that play is not just a fleeting escape—it's a lifeline. It connects us to our vitality, our creativity, and the deep well of resilience that allows us to navigate life's challenges with more grace and joy.

Reflections: Bringing Pleasure and Play into Your Life

Integrating pleasure and play doesn't require a major life overhaul. It starts with small, intentional choices—pausing to savor a moment, trying something new for the joy of it, or simply allowing yourself to rest.

Start Small

Take thirty seconds to notice and truly savor something beautiful—a flower, the texture of your coffee foam, the beautiful way sunlight dances on the wall.

Get Curious

- What activities bring you authentic joy? Certain songs? Activities? Hobbies?
- What did you love as a child?

Pleasure, Play, and Purpose

Pleasure and play are not distractions from purpose—they are its fuel. When we allow ourselves to feel good, we expand our capacity for creativity, connection, and resilience. We tap into a state of flow that draws us closer to our purpose, not through force, but through alignment.

> Imagine a life where success isn't measured by how much you've achieved but by how richly you've lived and where joy is not an afterthought but a guiding principle.

Pleasure and play offer us this possibility—a way to thrive, not just survive.

So take a deep breath. Pause. Laugh. Savor. Let pleasure and play light the way forward. The stage is set, and the spotlight is yours. Step into it fully, with joy as your guide.

REFLECTIONS:
RECLAIMING PLEASURE AND PLAY

1. What kind of stories have you been telling yourself about pleasure and play? Were you trained to think they're lazy, childish, or nice to have but not essential? Time to call that out and rewrite the narrative.

2. Think back to a moment when you felt pure, unfiltered pleasure— when you were totally present and lit up by something simple. What's one easy way you can bring more of that into your daily grind, like sipping your coffee without doomscrolling or letting yourself bask in the sun for five minutes?

3. How can you sneak a little playful mischief into your everyday life? Maybe it's experimenting with a funky dance move while folding laundry, cracking jokes in the middle of a boring meeting, or letting curiosity lead the way on your next errand.

4. If play didn't have to involve board games or sports, what could it look like for you? Think spontaneous kitchen experiments, weird doodles on sticky notes, or blasting your favorite song and belting it out like no one's watching.

5. What would change if you ditched the guilt and decided that pleasure and play aren't luxuries—they're fuel for your badassery? Pick one small thing to savor or one playful thing to try today. Go ahead—permission granted.

Chapter 22
E—Embodied Alignment:
Thriving as Your Authentic Self

Before You Dive In

How would you describe your relationship (and relationship history) with your body? Is it a relationship of control, curiosity, suppression, devotion, or mistrust?

This is where the magic of the PROSPER framework clicks into place. So far, we've been building the foundation: finding clarity around your Purpose, reclaiming your power with Response-Ability, opening up to Openness, standing tall in your Self-Worth, and rediscovering the vitality of Pleasure and Play. Each piece has offered insights, tools, and reflections to help you see yourself and your life in a whole new light.

But here's the truth: Insights alone won't transform your life. Simply knowing something doesn't automatically shift the way you live, love, or lead. Real change happens when what you know in your head sinks into your body, your choices, and your daily rhythm. That's the heart of Embodied Alignment.

It's the difference between a fleeting *aha!* moment of clarity and a deep *oooooh* that reverberates through your entire being. Embodied alignment moves you from understanding your purpose to living it. It's about syncing your thoughts, actions, and values so they're in harmony—not as a performance, but as an authentic, seamless way of being.

Think of it like this: You can read all the swimming guides in the world, but it's not until you're in the water, feeling the waves around you, that you become a swimmer. Embodied alignment is stepping into the water and trusting the rhythm of the stroke. It's where the theory you've learned becomes the transformation you've been waiting for.

This is the moment when your values, purpose, and authentic self stop being abstract ideas and start shaping the way you navigate every part of your life. It's the integration of all the work we've done so far. It's where you move from knowing who you are to being who you are, fully and unapologetically.

What Is Embodied Alignment?

Embodied Alignment is the natural outgrowth of everything we've explored so far in the PROSPER framework. It's the process of grounding your insights into your body, emotions, and daily life. It's the shift from concept to lived experience, where your Purpose, Response-Ability, Openness, Self-worth, and Pleasure are no longer abstract ideas but active forces shaping the way you move through life.

This work matters because authenticity—living in alignment with who you truly are—is far less stressful than trying to fit into molds that don't belong to you. When we mask ourselves to meet others' expectations, our nervous systems bear the cost. Misalignment creates chronic stress, tightens our bodies, and depletes our energy. But when we step into authenticity, we experience ease, connection, and a sense of being truly at home within ourselves.

Embodied alignment is about claiming that ease. It's the integration of mind, body, and spirit. It's living as the truest version of yourself, not just in flashes but consistently, with intention and grace.

From *Aha* to *Oooooh*: Moving from Insight to Aligned Action

Each stage of the PROSPER framework thus far has given you tools for self-discovery and growth. Along the way, you've likely experienced moments of clarity—an aha moment where a new insight lands and something clicks. Maybe you recognized a conditioned belief that no longer serves you. Maybe you identified the misaligned habits draining your energy. These aha moments are exciting, but they're only the beginning.

Embodied Alignment takes those sparks of insight and transforms them into lived truth. The oooooh moment happens when your body catches up to your mind—when the lesson becomes something you feel, act on, and integrate. This is the shift from intellectual understanding to deep, authentic living.

Here's an example. Let's say you've realized that chronically overgiving and overcommitting yourself lead to burnout and resentment. That's the *aha*. The *oh* comes when you feel your body's signals—your gut clenching at another yes you didn't mean—and pause to choose differently. The *oooooh* sometimes feels like a moment of humbling ick.

> Embodied Alignment means practicing that pause, gathering a couple heaping scoops of compassion and courage, realigning your actions with your truth, and slowly rewiring your nervous system to prioritize what actually feels right.

This process isn't about perfection; it's about progress. Every small, un-sexy step toward alignment reinforces your ability to live authentically.

The Role of Creativity and Curiosity

Creativity and curiosity are essential tools for embodiment. Earlier, in the Openness chapter, we explored how creativity allows us to imagine new possibilities and think beyond habitual patterns. Here, creativity helps us experiment with what alignment feels like in our bodies and lives.

Curiosity, meanwhile, invites us to approach this process with compassion rather than judgment. It's the gentle nudge that says, "What would it take to try this differently?" or "What could alignment look like here?" Instead of beating ourselves up for old habits, curiosity opens the door to experimentation and discovery.

Engaging with these tools activates neuroplasticity—the brain's ability to rewire itself. As we approach alignment creatively and curiously, we shift from old patterns of misalignment into new, supportive ways of being.

Authenticity and the Nervous System

Authenticity isn't just a conceptual ideal; it's a physiological necessity. When we live out of alignment—constantly censoring ourselves, people-pleasing, or pursuing goals that don't resonate—our nervous system registers this dissonance as a threat. This activates our stress response, keeping us in fight-or-flight mode and draining our resources.

Chronic stress, as we've discussed, can wreak havoc on every system in our body. But alignment offers an antidote.

> When we live authentically, we communicate safety to our nervous system.

This shifts us out of survival mode and into the parasympathetic state of rest, repair, and regeneration.

Practicing embodied alignment might mean setting a boundary, speaking your truth, or choosing rest when your body needs it. Each time you honor your authenticity, you reinforce the nervous system's connection between truth and well-being. Over time, this creates a foundation of resilience, trust, and ease.

The Interconnection of Embodiment and the PROSPER Framework

Embodied alignment isn't just another concept to check off your personal growth to-do list—it's the bold, messy, courageous weaving together of everything we've explored in the PROSPER framework so far. It's where the aha moments become a way of being not just fleeting insights.

- **Purpose** handed us our North Star, our why behind everything we do. Embodied alignment roots that purpose in the way we walk, talk, work, and connect with others.
- **Response-Ability** showed us how to replace knee-jerk reactions with thoughtful, empowered choices. Embodied alignment means showing up authentically when life throws its curveballs.
- **Openness** invited us to stay curious and say yes to growth, even when it felt uncomfortable. Embodied alignment asks us to stay connected to our heart space and lead with curiosity.
- **Self-Worth** reminded us that we're valuable, not because of what we do but because of who we are. Embodied alignment lets that worthiness sink deep into our bones, shaping every decision from a place of confidence, not fear.
- **Pleasure and Play** gave us permission to savor the sweetness of life, guilt-free. Embodiment transforms that permission into practice, making alignment feel as good as it looks on paper.

- **Embodiment** takes that purpose and choice and turns it into action—an everyday practice of courage and expansion.
- **Resonance** is the culmination of all of these qualities playing out cocreatively in life, but we will get to that in a minute.

Embodied alignment is the magical glue. It ties every piece of the framework we've explored together, transforming insights into real-deal, lived truth. And it's what we see missing from the vast majority of personal growth work. It's not about thinking your way into alignment—it's about feeling it, living it, and letting it ripple through every corner of your brain, body, and life.

Reflections: Listening to and Learning to Decode the Body's Signals

Good-bad news: Your body has been communicating with you all along—sending signals of alignment, authenticity, and safety, as well as tension, resistance, and misalignment. Unfortunately, and for a lot of reasons that we've already explored in this book, we learn to suppress or overlook them. But it's never too late to listen.

- Looking back, what moments or memories can you recall when your body felt at ease, open, energized, or safe?
- What about times when you felt drained, tense, tight, or disconnected?
- In hindsight, what can you learn about how your body is responding to each?
- How can you learn and use these physical responses as guideposts moving forward?

CHAPTER 23
R—RESONANCE:
TAPPING INTO ABUNDANCE

BEFORE YOU DIVE IN

How do you define *enough*? When you look through the lens of money, status, achievement, love, impact, success, etc., what is enough?

We've arrived at the final pillar of the PROSPER framework: Resonance. This is where all the work we've done—exploring Purpose, cultivating Response-Ability, expanding into Openness, reclaiming Self-Worth, embracing Pleasure, and Embodying alignment— culminates in a way of being that magnetizes abundance. Resonance is the flow state, the magic, the deep synchronicity that occurs when we align with who we are at our core and trust in the natural unfolding of life.

Resonance isn't something we force; it's something we tune into. It's the energy that hums through us when we're aligned with our purpose, grounded in self-worth, open to possibilities, and living in a state of embodied authenticity. Resonance is a natural result of living into our authentic design and moving through life with a harmonized nervous system. It's not about chasing resources, relationships, or opportunities—it's about attracting them by becoming the kind of person they naturally gravitate toward.

Redefining Resources and Abundance

Before diving deeper, let's clarify what we mean by resources and abundance, because these words can carry preconceptions.

- **Resources** are not just financial. They encompass time, energy, creativity, relationships, insights, and spiritual alignment—the elements that nourish and sustain us.
- **Abundance** isn't merely about accumulation; it's about the felt experience of having enough and trusting in the replenishing flow of life. It's the sense of being connected to an infinite source of support and possibility, even in the face of challenges.

Resonance, then, is the energetic state that attracts these resources and abundance into our lives. It's not about wishful thinking or passive waiting; it's about aligning so deeply with our purpose and truth that we naturally harmonize with opportunities, support, and flow.

Quantum Potential and the Science of Resonance

As we discussed in the introduction to the Leadership Types and our introduction to the PROSPER framework, quantum science shows us that the universe is not a collection of static objects but a vast field of energy in constant motion. Everything, including us, exists as a dynamic interplay of particles and waves, oscillating between potentiality and practical manifestation. In quantum terms, we are not fixed beings but energetic systems continually interacting and cocreating with the world around us.

When scientists first explored the subatomic world, they discovered something astonishing: Particles didn't behave like tiny solid marbles as once believed. Instead, they could exist as both particles (matter) and waves (energy), sometimes behaving like one, sometimes the other. This is called *wave-particle duality*—and it means that, at a fundamental level, reality is both potential and physical form at the same time. What we experience as solid matter is really concentrated energy that has temporarily taken shape.

But it doesn't stop there. The more scientists studied these particles, the more interconnected they appeared. In certain experiments, two particles that were once connected could continue to affect each other instantaneously, even when separated by vast distances—a phenomenon called *quantum entanglement.* In simple terms, everything in the universe remains deeply connected through these invisible energetic threads. You are not separate from the world around you; you are participating in an interconnected field of energy, always in communication with the whole.

This is where resonance becomes so important. Resonance is about aligning our internal state—our beliefs, emotions, beingness, and choices—with the frequency of who we truly are, how we're designed to thrive, and what we want to experience. In much the same way that quantum particles collapse into a specific state when observed, our embodied alignment focuses the infinite possibilities surrounding us into tangible outcomes. You can think of this as standing in a room full of countless possible songs, but your unique frequency determines which song begins to play.

This process isn't mystical; it's simply how energy behaves. When our internal energy (our embodied alignment) matches what we're consciously calling in, we create a state of *quantum coherence*—a kind of harmony between our inner system and the field around us. Coherence happens when your mind, emotions, nervous system, and energetic blueprint are all vibrating in sync. When this occurs, your energy field becomes clear, efficient, and magnetic. You're no longer scattering energy in different directions through inner conflict, fear, or conditioned programming—you're broadcasting a steady, coherent signal that amplifies your ability to attract what you truly need to thrive, create, and serve.

> Resonance is the state of living in this coherence. It's what happens when your thoughts, emotions, and authentic being-ness vibrate together, allowing you to participate fully in the creative field of life.

This is often where people confuse the Law of Attraction with the deeper science of the Law of Resonance. The Law of Attraction is often simplified into the idea that if you think positive thoughts, good things will come. But it's not simply about what you think—it's about who you are *being*. Thoughts without embodied resonance are like radio signals too weak to reach their destination. The Law of Resonance reminds us that we don't attract what we want; we attract what we are in coherent alignment with.

Take a moment to ponder that.

When you are aligned with your true design, you become that clear signal. Your nervous system stabilizes. Your creativity expands. Your energy becomes magnetic—not because you're forcing outcomes, but because your frequency naturally draws in the people, opportunities, and experiences that match your unique resonance.

You're no longer chasing.

You're no longer forcing.

You're no longer hustling for your worth.

You're simply allowing what was always trying to find you to finally arrive.

> Human Design offers us a profound map for this work—not simply a personality tool, but a quantum technology for alignment. It helps you identify your optimal frequency, teaches you how to maintain coherence, and ultimately allows you to cocreate your life with greater ease, clarity, and purpose.

Scarcity Versus Abundance: A Shift in Mindset and Biology

As we explored in the GRIND framework, many of us are conditioned to operate from a scarcity mindset. We worry there isn't enough—time, money, talent, opportunities—or that *we* aren't enough to deserve them. This belief narrows our perspective, creating a sense of competition and constriction. It's like living in a tiny, dimly lit room, convinced the walls are closing in.

An abundance mindset, on the other hand, acknowledges challenges but also trusts in the vast field of possibilities beyond what we can immediately see. It expands our perspective, allowing us to breathe and approach life with curiosity and trust.

From a neurological perspective, scarcity and abundance are more than just ideas; they're states that affect how our nervous system functions.

- **Scarcity** triggers the brain's stress response, keeping us in a state of vigilance. Elevated cortisol levels narrow our focus and limit creative problem-solving. The brain's reticular activating system (RAS)—responsible for filtering what we notice—becomes hyperattuned to evidence of lack, reinforcing the belief that we're stuck.
- **Abundance**, in contrast, activates the parasympathetic nervous system, allowing us to relax, restore, and think more flexibly. The RAS begins to highlight opportunities, connections, and solutions that align with our open, trusting state of being.

This shift isn't just theoretical—it's a neurobiological and energetic change that influences how we perceive, respond to, and create opportunities.

Resonance: Tuning to the Frequency of Abundance

As we have said, resonance occurs when one vibrating system causes another to vibrate at the same frequency. Picture striking a tuning fork and seeing another fork across the room begin to hum in response. The two systems have entered harmony—not because they touched, but because their frequencies matched.

Now imagine yourself as that tuning fork. You are constantly broadcasting a frequency into the quantum field, shaped not only by your thoughts, but by your emotions, beliefs, nervous system state, and subconscious meaning-making. Every experience you've ever had—every story you've inherited or absorbed—contributes to the particular energetic signal you're sending out at any given moment.

When your internal state is aligned—when your beliefs, emotions, nervous system, and actions are coherent—you emit a clear, stable frequency that naturally harmonizes with opportunities, relationships, and outcomes that resonate with that frequency. Like calls to like. You're not forcing outcomes; you're becoming magnetic to those outcomes because you are embodying the energetic signature that matches them.

This is the true essence of resonance. It's not about controlling every step or hustling to make things happen. It's not about trying to think positively while still feeling anxious underneath. Instead, it's about aligning so deeply with your purpose, your design, and your authentic being that you become a natural match for the resources, connections, and possibilities that are already present in the quantum field, waiting to be drawn in.

When you are in resonance, life feels less like an uphill battle and more like a dance—fluid, responsive, and often surprising in its generosity. You're no longer driven by fear or the need for constant external validation. Instead, you show up in aligned action and allow the coherence of your energy field to do much of the heavy lifting. The work you've done—cultivating clarity, worthiness, openness, nervous system regulation, and energetic alignment—becomes the signal that organizes the field around you.

Often, what arrives isn't what your mind could have predicted or planned—but it's exactly what your soul has been preparing for.

Living Your Purpose to Tap into Abundance

Purpose sits at the heart of the PROSPER framework. It's the guiding star that orients us toward what matters most, the unique contribution we're here to make. When we're living (and *being*) our purpose, we create a magnetic field around us. This doesn't mean challenges disappear, but the effort feels fluid, like we're being carried by a current rather than swimming upstream.

Quantum theory tells us that energy follows focus and intention. When we consistently align with our purpose, honor our design, and trust in our inherent worth, we "collapse" the field of infinite possibilities into tangible experiences that match our energy. Opportunities, resources, and connections seem to flow toward us—not because we're lucky, but because we're energetically resonating with them.

Practices for Resonance

1. **Anchor in Gratitude**
   Gratitude is like resetting your internal station to Abundance FM. Take time each day to notice what's working, no matter how small, and let it expand your perspective.

2. **Act from Alignment**
   Before making a decision, ask yourself: Does this align with who I truly am and what I want to create? Pay attention to how your body feels when you consider your answer.

3. **Trust the Flow**

   Stop gripping so tightly. Life unfolds in ways we can't predict. When you release control, you make room for surprises that align with your highest good.

4. **Celebrate the Small Wins**

   Each time you notice even a whisper of resonance in your life—a kind word, a moment of ease, a spark of inspiration—celebrate it. These are signs you're on the right frequency.

5. **Reconnect to Your Purpose**

   When doubt creeps in, anchor back to your purpose. It's your North Star, the steady guide that keeps you aligned with what truly matters.

The Magic of Resonance

Resonance is the culmination of the PROSPER framework—a state of being where purpose, alignment, and abundance converge. It's not magic in the mystical sense (although it *does* feel pretty damn magical when it happens); it's the natural result of living in harmony with the quantum potential of who you truly are.

As we align with our truth, we stop forcing and start flowing. We become attuned to opportunities that match our frequency, living with greater ease, joy, and abundance. In resonance, life doesn't just happen to us—we cocreate it, moment by moment, from a place of authentic alignment. We live life at the intersection of authenticity and possibility.

The PROSPER framework has been a journey of rediscovery, inviting you to reclaim your purpose, embody your worth, and trust the process. Resonance is the reward, the natural outcome: a life that feels abundant, meaningful, and profoundly alive. Now, it's your turn to tune in, align deeply, and let your unique frequency shape the world around you. Abundance is already within you, waiting to flow. Let it.

Reflections

1. **Tuning Your Frequency**

    When in your life have you felt most in flow, like opportunities and resources were drawn to you with ease? What were you doing, thinking, and feeling at that time?

2. **Scarcity Versus Abundance**

    What are the stories you've been telling yourself about scarcity—what there's "never enough" of? (money, time, energy, opportunity) How might those stories shift if you trusted that there's always enough (and *you're* always enough) for what truly matters?

3. **Amping Up Your Magical Magnetic Field**

    How aligned do you feel with your purpose, values, and truth right now? What's one step you can take today to bring your inner frequency closer to what you want to attract?

4. **Gratitude as a Practice**

    What are three things you're grateful for in this moment? How can you let gratitude guide your focus toward abundance rather than lack? (Bonus points if you can find gratitude or purpose in a current or past challenge.)

5. **Resonance in Action**

    Imagine living fully in resonance—your actions, thoughts, and emotions humming in harmony with truth, possibility, and enoughness. How would your daily life, thoughts, and relationships shift if that was your default state?

Chapter 24
Storytime: Bringing PROSPER to Life

By now, you've been introduced to the PROSPER framework—and maybe some parts of it already sparked insight or recognition. These seven pillars offer powerful direction when you're feeling stuck, disconnected, or caught in cycles that no longer serve you. But before we guide you deeper—into the Integrative Somatic Experience (ISE) process we've created to help you shift the stories holding you back on a conscious and unconscious level—we want to bring it all down to earth.

Because concepts are helpful. But lived examples? They're where things get real.

What follows are stories from each of us—honest, unpolished glimpses into what it has looked like to practice living the PROSPER way in our actual lives. These stories show how we've failed forward, circled back, and slowly reclaimed our energy, purpose, and prosperity one imperfect choice at a time.

We've learned through both personal experience and our work with clients that true transformation isn't just about mindset. It's not just about doing more (or less). It's not even just about having the right tools. It's about working on multiple levels: shifting the way you see the world, changing the way you relate to yourself in the everyday moments, and addressing the deep, often hidden stories that live inside your body and nervous system.

That's where the PROSPER framework and the ISE™ process that follows work hand in hand.

PROSPER helps you name what to shift—what to do (or stop doing) to reclaim your energy, clarity, and life force.

ISE helps you untangle what's still holding you back beneath the surface—those subconscious patterns, stuck emotions, and energetic tethers that often keep you repeating old loops, even when your conscious mind wants and knows better.

We're going to walk you through that full process soon.

But first, we want to make it human… to show you how the PROSPER pillars have been lived out in our own lives. Our hope is that in reading our stories, you'll begin to see your own patterns more clearly—and begin to imagine new ways of choosing, living, and leading from a more prosperous place.

A Story About a Sorceress Who Lost Her Light (but not really)

Alright y'all, Laura here. It's time to see how the PROSPER framework has played out in real life for me in my journey through burnout. I have woven each of the principles throughout the story and denoted them in parentheses for ease—think of them like a little nod. Hopefully, it will help you to see how they are more than just ideas, these are the very values that help us to see our patterns and shift our stories.

I've already shared the time I was diagnosed with adrenal fatigue—that space between my life as an art jeweler and stepping into my path as a healer and coach. But let's linger there for a minute. In that liminal pause, as I began to heal my body, my mind, and my spirit, I could literally feel my Master Builder energy coming back online. That feeling can be like pressure to seek out something, or like a restless leg of the soul. I wasn't ready to jump into something full time, but I started to wonder, to get curious about what might be next.

As I started to look for a "job," my weary little being just wanted something simple compared to running my own company. I fantasized about clocking in, smiling at everyone, maybe even whistling while I worked (*um, fantasize much, Laura?*), then heading home to enjoy quiet evenings with my family. Dreamy, right?

Except there was this little voice inside—every time I looked at that Trader Joe's application (and honestly, I believe every creative entrepreneur secretly dreams of quitting it all and working at Trader Joe's, probably because everyone there is smiling)—this voice would stop me and whisper that I was here for something else.

And, true to my well-practiced tendency of avoiding uncomfortable emotions, I tried not to listen. But I knew this part of me. I had met her as a child—and again as a young adult when a traumatic event cracked me wide open. So when I felt her this time, I wasn't surprised. Just frustrated. I wanted life to be easy... and fun. And it felt like I couldn't have both and live on purpose. (Spoiler alert: I'm designed in Human Design to use joy as my North Star and course correct when I've lost my way, so of course life was going to hand me plenty of practice rounds.)

So there I was in this void, knowing I was here on purpose because that little soul whisper wouldn't leave me alone. My only real choice was to surrender to it. So, I opened. I got curious. I began to wonder—*What is next? How will I find it? Would I find it? When?* You get the point. And thankfully, I didn't have the bandwidth to push or force my way there. I was too tired for that. So, wondering (Openness) worked.

That's when I found the field of Brain Integration. Well technically, my child did—but I needed it just as much, maybe more. Because while I was spending my days with *Murder, She Wrote* and naps, I was quietly falling apart. Adrenal burnout had flattened my body. But my mind? My mind wouldn't rest. My old patterns of proving, fear, and hustle were flaring up in the silence. I was in the void after a major disruption with zero tools and a whole lot of thrashing. So when I landed in a modality that helps regulate the nervous system and rewires unconscious thought patterns? Not a coincidence.

Brain Integration helps the brain create new responses—to breathe, to choose. It brings the executive functioning part of the brain back online, slowing things down enough to create space between trigger and action, which is literally the definition of Response-Ability. Can you imagine a world where everyone could do that? I mean… *hello, life purpose.* I felt the rightness of it, the way it all clicked into place, and the feeling I had known as a little girl came rushing back.

The first time I felt that sacred tug, I was playing (Play). Literally. A storm was coming, the sky wild and electric. I ran inside, threw on my mother's nightgown (because obviously you need the proper attire), and raced onto the deck. Arms open, hair whipping in the wind (Pleasure), I became my inner Sorceress. I knew—deep in my bones—that I could speak to the wind, call the water, connect with the stars, the trees, all of life. That power swirled through me, pooling in my belly. I just knew I could shape the universe, for good of course.

And then my mom screamed my full name from the back door because I was standing barefoot in the rain, in her favorite nightgown. Just like that, I was yanked back into reality. But the feeling—the quiet knowing that a power lived just under the surface—stayed with me.

Then, of course, I hit puberty and lost touch with the magic. *My* magic.

Like so many, my teenage years tangled into insecurity and father wounds. I searched for my value everywhere but within. At nineteen, I became pregnant. One day I'll write the full book on that chapter—it was bursting with transformation. But for now, I'll simply say: It was the second time my inner sorceress woke me up. And through that, I realized I had a choice. I had a purpose. I was here to live it, seek it, return to it.

I would love to say I came out of that fully awake and ready to live my purpose. But... I didn't. I did meet my husband in magical, guided ways, had two incredible children, built a family—which was absolutely part of my purpose. And then I built my jewelry career, which also felt like purpose. Until it didn't. Until I found myself in the fetal position wondering how I had gotten the American Dream so terribly wrong.

Because I kept trying to find my purpose in what I was *doing*, not who I was *being*. I hadn't yet learned to fully value myself. So I spent a lot of those years, especially in jewelry, trying to prove my worth (Self-Worth) through knowing, learning, and doing. And I completely burned myself out.

When Wes sold me the company and left, I inherited a massive workload. There are so many people struggling with ADD, ADHD, learning differences—and not enough trained professionals to help. I had a six-month wait list. I loved the work, but the modality, rooted in applied kinesiology, was rigid: lie on the table, follow the protocol, voila—cured. Except... have you ever tried to keep a six-year-old with severe ADHD still? It's like massaging a squirrel.

It was a lot. And my entrepreneurial brain saw the gap and tried to fill it.

So I expanded. I trained five new practitioners, built a clinic, created resources, ran trainings, pursued my 2000-hour Energetic Kinesiology certification, began studying Applied Neurology, helped build a school, managed a business, mentored staff...

It was too much. And still, we were going into debt.

Referrals kept coming to me, not my team. The work was sacred, but I couldn't keep the ship afloat. I didn't understand how to run a business. I tried—books, coaches, mentors—but what I really needed was to believe in my worth.

My core wound healing is about boundaries and devotion (yes, this insight is actually in my Human Design chart too). So a central part of my soul school is about learning to say yes only when I mean it, and committing only to what I can give my full heart to. But I'd been shaped by proving, fear, and a desire to be seen as smart and capable. And the only path to healing worth? Stillness. Curiosity. Going inward.

This is dragon-slaying work. And you can't do it alone.

Every hero's journey has allies. Mine included community and my relationship to Source. Always. Even in death, we return to Source. Connection is the foundation. From there, we learn to see differently, to forgive, to open.

When I first started training, my mentor asked if I had a spiritual practice. I said, "I had my chakras balanced in college once..." So, not really. He encouraged me to find one. And I listened.

I found my spiritual home at Unity of the Blue Ridge just outside Asheville. On day one, Reverend Darlene Strickland said, "This is the church for people who don't like churches," and gave one of the best talks I'd ever heard on the difference between spirituality and religion. From that moment, I knew I had found my place.

I started meditating. If you've ever tried meditation as a beginner, you know—it's hard. You try not to think, but thinking is the water we swim in. What we're really avoiding is feeling. As long as we stay busy, we don't have to feel. But true fatigue lives in the soul. And the only antidote? Re-Sourcing (reconnecting with Source).

I had spent my whole life doing. Builder energy. But I needed to learn how to *be*.

That's when I found Dr. Joe Dispenza. His work blew my mind—the intersection of thoughts, emotions, physiology, and Spirit. I learned to meditate deeply, to connect with Source, and to rewrite my stories about worth.

That work returned me to the little girl who called the wind. It helped me feel again. Not just the joy, but the pain. Because to feel pleasure, you must first feel your pain—you can't selectively numb or avoid emotions. Trust me, I tried.

So, I reclaimed my relationship with Pleasure. And pleasure lives in sensation. I learned to feel the sun, the water, the ground, the taste of food. I took somatics classes to reconnect through Play.

I built a sacred space in my closet—a fort of play. I wrote poetry, colored, solved puzzles, sang made-up songs, painted poorly. And slowly, I healed the parts that were afraid to be seen.

I danced. I swung at the park. I waited for joy to return, and I trusted the process. And in that waiting space, I discovered that pleasure lives in the gap—between desire and fulfillment. That waiting space? That's the Builder's sweet spot. The sacred tension of what is becoming.

The more I played, the more I healed.

And then... things began to shift. I started to *feel* into what was right for me—and what wasn't. Which (spoiler) can be life-wrecking. Boundaries rearrange everything. But this time, I had the tools: spiritual practice, meditation, play, trust in Source. I could stay grounded even in the storm.

Curiosity, Source, and Play brought me home to myself.

Pleasure became my compass. I started responding to aligned opportunities. One of those was an email about a speaker program. I felt a full-bodied yes. It was pricey. I didn't have the money. But I sat with it in wonder. I asked, "What would it take?"

Eventually, I called my mom—my rock. She's a Possibilitarian Guide. I asked if she thought this was right for me. She said yes without hesitation. She offered to pay the deposit. Then the second payment too. I cried. I received. I surrendered.

That program changed everything. We clarified our message. Wrote our keynote. And we even got our book deal (but Meghan will tell you more about that in her story!).

This is the magic of Resonance. You can't will it. You align with it.

I realized that I had been forcing things for years. But when I finally surrendered to Source, my true worth and wonder—they simply unfolded.

When Meghan and I talk about the resonance that comes from living your design, this is what we mean. When Dr. Joe says that the expected is the known, and true manifestations come from the unknown—this is what he means. Prosperity is the harmony between money and well-being. You can have abundance out of balance; you can have wealth without harmony. But true prosperity? That requires resonance with your true purpose, where being and doing finally dance together.

There is nothing you have to figure out. You simply have to be who you are designed to be—and then put your feet on the ground and walk that in service to something bigger than your ego: your heart.

I would love to say that I'll never burn out again—that I've finally learned the lesson. But I know better. Life will keep inviting me back to these edges: worth, boundaries, joy. The classroom never really closes.

But something is different now.

The fight has softened. The grasping has loosened. I don't need to force or prove or chase. I know how to listen for the quiet *yes* that lives in my belly—my Sacral response. I know how to sit in the in between, where desire hasn't yet become form, and trust that life is still moving beneath the surface of what I can see.

I know now that alignment isn't something I earn—it's something I return to.

I've learned to let joy lead me home, again and again.

And if I ever forget, I know that I have that inner Sorceress within me, ready to guide me back to my path and into the unknown.

REWRITING MY PROSPERITY NARRATIVE: HEALING MY MONEY STUFF AND LIVING BEYOND THE GRIND

Meghan here with another heaping scoop of (hopefully affirming and inspiring) humanity for you...

I spent decades thinking *prosperity* meant making money, performing success externally, and proving my worth to... everyone. I believed that if I worked hard enough, hustled long enough, and made myself useful and valuable to everyone around me, I'd eventually feel fulfilled, secure, and blissfully lit up by the sweet feeling of finally "making it."

Spoiler: That formula didn't work. At least not in any sort of sustainable or feel-good way.

Even while building a meaningful business and supporting others in beautiful ways, I often felt like I was failing—especially when it came to money. I was overgiving, chronically second-guessing myself, and caught in a loop of exhaustion and self-doubt. My nervous system was in a constant state of overdrive, and no matter how many hours I worked, how powerful my sessions with clients were, or how much I cared, I *still* felt like I was falling short. If you want opportunities to heal your money stuff (which is rarely just about money), become an entrepreneur. It will *always* reflect your blind spots.

Now I see it clearly: I was deep in the GRIND—living out the very patterns this book helps you name and shift. Sometimes, we have to live fully into what doesn't work long enough to finally realize what does.

And that's where the PROSPER framework comes in. These seven pillars aren't a checklist or a one-size-fits-all formula.

They're not something you master once and for all. They're invitations—anchoring principles that have become a trusted compass to step out of the swirls of my conditioning and back into the life I actually want. When I feel disconnected from my energy, clarity, self-worth, or truth, I return to them. They guide me back to myself and what's most nourishing.

And as I've lived these principles, they have invited me to redefine prosperity in some pretty huge ways. Now I know that it's not the size of my bank account or how many people approve of me that make me successful. It's not something that comes from chasing success or relentlessly trying to prove I deserve it. Prosperity, I've learned, is actually a way of life, a state of *being*. A relationship with life that is rooted in truth, fueled by what feels good, and a courageous willingness to be open to the unexpected. When I live in that way—when I embody these principles—abundance flows in ways I could never have controlled, planned, or strategized.

What follows are bits and pieces of stories from my own journey—moments where I practiced these concepts, sometimes clumsily, sometimes courageously, and always imperfectly. I offer them not as a prescription, but hopefully as a sort of mirror. My hope is that you'll begin to notice where PROSPER is already alive in your life—and also where you're being invited to trust deeper, open wider, and step into a more resonant, sustainable success.

P – Purpose

As I mentioned earlier in the book, from a very early age I've known I was here for some sort of big calling, responsibility, or purpose. But for a long time, I was confused by it. My strong sense of purpose often became conflated with the stories I learned about success and worthiness. So, I unknowingly tried to express (and prove) that purpose through a cultural lens that simply didn't fit my authentic design. I was always surrounded by people who prided themselves on productivity, enduring, and pushing through—and I internalized the belief that my worth depended on how much I did, how much money I made, and how much I suffered or endured in the process. Ugh. Exhausting.

Discovering my Human Design was the first domino. It gave language to something I had always sensed: I wasn't here to hustle—I was here to see, sense, and guide. That my deepest work happens in the energetic, the relational, and the intuitive realms. When I learned this, I felt both wildly affirmed and... pissed off! Parts of me really wanted to fit in with those stories I had learned, to be the badass that did all of the things, and to continue earning gold stars for being a good little achiever. I'll be very transparent with you in saying that I had to grieve the truth of not being who life taught me I should be for a while before I could even begin to embrace my design. And I definitely wouldn't have been able to embrace it through practical choices in my life... and finally detox from the GRIND (because that adrenalized way of life is pretty addictive and compelling) without support from aligned people (like Laura), who kept reminding me that my deep presence *was* the gift and the "work"—NOT my productivity or output.

This untangling of beliefs has been... a process!

It has taken *years* to trust the purpose of my design more than the "uncomfortable comfort" of my conditioning.

But the thing is, when I reconnect with my true sense of purpose—not the one I was conditioned to chase, but the truth that lives in my cells—I remember that, as a Possibilitarian Guide, I'm here to be wise about energy far more than about matter. I'm designed to sense what others often miss, to feel deeply, to witness patterns and stories, and to help guide people back to themselves and their full potential. I'm here to be valued for *that*. Through understanding deeper aspects of my Human Design (beyond what we explore in this book), I've also come to understand that some of my most challenging life experiences weren't obstacles to my purpose at all—they were necessary compost to grow me *toward* my purpose. They broke me open in just the right ways to grow the wisdom I'm now able to offer others. The painful events, losses, and disappointments were actually perfect catalysts for clarified purpose, empowerment, and service to the world—wisdom and guidance that's rooted in the integrity that can only be gained through lived experience. This deeper understanding of my "soul school curriculum" has helped me reframe countless moments that could have left me stuck in shame, victimhood, or struggle. Instead of seeing them as failures, I now see them as part of the Divine unfolding. Purpose, for me, is no longer a goal to achieve—it's a way of being that keeps calling me home to myself. And when challenges arrive on my doorstep, I don't necessarily invite them in for tea with a smile on my face, but I know without a doubt that there's a gift waiting to be unwrapped within them... and that perspective alone has transformed my life in some pretty incredible ways.

But those old stories around success are persistent—and having a sense of purpose is essential, but often isn't enough. Without creating safety, ease, openness, and trust in the body, it's nearly impossible to move toward truth and be brave enough to actually *live* it.

R – Response-Ability

I spent a lot of time in my life trying to force and control things—not necessarily in the overt control freak, bossy pants sort of way (although I have absolutely played that role), but where I tended to find myself stuck more often was in the "If it matters, then make it happen" camp. I thought that if something mattered—my work, my personal growth and healing, my relationships—I needed to push it forward in the desired direction and use my will to bring it into form. I thought it was noble. I thought that I was honoring my sense of purpose through drive. But the truth is, control always has fear pulling the strings beneath the surface, and on a nervous system level, I was living in a consistent stress response. The more

I tried to force clarity, fix things, or out-hustle my fear of failure, the more depleted I became. I kept thinking if I could just find the right strategy or work a little harder (i.e., have more control), I'd finally feel safe to move forward—toward success, toward relief, toward what would really make me happy. But what I really needed wasn't another plan—I needed to pause.

And I really, *really* didn't want to pause. Adrenalized momentum had become like a security blanket for me. It kept me from having to feel the tender feelings like helplessness, grief, and fear directly. If I stayed busy, then I could somewhat outrun the parts of my humanity that felt overwhelming.

So, not only did learning to slow down and pause not come naturally, but at first it was wildly uncomfortable, cringey, even scary at times. My nervous system had been trained to equate stillness with danger or failure—if I let my guard down, and stopped controlling life, who even knows what could happen?! But eventually, as I built capacity for moments of stillness and quiet (literally setting a timer for five to ten minutes at a time at first because that's all I could handle), I started noticing the signals my body was sending me—tight jaw, racing thoughts, that familiar urge to overfunction. And instead of powering through, I began treating those signals as invitations.

Not invitations to do more, but to *be* with myself differently. To get curious. And to do the opposite of what I'd always done.

I began practicing small, radical acts of reset: lying down for five minutes in the middle of the day, putting my hand on my heart and breathing for several seconds before answering an email, and going for a short walk to shake out some energy instead of pushing through my to-do list without a break. These weren't flashy or impressive choices, but they were life changing. Bit by bit, they incrementally rewired my relationship to stress. They helped me shift from the constant adrenalized momentum of reacting to life out of fear to responding from a place of intentional choice.

This, to me, is true personal responsibility—the ability to *respond* to life in a way that honors my energy, my nervous system, and my well-being. Checking in with my nervous system and overall stress is something I return to countless times daily—especially when the old patterns try to sneak back in and convince me that doing more is the way to feel safe again.

O – Openness

In early 2023, I followed an unrelenting, totally illogical, but undeniably strong intuitive call to take a month off and drive across the country—alone. I didn't have a perfectly planned itinerary or a spreadsheet of stops—control had left the building! What I *did* have was a deep sense that I needed to meet the Pacific Ocean, to step out of the patterns of the life I was living in order to allow something to shift deep within me, and to let life show me what else was possible. So I made plans for my pup and my kiddo, told my clients I'd be on a short sabbatical, and within a couple of months I was packed up in my car, whispering a quiet prayer, and hitting the road with snacks, new tires, and one central guiding mantra: *I wonder what magic will happen for me today?*

And magic *did* happen! Strangers showed me unexpected kindness and generosity. Old pressures and fears softened while driving long stretches of expansive landscapes. Countless moments of synchronicity reminded me that no matter how alone or overwhelmed I felt, I was *always* being supported and guided.

That trip became a living initiation in whole-hearted surrender. It taught me what it feels like to live with open palms instead of a white-knuckled grip. To trust not just in the Universe, but in my own capacity to meet the moment with curiosity instead of relying on control. That lived experience of openness rewired something deep in me, and it has become a sort of golden thread I've been weaving into my everyday life ever since—a trust that I don't have to have it all figured out to be on the right path. And what a relief that has been!

Openness, I've learned, isn't about recklessness or blind faith. It's about choosing to believe that life is conspiring in your favor, even when you don't yet know how. It's not about denying the disappointments, injustices, or pain of life, but instead balancing all of that out with a sense of wonder, faith, and openness. And in this world, choosing faith over fear is a pretty radical act.

S – Self-Worth

Old stories die hard. Mine told me that rest had to be earned. That value came through sacrifice. That being small was the safest way to belong. These stories weren't just beliefs—they were survival strategies shaped by culture, family, and lived experience. And even now, I'm still in the process of rewriting them.

But here's what I've learned: Rewriting doesn't always look like a grand revelation. Sometimes, it looks like choosing to lie down in the middle of the day—even when the dishes aren't done. Sometimes, it's saying no to a client who doesn't feel aligned even though I "need" the money or walking away from a relationship that drains my energy. Each time I make a self-honoring choice, I plant a seed of a new truth: *I am inherently worthy.* Nothing to earn or negotiate. Nothing to prove.

I matter not because I'm useful. Not because I worked hard enough. But because I *am.*

This is the sacred, gritty work of healing. It's unglamorous and revolutionary all at once. And over time, these choices add up. They build a new internal ecosystem rooted in deep self-trust which is the necessary foundation for authentic self-confidence. And by living this way, I hope to be a sort of embodied permission slip for others, reminding them that worthiness isn't something to chase—it's something I come home to, again and again… and they can too.

P – Pleasure and Play

Focusing on pleasure and play didn't come naturally to me. I am an old soul, parentified kid—conditioned to feel more at home in responsibility than in silliness or ease. I learned early on that being helpful, thoughtful, and mature earned me praise. And praise, as it turns out, can be a bit like a drug—so I got really good at chasing the next "hit." Play, on the other hand, felt foreign. Awkward. Even when I wanted to join in and play like other kids, it was as if I was a computer missing that program entirely. I could be crafty with my hands and always had a quick, witty sense of humor—but when it came to letting go, being silly, or simply following joy for no reason, I was at a total loss.

In my thirties, I realized that if I wanted to feel alive—not just functional—I had to learn how to play. Not in the forced fun way. Not as a concept, but as a lived, embodied experience of letting go and following what felt good. I had to let my nervous system know that pleasure was safe. That delight didn't have to be earned and that joy wasn't a distraction from my purpose—it was actually a necessary part of it.

So I started small: I went to a theme park with two of my best friends, paninis packed in a cooler (because I'm still bougie), with the clear intention of reclaiming space to play. I committed to showing up at the dance studio regularly and even started to (gasp!) perform—yes, I was that thirty-something woman shopping unapologetically at Forever 21 for performance costumes. I began embracing more of my natural sass and quirkiness in the little moments of daily life. I let myself read romance novels in the middle of the day. I blocked time just to follow what felt good, without any plan. I prioritized spending time with people who made me feel free—people who were naturally more playful than I was (because let's be honest, we all need examples and models sometimes). I practiced following what felt light and alive, even when it didn't make logical sense.

And the more I practiced, the more I noticed how play became a portal—a way back to myself. A way to remember that pleasure isn't frivolous—it's fuel. It's how we reclaim our creative power and call back our life force after being depleted by the grind of traditional adulting. The more I wove the magic of play into my life, the more creative energy I had to do my work.

And I've found that when I follow what feels joyful, life has a funny way of opening up new, unexpected paths—ones I could never have strategized my way into. I can't tell you how many client inquiries, unexpected opportunities, or other forms of abundance have showed up as I was traveling home from the pleasures and play of vacation. And if you need proof, remember Laura and I met in the epicenter of joy and play—the dance studio! That's undeniable proof that big purpose loves to emerge from what feels good.

E – Embodied Alignment

My body has always been wise—but for a long time, I didn't know how to listen. Or rather, I didn't know how to *trust* what I heard. I was skilled at overriding—at pushing through headaches, fatigue, tight shoulders, gut flutters—chalked up as "normal" or "not that bad." I had internalized the belief that logic was more reliable than sensation, and that being a good, successful, likeable person meant tolerating discomfort instead of honoring it.

But ignoring my body always came at a cost.

Over time, I began to realize that my body wasn't trying to sabotage me—it was trying to *save* me. Save me from burnout, from misaligned decisions, and from abandoning myself. I started to pay closer attention: to the ache in my jaw when I wasn't speaking my truth, to the heaviness in my belly when something was off, to the flutters of intuition in my body that whispered "this way" when something was aligned but beyond my comfort zone.

Embodiment, I learned, isn't just about sensing the body—it's about taking courageous action in life. It's about trusting the truth of your body enough to *act* on it. Even when that truth disrupts your plans. Even when it disappoints people. Actually, especially then.

And let me tell you—choosing embodied alignment over approval has changed everything. It's been both terrifying and liberating. But it's brought me into a felt sense of integrity and internal fortitude that no external validation could ever replicate. Every time I choose embodied alignment over performative perfection, I reclaim a little more of myself.

And that congruence of living what my body knows to be true has become a powerful compass that I've learned to trust more and more over time. That alignment between my body's yeses and noes, and my choices in life has made me like a radio station that emits a frequency that not only feels like home to me, but one that the universe unmistakably responds to… like magic.

R – Resonance

I'll never forget the moment we got our book deal (*this* book deal).

We had flown across the country to speak at a conference—not to pitch, not to hustle, but simply to serve. Just days before, I had been in a car accident with a semitruck (thankfully I was okay but was definitely navigating some trauma from the close call). After the accident, when I arrived home, my body clearly told me that my marriage was over… even if my mind wasn't ready to embrace that fact. I offer this context because I don't want you to think that we get to do this work without navigating the stuff of life. On one hand I showed up to attend and speak at this conference feeling like a total mess, swirling with trauma recovery and grief. Yet, my sense of purpose, passion, and a desire to serve everyone attending that conference got me out of my own stuff and into my heart. It's powerful what purpose can do to keep us afloat during hard times. So, I showed up as a wildly imperfect human with an open heart, rooted in purpose. No attachment, no performance. Just presence. And after our talk, we could feel the resonance through the room. People were affected by what we offered. They came to give us hugs and offer thank yous—some with damp eyes rooted in relief and release. *That* is our purpose, and we felt it fully alive.

And then, as we were walking out of the conference room where we had just presented, Michelle—the owner of the publishing company who also hosted the event—approached us and asked, "Have you two ever considered writing a book?" Without hesitation, we said, "Yes, absolutely." We'd both dreamed of it for years. We had taken the courses, worked with book coaches, researched our options... but deep down, we knew we weren't meant to self-publish a quick e-book. We were waiting for the *right* opportunity—the right partnership—to support us in bringing our message into the world with the integrity and reach it deserved.

Michelle smiled and said, "Well, we think you've got a great book waiting to be written and we'd love to publish it."

What she shared next sealed the moment as something truly magical. She told us that, while we were presenting, Dr. Karen Parker—a Human Design thought leader we respect deeply—had walked over to her and asked, "Why haven't I been asked to write the foreword for their book?" Michelle responded, "They're not under contract." And Karen simply said, "Well, you need to change that."

So not only were we offered a traditional publishing deal—we were simultaneously supported and affirmed by someone whose work had profoundly shaped our own. And the best part? We didn't even have to ask her to write the foreword. She offered! Unprompted. Aligned. Resonant.

If that's not an example of frequency meeting opportunity, of purpose meeting possibility, I don't know what is.

I've seen it again and again. A friend describing her dream home that she just couldn't find, and realizing it was *our home* that we hadn't even put on the market yet! A client "accidentally" landing on my website after I let go of trying to market and focused instead on being deeply present to doing the work. Invitations, relationships, resources—they seem to arrive not when I chase them, but when I become a clear enough signal for them to find me—when I'm too busy *embodying* my purpose to worry about failing at it.

That's the magic of resonance. It's not passive, and it's not luck. It's the result of doing the inner work to clear out what's not yours, to return to your own truth, and to live in integrity with that truth. It's what happens when you stop outsourcing your worth and start radiating your essence.

This framework has become deeply embedded in my way of life—especially when things feel uncertain, when old stories get loud, or when I'm tempted to slip back into the GRIND. Living the PROSPER way doesn't mean I never wobble or get scared. It doesn't mean life is without challenge. Let's be honest: life's always gonna life. Conditioning doesn't vanish overnight. And fear doesn't disappear just because you've found your purpose (if only!)

But what PROSPER gives me is something more powerful than perfection. It gives me a way home.

When I remember why I'm here…

When I take responsibility for how I show up…

When I stay open, make choices that honor my worth, dare to follow what feels good, listen to the (often inconvenient but unapologetically honest) wisdom of my body, and trust that resonance—not force—is the real-life flex…

That's when I get unstuck.

That's when I feel free.

That's when the unexpected abundance, aligned opportunities, and soul-nourishing connections arrive—not because I chased them, but because I became available for them.

And every time I choose presence over proving, trust over tension, and inner alignment over external approval, I take one more step toward the kind of prosperity I always longed for and the inspired life I truly want to live.

Section 4: From Insight to Integration

By now, you've explored how the GRIND framework can illuminate the deeper cultural stories that shape how we relate to success, purpose, worth, and well-being—often without realizing it. Seeing these patterns is powerful. Because once you see a story, you can start to get curious:

What else might be possible?

What stories do I no longer want to consent to?

What choices might be a better fit for the life I want to create?

That's where the PROSPER framework comes in.

If GRIND reveals what's no longer working, PROSPER shows you what to move toward. These seven pillars offer a new perspective—a more nourishing, aligned, purpose-guided path that helps you get unstuck and reconnect with what truly matters. And in the stories we just shared, you saw how we've each practiced (and continue to practice) living into those pillars in real, imperfect, human ways.

But here's the thing:

Even when you know what's no longer working…

Even when you know what would serve you better…

Insight alone often isn't enough.

Neither is action, if it's not also integrated at the level where your most deeply held patterns and beliefs live… below the surface.

That's why we developed the Integrative Somatic Experience™ (ISE) process—a holistic, body-based method of deconditioning and re-storying that supports change not just in your thoughts or behaviors, but in your nervous system and subconscious.

ISE is the missing piece. It's the bridge between clarity and capacity—between knowing your potential and finally becoming the kind of person who can live it.

> Because the stories we carry—about who we are, what we're worth, and what's possible—don't just live in our minds, they live in our bodies, in our stress responses, in the way we contract or expand in response to life.

If we want to truly get unstuck, we have to rewrite those stories not just mentally, but somatically (or as Meghan likes to say, "So-magically").

What comes next is an introduction to the ISE process—a step by step practice that supports your whole self in becoming more safe, comfortable, and sturdy in the stories of potential and possibility you most long to live.

Chapter 25
Embodied Purpose and Choice: The Practice of Integrative Somatic Experience

We're so excited to share this with you! It is through decades of our own lessons, experimentation, and learning that we've crafted this holistic model, and we hope that it helps you get unstuck and lean more powerfully into your purpose as much as it has supported us and our clients. *This* is where the magic happens—where the limiting stories you've inherited are fully transformed—on all levels of your being—into the stories you choose.

This is the heart of Integrative Somatic Experience: a practice and process that we designed to support you in moving from cool insight to sustainable energetic, neurological, full-body shifts. It's a process that bridges the gap between knowing and living. ISE is designed to help you integrate the insights you've gained throughout this book, supporting you in aligning your mind, body, and spirit with the life you want to create. It's not just about understanding your patterns or recognizing where you've been stuck; it's about rewiring those patterns and building new, embodied pathways to a thriving, purposeful life.

What Is Integrative Somatic Experience?

ISE is a multidimensional process that weaves together powerful, evidence-based practices to help you:

- move through unconscious blocks
- regulate your nervous system
- reconnect with your body's innate wisdom
- align with the stories, beliefs, and choices that resonate with your truth to get you unstuck… over and over again

Drawing from neuroscience, somatics, Internal Family Systems or parts work, energy psychology, guided visualization, and the wisdom of the five elements, ISE creates a holistic framework for sustainable, whole-self positive change. Each element of the practice is backed by science and grounded in years of experience, making the process both effective and deeply impactful.

The Core Elements of ISE

1. Breath

Breath is the most fundamental component of ISE. It's also one of those tools that might seem so simple, so un-sexy, that it's easy to overlook. But don't let its simplicity fool you; breath is a game-changer. This seemingly basic act directly impacts the body's autonomic nervous system (ANS)—the system that governs everything from our stress response to our heart rate and digestion. Conscious breathing techniques have been shown to calm the sympathetic branch of the ANS (the fight-or-flight system) and engage the parasympathetic branch (rest and digest), fostering balance, relaxation, and emotional regulation.

When we slow down and deepen our breath, the brain gets a clear signal: It's safe to let go of high alert. This shifts us out of survival mode, gently reducing stress hormones, lowering our heart rate, and supporting mental clarity. The breath's influence on the vagus nerve—a key player in emotional stability and resilience—is well-documented. Practices like box breathing or slow diaphragmatic breathing regulate this vital nerve, creating a cascade of calm and balance throughout the body.

Breath may not come with bells, whistles, or flashy Instagram-worthy moments, but its power lies in its ability to create a stable foundation for everything else. By integrating mindful breathing into our daily routines, we lay the groundwork for all other ISE modalities to take root and flourish. In its simplicity, breath offers profound transformation, reminding us that sometimes the most understated tools are the ones that hold the most magic.

2. Heart-Brain Coherence

Heart-brain coherence involves aligning the rhythms of your heart with the patterns of your brain, creating a state of physiological harmony and heart-centered wisdom. Research from the HeartMath Institute has shown that when the heart and brain are in coherence, the nervous system becomes more regulated, stress response decreases, and greater clarity, emotional resilience, and connection to intuition are experienced.

The heart's electromagnetic field is the strongest in the body, and when it's in coherence, it sends signals to the brain that promote calm, focus, and creative problem-solving. By practicing heart-focused breathing and cultivating positive emotional states (like gratitude or love), we create the physiological conditions for deeper integration and alignment.

3. Somatics

Somatics is the practice of tuning into the body as the primary site of transformation. Traditional talk therapy, or achievement-focused coaching, focuses largely on the mind, but somatic practices recognize that our experiences—especially those related to chronic stress and trauma—are stored (and often hidden) in the body. By working with the body, we access a deeper layer of healing and more sustainable and whole-self change.

Principles of somatic therapy and coaching allow us to process stuck energy, release tension, and reconnect with our most authentic selves. Neuroscience supports this approach: Research has shown that the body's interoceptive system (its ability to sense internal states) plays a crucial role in emotional regulation and self-awareness. And we love that!

4. PARTS WORK (IFS)

Internal Family Systems (IFS), or parts work, developed by Dick Schwartz, is based on the understanding that we all have different parts within us—distinct voices, feelings, or roles that make up our inner world. For example, one part might be a perfectionist, while another part carries the wounds of a younger self. IFS helps us identify, understand, and integrate these parts, fostering inner harmony and self-leadership.

This process is particularly powerful for moving beyond limiting narratives. By getting to know the protective parts that hold onto old stories and patterns, we can offer each part the love, compassion, and recognition it needs, gently guiding all parts toward releasing their grip. Neuroscience shows that integrating conflicting aspects of ourselves, embracing the "holy both-and," as we like to call it, reduces inner tension and strengthens emotional regulation.

5. ENERGY TOOLS

Emotions are literally energy in motion: "e-motions." They are part of our internal experience and the energy field surrounding our physical body; thus, they are key players in what we are putting out into the world and resonating with. So we want to be able to work with that energy. There are many modalities that address emotions, but we wanted to share the most effective and efficient—meaning, they are easy to learn, easy to use, and get the job done. So in our work, we use Emotional Freedom Technique and neurovascular holds. Let's take a quick look at these two techniques.

Emotional Freedom Technique

Emotional Freedom Technique (EFT), or tapping, blends ancient meridian-based practices with modern psychology to release emotional blocks and calm the nervous system. Developed in the 1990s by Stanford-trained engineer Gary Craig, EFT simplified Dr. Roger Callahan's Thought Field Therapy (TFT), an earlier method rooted in kinesiology and acupressure.

Tapping involves gently stimulating specific acupressure points while focusing on an emotion, thought, or belief. This process sends calming signals to the brain's amygdala, reducing the fight-or-flight response and lowering cortisol levels. Research has shown its effectiveness in reducing anxiety, improving emotional well-being, and rewiring stress responses.

As part of the ISE process, tapping is a powerful, accessible tool for shifting limiting patterns and creating space for alignment and growth.

Neurovascular Holds

Neurovascular holds (NV holds) trace their roots to the work of Dr. Terence Bennett, a chiropractor who, in the early 20th century, identified specific reflex points on the head. When lightly held, these points encourage blood flow and gentle warmth in the brain's emotional processing regions, helping to ease stress and support emotional regulation. Incorporating NV Holds creates a calming effect, offers a deep emotional release, and helps the body settle into a state of presence and balance.

In this book's introduction to ISE (coming so soon!), we will be focusing on a primary NV hold that was developed and used successfully to support regulation in patients with PTSD, as it has an incredible ability to disrupt the stress response.

6. Guided Visualization

The mind doesn't distinguish much between real and vividly imagined experiences. Guided visualization uses this principle to help rewire neural pathways and anchor new stories in the subconscious mind. By engaging the imagination, we create a bridge between the conscious and unconscious, allowing us to practice new ways of being in a safe, supportive space.

Visualization activates the brain's Default Mode Network (DMN), a concept we discussed earlier. When paired with somatic practices, it becomes a powerful tool for integrating insights and aligning with new possibilities.

7. The Five Elements

Inspired by traditional wisdom systems like Chinese medicine, the five elements—wood, fire, earth, metal, and water—offer a holistic framework for understanding balance and transformation. Each element represents a different aspect of life:

- **Wood:** Growth, creativity, and vision. Helps us move from anger and frustration to motivation and assertiveness.
- **Fire:** Passion, connection, and expression. Helps us move from panic and anxiety to joy.
- **Earth:** Nurturing, grounding, and stability. Helps us move from worry, martyrdom, and codependence to compassion, self-worth, and devotion.
- **Metal:** Clarity, focus, and release. Helps us move from grief, difficulty letting go, and victim mindset to inspiration and reflection.
- **Water:** Flow, intuition, and adaptability. Helps us to move from fear to curiosity, creativity, and hope.

By working with the elements, we honor the interconnectedness of all parts of ourselves. We are able to see the whole story of our experience and what we are trying to shift, the thoughts, emotions, feelings, beliefs, fears… all of it. When we collect the whole story, we are better able to use ISE techniques to ensure that the changes we make are sustainable and well-rounded.

Why This Approach Works

The Power of Integration

While each of these practices is impactful on its own, the way ISE weaves them together creates exponential results. It's not about addressing one aspect of yourself in isolation; it's about aligning your mind, body, and spirit in a unified way. Integration is what allows insights to become actions and actions to become lasting change.

The Science of Neuroplasticity

The brain's ability to change—known as neuroplasticity—underpins the ISE process. When we engage in practices like heart-brain coherence, somatics, and visualization, we activate the brain's plastic potential, creating new neural pathways and breaking free from old, limiting ones. Over time, these new pathways become default patterns, supporting more aligned, resilient ways of being.

The Role of Regulation

Regulation is the foundation of transformation. Without a regulated nervous system, change feels overwhelming or unsafe, and our bodies resist it. ISE emphasizes practices that calm the stress response, create safety, and expand our capacity to embrace change.

An Invitation to Embody Your Insights

This section of the book is where theory becomes practice, where insights meet action, and where you begin to truly live into the stories you choose. ISE isn't a one-size-fits-all process; it's adaptable to your unique needs, design, and journey. Some days, it might be a ten-minute practice of tapping or heart coherence. Other days, it might involve a deeper dive into parts work or guided visualization.

The goal isn't perfection; it's progress. It's about creating a sustainable, nourishing rhythm of embodiment that supports your continued growth and alignment. With ISE, you're not just healing old patterns—you're building a life that feels true, vibrant, and profoundly your own.

What follows is a kind of choose-your-own-adventure toolkit for managing stress and re-storying your life. We get it—you won't always have thirty uninterrupted minutes and a quiet room to do deep inner work. That's why we start with quick, accessible practices designed for those oh-shit moments—the ones where your nervous system is hijacked, and clarity feels out of reach. These short tools are powerful on their own and build even more impact over time, especially when used regularly. And when you're ready to go deeper—when you want to unravel an old belief, pattern or perspective that's been holding you back and replace it with one that's aligned with who you're becoming—that's when it's time for the full experience. That's when you'll dive into the complete ISE process (we refer to it as "The Full Monty") to decondition, re-story, and help your whole system—mind, body, and energy—embrace a new, more empowering way of being.

Ready?

We're so excited about the magic you're about to make in your life!

Chapter 26
Quick ISE Stress Management and Deconditioning Guide

In this section, we wanted to give you the right tool, for the right moment, to get the job done. An ISE session can help you really dive in and decondition a long-standing story. But we don't always have time for all that. Sometimes, shit is hitting the fan in real time, in front of us, and we need tools for every situation. We have included a resource pdf on our website unstuckyourselfbook.net so that you can print it out and keep it in your car, desk drawer, underwear… wherever you need it so that you can access your tools quickly.

The Oh-Shit Tool: When You're in the Thick of It (One to Three Minutes)

This is for the "I need to stay calm, but Uncle Bob is talking politics" moment. When you feel the heat rising, your stomach knotting, or your hands ready to throw something, you need one thing and one thing only: your breath.

This tool is fast, reliable, and scientifically backed. Plus, it's free, requires no equipment, and won't get you fired or arrested.

WHAT TO DO:

1. Close your mouth.
2. Breathe in through your nose for a count of six seconds.
3. Exhale slowly through your mouth for another six seconds.
4. Repeat at least three times. Bonus points if you notice the tiny pause at the top and bottom of your breath.

WHY IT WORKS:

- **Regulates your nervous system.** (Your brain loves a slow, steady breath.)
- **Stops your stress response before it takes over.** (No more spiraling into fight or flight.)
- **Gives you a tiny but crucial pause between your reaction and your response.** (So you don't say something you regret or make an exit that involves throwing mashed potatoes.)

Do this anytime, anywhere. In a meeting. At dinner. While waiting for someone to text back. It's your built-in reset button.

THE THREE-TO-FIVE-MINUTE RESET: WHEN YOU NEED TO SHIFT FAST

You made it to the bathroom. Or your car. Or that weird, semi-private corner at the office where you pretend to be checking your phone. Maybe you just dodged a conflict, felt an old pattern hijack your brain, or realized you're about five seconds away from saying something you'll regret.

This is your moment. You've got a few minutes to course-correct—let's make them count.

What to Do: The NV Hold Reset

1. **Start with your breath.** (Always. It's your built-in reset button.)
2. **Name what's happening.** What are you feeling?
   - Frustrated?
   - Anxious?
   - Shut down?
   - Just *off*?
3. **Hold the primary Neurovascular Hold.**
   - Hold one hand on your forehead (this helps bring emotions into the present moment instead of letting them run wild).
   - With your other hand, hold the NV points at the base of your skull.
4. **Breathe and hold.**
   - Stay here until you feel a shift.
   - If a new emotion emerges, name it and stay with it while you continue to hold until you return to a neutral state.

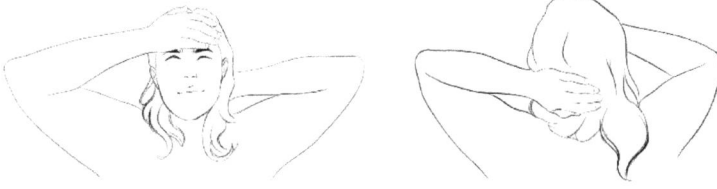

Why It Works:

- **Increases blood flow to the brain.** (So you can actually think instead of just react.)
- **Regulates the nervous system.** (Stops the emotional hijack and brings you back to center.)

- **Helps emotions move through instead of getting stuck.**
  (No more carrying that tension for hours—or days.)

This tool is a game-changer for catching yourself mid-pattern and shifting in real time. Use it before a big conversation, after an argument, or anytime your emotions feel like they're running the show.

And remember—this isn't about suppressing emotions. It's about giving them space to move so they don't control you.

The Ten-to-Fifteen-Minute Emotional Reset: Moving from Emotionally Stuck to Positively Shifted

Sometimes, emotions don't just pass through—they *camp out*. Maybe frustration has been sitting in your chest for days, or grief keeps sneaking up on you when you least expect it. Maybe anxiety has its claws in your stomach, or resentment feels like a weight pressing on your shoulders.

This practice isn't just about calming down—it's about getting emotionally unstuck. Instead of stuffing your feelings down or getting caught in the same reactive loops, this process gives your emotions space to move and integrate so you can shift into a more empowered state.

How To: The Heart-Brain Emotional Shift

1. **Get settled.**
   - Find a quiet space where you won't be interrupted.
   - Sit comfortably, letting your shoulders soften and relax.
2. **Breathe to create space.**
   - Inhale slowly through your nose.
   - Exhale slowly through your mouth.
   - Match the length of your inhale to your exhale, creating a steady rhythm.

- Do this a few times, allowing your body to settle.

3. **Tap into your heart-brain connection.**
   - Gently tap your fingertips on your heart space with one hand.
   - With your other hand, lightly tap the center of your forehead, the space between your eyebrows.
   - This helps synchronize your emotional experience with the part of your brain that can process and integrate it.

4. **Call in a high-vibe emotion.**
   - Focus on a feeling like joy, love, gratitude, or compassion.
   - If it feels hard to access, bring to mind a person, pet, memory, or place that makes you feel this way.
   - Let yourself fully feel that emotion in your heart—not just as an idea, but as a real, felt experience.

5. **Now invite in the emotion that's stuck.**
   - Whether it's anger, frustration, sadness, fear, or shame, let it be present.
   - Instead of fighting or analyzing it, just let it sit in the center of the high-vibe emotion you've cultivated.
   - Imagine your love, joy, or compassion holding space for the emotion—like a wise, steady presence that says, *You don't have to go anywhere, but you also don't have to take over.*

6. **Let the emotions interact.**
   - There's no need to force a shift. Just breathe and let your system integrate.
   - You may notice the emotion softening, dissolving, or shifting into something else.
   - If a new emotion emerges (like relief after anger, or sadness underneath frustration), let that be here too.

7. **Stay as long as you need.**
   - When you feel the emotion begin to release, let yourself return to neutral.
   - Notice how your body feels now—lighter? Softer? More open?

WHY IT WORKS:

- Emotions don't need fixing; they need witnessing. By letting them exist inside a field of love or joy, you allow them to integrate rather than control you.
- Your heart's energy field is powerful. When you activate it with high-vibe emotions, it coregulates your entire system, calming stress and shifting emotional stuckness.
- This rewires your nervous system over time. The more you practice, the more you train your brain and body to process emotions in a way that feels *empowered* rather than overwhelming.

This is a powerful tool for emotional transformation—not to bypass feelings, but to move through them with presence, self-compassion, and a deep trust that your system knows how to heal.

You don't have to stay stuck just because it's familiar.

THE FULL MONTY: WHOLE-SELF DECONDITIONING AND RE-STORYING PROCESS

This is it, y'all. For when you are really ready to go for it, to rewrite your narrative, to change how you are feeling and reacting, and to really, truly… and finally bust through that old, conditioned story (consciously *and* unconsciously). When you're really ready to do the damn thing. This is the full culmination of the ISE experience. For this you will need at least thirty to forty-five minutes.

What to do: This is a comprehensive process. So we will break it down into steps for you. Make sure to create a space to do this work. No noise, no distractions, just you (and all of your one million hamster-wheeling thought monkeys).

ISE Deconditioning and Re-Storying Process

First things first—this deep dive process might require some extra tools, resources, and support… and we've got you. As you move through the ISE (Integrative Somatic Experience) process, there may be moments when you hit a blank wall. You may be asked to name a sensation and your mind goes fuzzy. You try to identify an emotion and come up with… *meh*? You try to uncover a core belief and feel unsure of where to even start looking. Please know: *That's not a personal failing.* Most of us didn't grow up in environments that encouraged emotional literacy, body awareness, or curiosity about the stories pulling the strings behind our decisions. So of course this can feel unfamiliar. That's why we created a whole ISE Resources section—to give you language, examples, and supportive resources to help you get clear and dive deeper. If you get stuck or feel unsure, flip ahead. It's there to support you.

Okay, let's dive in….

Part 1: Deconditioning the Narrative

In order to decondition a narrative or long-time behavior pattern, we first need to gather the whole story. So grab your boots, and let's go deep!

Step 1: Get Grounded

1. **Find your breath, find your center.** Shake out your wiggles and let your breath travel inward.
2. **Connect to your heart.** Inhale and exhale, matching the length of the inhale and the exhale. Imagine, sense, or feel your breath move in and out of your heart. Relax your face, your head, your shoulders, arms, hands, ribs, belly, hips, legs, feet, and every single toe.

3. **Visualize the energy of your thoughts dripping like honey** from your head down your spine, through your legs, and out the bottom of your feet.
   - Feel yourself rooting into the earth, letting your roots dive deep through soil, rock, and caves until they reach the healing waters at the center of the earth.
   - Let your worries drain into these sacred pools.
   - Now allow those roots to drink deeply. Feel the rush of nourishment rising up into your feet, legs, hips, belly, and heart. Breathe into this cycle of release and renewal.
4. **Bring your awareness from your heart up through your head and beyond,** maybe 300 feet above you. Breathe into that expansive space—into the unlimited potential that exists beyond your physical form.
   - Connect here to your higher wisdom and any universal intelligence that guides you.
   - Feel your heart pull that energy down through the top of your head and back into your heart, like a flock of birds softly coming to roost.
5. **Breathe. Continue to breathe.** Feel the sweet nourishment of being grounded and connected to your higher wisdom. Gently open your eyes, staying in this place of calm and deep connection.

Step 2: Clarify Your Focus

1. **What do you want to work with today?** Is it an emotion? An experience? A repetitive behavior or pattern? Name it.
2. **What kind of stress does it cause?** How is it disruptive in your life, relationships, or health?
3. **Who would you be without this challenge or story?** What would your life look like? What would shift in your

relationships? If you could wave a magic wand and change it all, what do you truly desire?

4. **When you think about living beyond this challenge, what stories do you tell yourself?**
   - When we picture what we truly desire, we usually get a whole host of thought-based objections about why we can't. We call this the "Ship of Saboteurs." Hello, Captain!
   - Let those saboteurs shout their reasons it's impossible—you can't, shouldn't, it won't work because…
   - Make notes of every story or thought that arises.

5. **How do these thoughts make you feel physically?** Where do you feel them in your body? (Sweaty hands, tension in your jaw, tightness in your belly?) Just notice the sensations that arise when you think those thoughts—no need to fix anything, just notice. On a scale of one to ten, how intense is the feeling?

6. **Can you name the emotions tied to these feelings?** Emotions bridge our thoughts and physical sensations. If you're stuck, skim the emotion chart in the ISE resources section.

7. **Look for deeper beliefs.** Beneath thoughts and emotions lie wounds, stories, conditioning—beliefs and perceptions from our own experiences or from our people: family, childhood influences, culture. Listen for guilt or shame, should statements, or "I am / I am not" language (like "I am not good enough").

8. **Pause if it's intense.** Come back to your breath or the primary NV hold to help move the emotion—but don't avoid it. Remind all parts of yourself that it's safe to keep listening.

9. **Identify the primitive fear.** Often, underneath everything, there's a fundamental fear of rejection, abandonment, punishment, or pain. Glance at the fundamental fear list if you're unsure.
10. **Celebrate your courage.** Give yourself a big pat on the back for being willing to gather your entire story, raw and real. That alone is huge.
11. **Scan for blame.** Are you wishing your boss/partner/government/[fill in the blank] would just do something different so your story would vanish? Write it all down—don't hold back.
12. **Give your story a symbol.** It can be a letter, an image, a shape, a color—something quick and easy to visualize.

Step 3: Let It Go

1. **Come back to your breath, to your earth connection, to your higher wisdom, and to the pure source energy in your heart.** Breathe here for a few moments.
2. **Bring your symbol to your heart.** Imagine or sense it wrapped in the light of your heart.
   - Breathe love, understanding, and compassion into this story.
   - Affirm that it makes sense you think or feel this way.
   - Stay here as long as needed—at least thirty seconds.
3. **Place your hands in the primary NV hold position.**
   - Place one palm on your forehead (facing your face) and the other hand on the back of your head where it meets your neck.
   - This helps bring the old narrative into the present moment so it can be integrated.

4. **Hold the energy of love and compassion as your focus** and maintain this hold for thirty seconds to two minutes—until the emotional charge around the story releases and you feel more neutral.
5. **When it feels right, slowly release your hands.** Take a few deep breaths and flutter your eyes open. Notice how your body feels. Notice if the emotions or sensations have shifted in intensity. Go back to your one-to-ten scale—where are you now?
6. **Stand up and shake it off!** Shake out your feet, hips, shoulders, hands, and head.

Part 2: Rewrite It

Take a few breaths. Close your eyes and take a few breaths. Let yourself sink into that delicious space between what was and what could be. Resist the urge to barrel forward—there's real magic in this liminal moment. Invite every one of your senses to the party. There's a deep pleasure here, so let yourself linger.

When you're ready, open your eyes. From this more integrated perspective, look at your entire narrative:

- What have you learned from this experience?
- How have you grown?
- What unexpected gifts or blessings have come your way?
- What's changed for the better?

Craft Your New Story

Now let's rewrite your narrative. Let these questions guide you:
1. **What is the new potential that wants to emerge?**
2. **Project yourself six months to a year into the future to create a mental movie of you navigating life after this challenge is resolved.**
    - How does life look now that you're Unstuck from this pattern?

- What's different?
3. **What new thoughts are you having in this reality?**
4. **What sensations are you feeling in your body?**
5. **What emotions are here?**
6. **What core belief feeds this new possibility?**
    - *Example: I'm inherently worthy of love, success, support. I can trust myself. I matter.* (See the resources section for inspiring examples to pick from if you can't identify it right away.)
7. **How does this story or version of you create or change your life?**
    - What shifts in your family, relationships, career, health, etc., in this new story?
8. **Give this new story a symbol, color, character, or texture**—whatever helps you hold the vision. Trust what your imagination conjures here (sometimes the more unexpectedly weird, the better!)

Anchor It In

1. **Put down your pen, close your eyes, and return to your breath and heart.**
2. **Feel the emotions of your future self** in your heart and body. Turn up the dial on them—big time! (Your brain doesn't know the difference between now and then, but it does speak fluent "feels.")
3. **Focus on the symbol in your heart** while dialing up those high-vibe emotions—joy, bliss, love, gratitude.
4. **Stay here as long as you want**—at least two minutes—just feeling with your heart.
5. **Gently tap on your heart and forehead** to lock in this new reality.

When you feel complete, relax your hands, take a few more slow breaths, and when it feels good, open your eyes. Now, with your eyes open, **keep those high-vibration emotions active**. Anchor them in the present moment.

Ask yourself: **How can I move through my day holding on to this emotional state?** Because guess what? Magic happens when we actually commit to staying in this higher vibe.

Your Twenty-One-Day Practice

- This session might be done for now, but the real work continues. Studies show it takes about twenty-one days for our brains and bodies to build new neural pathways and shift old habits or conditioning.
- **Your homework:** For the next twenty-one days, set aside three to five minutes daily. Close your eyes, hold your symbol in your heart, and crank up those good feels.
- **Then open your palms**—and receive *all* the magic. Watch how your life begins to change because you're stepping up to do the work and release what no longer serves you.

You've got this—and your future self is already thanking you.

Chapter 27
Final Storytime: The Magic of Cocreating in Alignment

We've come to believe that the deepest form of leadership isn't about having all the answers. It's about having the courage to live the questions, embody the truth of who we are, and stay in integrity with the wisdom that lives within us—*especially* when the world tries to convince us otherwise.

We didn't write this book from the mountaintop of having it all figured out. We wrote it from the inside of a journey we're still on. A journey that has required us to unlearn so much of what we were taught about worth, leadership, and success. And perhaps most importantly? It's a journey we've chosen to take *together*.

Years ago, when we first started collaborating, we were both still trying to prove our worth through the lens of conditioned shoulds. We were focused on being fair, doing equal amounts of work, and trying to force good ideas into form. Meghan was *acting* like a Master Builder, trying to keep up with the doing and productivity pace she'd internalized from her upbringing and past professional roles. Laura, true to her Master Builder nature, was caught in the momentum of trying to *build* every idea that sparked between us—even if her Sacral was a clear no. It wasn't that we didn't have good intentions; it's that we were still living out old patterns rooted in scarcity and overefforting.

What changed? We started truly living our Human Design.

We began assigning tasks and shaping our roles based not on what was fair, but on what was aligned. We learned to honor our energetic needs—Laura, needing rest and genuine yeses *within* her workdays to keep her energy buoyant and joyful; Meghan, needing full-on spaciousness to restore after deep output. We've stopped pretending that our gifts need to look the same in order to be equally valuable. And because we respect the hell out of each other's designs, we can see clearly when one of us is starting to drift into old, conditioned territory—and we lovingly call each other back.

This book itself is a reflection of what becomes possible when two people align with their design and *trust the ecosystem of their collaboration*. Meghan's Possibilitarian Guide energy helped shape the narrative, tone, and relatability of the content while Laura's Master Builder brain foraged through endless sources of knowledge and research to construct the foundation. Every page in this book has been cocreated through a sacred balance of vision, strategy, reverence, and rest.

But the only reason we could do this without burning out is because we've built a relationship where authenticity and nervous system safety come before productivity. Our rule is simple: human first, business second.

We've had meetings that looked more like coffee shop breakups—where tears were shed and truth was spoken—not from a place of drama, but the tenderness that comes from sharing what's real. We've created space to process when life has been life-ing hard. We've learned to say, "This doesn't feel right" or "I just don't have it today," and trust that the other will not only understand, but honor it. We've held the mirror for each other countless times when one of us started slipping into martyrdom, overefforting, or fear.

We've had hard seasons—like the time we were finishing the rough draft of this book while prepping for a big facilitation gig and Laura was navigating a brutal month-long respiratory infection. Her body was screaming for rest and recovery, but the pull to *do* was loud. Meghan, energized by the right invitation and able to carry the load that week, said gently (but firmly), "Go take a damn nap." And she meant it. And Laura did... in spite of her resistance. She ended up having enough energy to colead the workshop and then went back to healing.

But alignment goes both ways.

Just a few days later, Meghan showed up to cowork and tears started flowing as soon as Laura asked how she was. All she could say was, "I'm just... so... tired." She put her head down on her desk and sobbed. She had run out of steam, just as Laura's Builder battery was coming back online. And Laura, from her rested clarity, said: "I've been waiting for this moment. You've carried us in such a beautiful way. Now it's time to rest." She booked Meghan a hotel and planned a spa day for total restoration. That moment—no big launch, no big payout—was one of the biggest wins in our work together. Because it reflected the *real* success story: two women in a collaboration where it is truly safe to *be fully human.*

Through this partnership, we've deconditioned hustle culture, learned to feel safe in receivership, and rewritten our stories around worth, success, and collaboration. We now move through our shared work with reverence—for each other, for our own energy, and for the sacred purpose we're here to fulfill. And as we've shared in this book, purpose isn't a title or a job. It's a state of being. One that we each access more fully when we stop trying to be everything and start truly being *ourselves.*

We hope this story reminds you that aligned success isn't a solo sport. It's not about perfectly executing some shiny five-year plan. It's about showing up, one choice at a time, in integrity with your design, your values, your body, and your truth.

You now have the frameworks. You have the tools. You have a map, a compass, and a blueprint.

And most importantly, you have *you.*

May your leadership, healing, and authenticity ripple out into the world as your own powerful form of activism.

Because when we live in alignment, we don't just change our lives. We change what's possible for *all* of us.

CHAPTER 28
YOUR ISE RESOURCES

Welcome to your ISE toolbox! In the pages ahead, you'll find helpful resources to support you in the full monty deconditioning process—including a step-by-step outline of the process itself, plus quick-reference cheat sheets to help you more easily identify sensations, emotions, and core beliefs as they arise. We know that getting stuck on "what am I even feeling?" or "how do I name this?" can derail the deeper work, so we've gathered these supports to help you keep moving. Use this section as your go-to guide for clarity, momentum, and embodied transformation as you re-story your life, one breath and one brave and honest reflection at a time.

THE ISE PROCESS PART ONE: RELEASING THE OUTDATED STORY OR PATTERN

This visual map is your guide through the brave and powerful process of release. Use it to untangle the web of stuckness—not with force, but with curiosity, compassion, and presence. You'll move through the questions in a circular flow, not to analyze your way to clarity, but to *feel* your way through what's been holding you back. Let this page be your playground of insight—jot down sensations, sketch symbols, scribble in the margins. This isn't about being neat or linear. It's about tuning into your body's wisdom, identifying the old stories you're ready to release, and creating space for something new. Your job here is simple, but sacred: notice, name, and let it go.

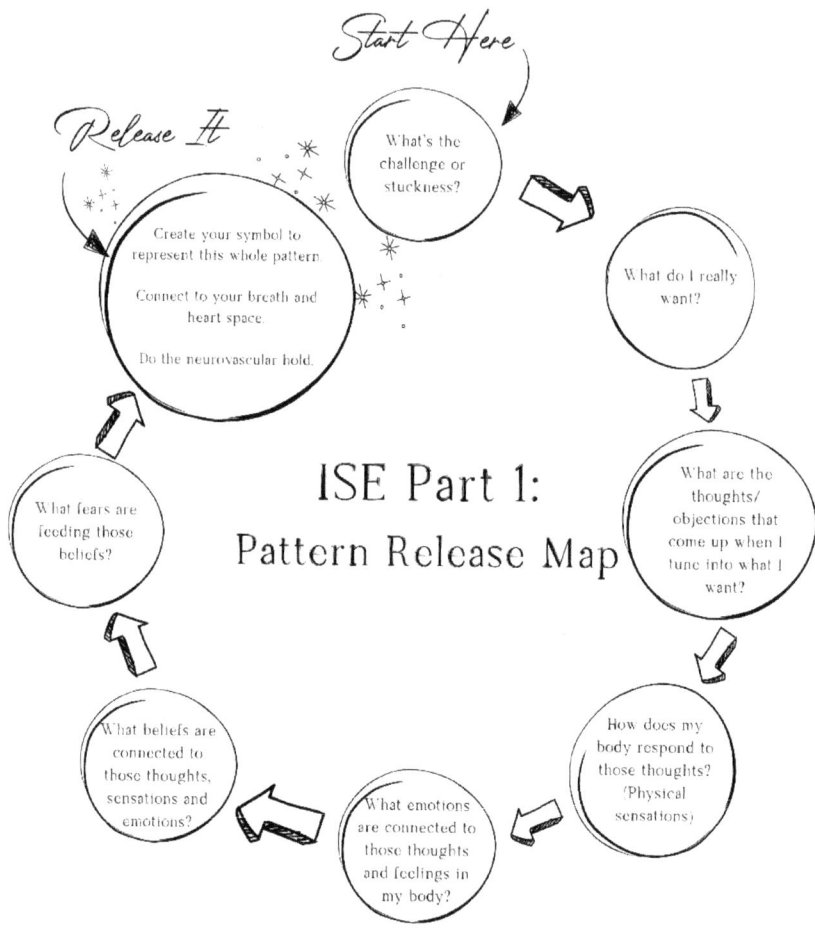

THE ISE PROCESS PART TWO: ANCHORING IN THE NEW STORY AND POSSIBILITY

Now that you've made space by releasing the old pattern, it's time to courageously choose what comes next. This map is your invitation to step into the magic of possibility—not just in your mind, but in your whole body. Imagination isn't fluff—it's a creative force that rewires your brain, shapes your nervous system, and anchors in new truths. So before you start writing, take a moment to *feel* the version of you who's already living this new story. Let your senses guide you. This is your chance to embody a new reality before it even arrives—because that's how we shift from stuck… to unstoppable.

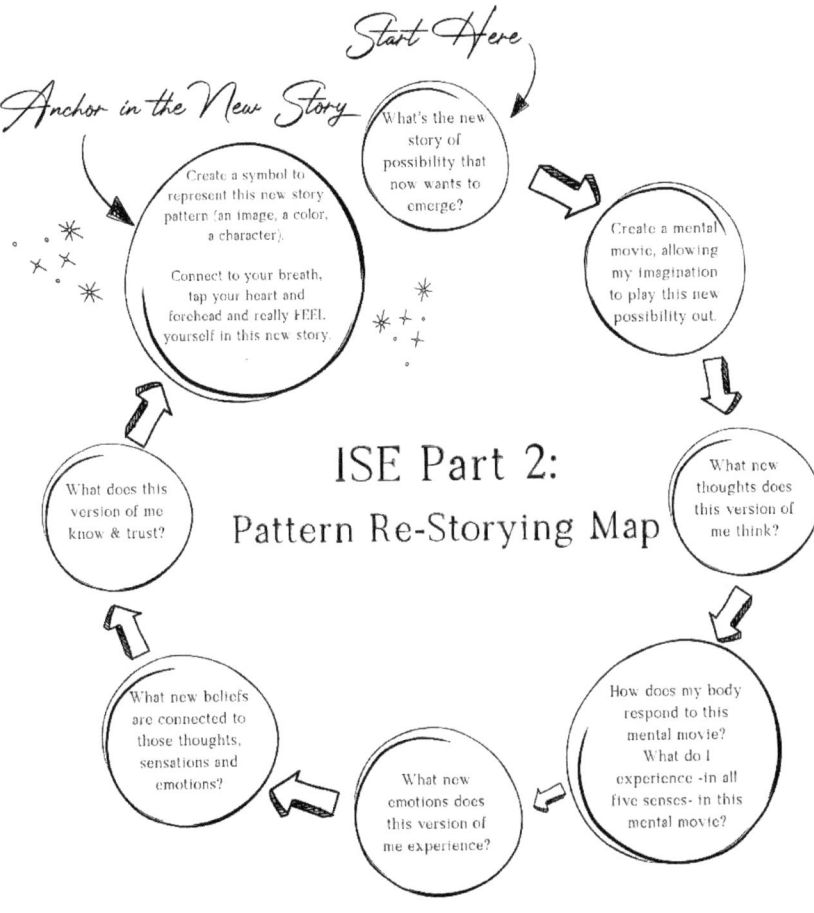

Sensations/Feelings Cheat Sheet

We're often so used to living in our heads that we miss the subtle (and not-so-subtle) cues our bodies are offering. But your body is always responding—often with unfiltered wisdom—whether you're aware of it or not. Use the list below to begin noticing how your body is reacting to a particular thought, memory, or belief.

Achy	Foggy	Sensitive
Airy	Fragile	Settled
Agitated	Frozen	Shaky
Blocked	Full	Shivery
Breathless	Gentle	Slow
Bruised	Hard	Smooth
Burning	Heavy	Squishy
Buzzy	Hollow	Soft
Clammy	Hot	Sore
Clenched	Icy	Spacey
Cold	Intense	Spacious
Constricted	Itchy	Sparkly
Contained	Jumpy	Stuck
Contracted	Knotted	Still
Delicate	Light	Suffocated
Deep	Loose	Sweaty
Dizzy	Nauseous	Tender
Drained	Numb	Tense
Dull	Pain	Throbbing
Electric	Pounding	Tight
Empty	Prickly	Tingling
Expanded	Pulsing	Toxic
Fizzy	Queasy	Trembly
Flowing	Radiating	Twitchy
Fluid	Relaxed	Vibrating
Fluffy	Relieved	Warm
Fluttery	Rigid	Wobbly

Emotions Cheat Sheet

Sometimes it's hard to find the words when we're in our feels. This cheat sheet may serve as an easy way to identify what's going on emotionally when your brain isn't feeling too "wordy."

Accepting	Edgy	Lethargic
Adventurous	Energized	Lively
Aggravated	Engaged	Loving
Agitated	Encouraged	Moody
Amazed	Embarrassed	Numb
Angry	Empty	On edge
Annoyed	Enthusiastic	Open
Apprehensive	Excited	Optimistic
Ashamed	Exasperated	Overwhelmed
Bitter	Exhausted	Passionate
Blissed out	Exploratory	Patient
Bored	Fascinated	Peaceful
Brave	Free	Perplexed
Burned out	Frazzled	Pissed
Calm	Frustrated	Playful
Capable	Fulfilled	Powerless
Caring	Furious	Present
Centered	Grounded	Proud
Confident	Grumpy	Questioning
Confused	Guilt	Radiant
Concerned	Happy	Reflective
Content	Hesitant	Refreshed
Curious	Hopeful	Rejuvenated
Cynical	Hostile	Rejecting
Daring	Humiliated	Reluctant
Delighted	Impatient	Renewed
Depleted	Indifferent	Resentful
Determined	Inhibited	Resistant
Dissatisfied	Inspired	Relaxed
Distant	Interested	Sad
Disconnected	Intrigued	Satisfied
Disturbed	Involved	Scattered
Doubtful	Irritated	Self-conscious
Eager	Isolated	Serene

Shocked
Shut Down
Skeptical
Strong
Suspicious
Thrilled
Trapped
Trusting
Uneasy
Ungrounded
Unsettled
Unsure
Victim-y
Vulnerable
Warm
Weak
Worried
Withdrawn
Worthy
Worthless

Examples of Stuckness—Inducing Core Beliefs

I should be further along by now.

I should be able to handle this on my own.

I should always say yes when someone needs me.

I should be grateful (so I shouldn't want more).

I should push through.

I should always be doing something productive.

I should know what to do by now.

I should never make mistakes.

I should always keep it together.

I shouldn't need help.

I shouldn't rest until everything is done.

I shouldn't feel this way.

I shouldn't speak up.

I shouldn't want more than I have.

I shouldn't take up so much space.

I shouldn't feel overwhelmed.

I shouldn't ask for what I need.

I am not enough.

I am too much.

I am lazy.

I am weak if I rest.

I am behind.

I am a failure.

I am responsible for everyone else's feelings.

I am not allowed to make a mistake.

I am only valuable when I'm useful.

I am only lovable when I'm successful.

I am not allowed to slow down.

I am selfish if I put myself first.

I am bad if I say no.

I am not allowed to need support.

The world is unsafe.

People will only value me if I prove my worth.

If I stop performing, I'll be forgotten/ overlooked.

People will leave if I'm not useful.

If I show who I really am, I'll be rejected.

Vulnerability is dangerous.

If I don't do it, no one else will.

Asking for help is a burden.

If I rest, I'll fall behind.

Slowing down means giving up.

My value depends on what I produce.

If I stop, everything will fall apart.

Rest is earned.

I have to hustle to succeed.

There's no room for error. Perfection only.

My needs don't matter.

There's never enough time, money, or support.

Success means self-sacrifice.

If I'm not constantly improving, I'm failing.

I have to fit in to be safe, loved, or successful.

I'll only be loved if I'm easy to be around.

I'm too sensitive for this world.

My gifts don't really matter.

I have to hide parts of myself to be accepted.

If I take up less space, I'll be more liked.

Being authentic is too risky/unsafe.

Examples of Core Fears

Fear of not being enough
Fear of being too much
Fear of being misunderstood
Fear of failure
Fear of success and what it might cost
Fear of disappointing others
Fear of being judged or criticized
Fear of losing love or approval
Fear of being truly seen—fully, honestly, vulnerably
Fear of being invisible or irrelevant
Fear of letting go of control
Fear of not doing enough
Fear of asking for help
Fear of being rejected for who we really are
Fear of being abandoned
Fear of being stuck forever
Fear of making the wrong choice
Fear of losing security or stability
Fear of starting over—again
Fear of being selfish for honoring our needs
Fear of being perceived as weak, emotional, or too sensitive
Fear of success (and what it might change)
Fear of becoming unrelatable to those we love
Fear that our dreams are unrealistic or irresponsible
Fear that nothing will ever really change
Fear of not fulfilling our potential
Fear of being excluded or left out
Fear of getting it wrong—even with good intentions
Fear that if we slow down, we'll lose everything we've worked for
Fear of being "too woo" or "not spiritual enough"
Fear of being misunderstood
Fear of stepping into leadership and being seen as arrogant

Fear that if we speak the truth, we'll hurt someone

Fear that our softness will be used against us

Fear that our strength will make others uncomfortable

Fear of being forgotten

Core Beliefs to Help You Get Unstuck and Thrive

I am enough, exactly as I am.

I don't need to earn my worth—I'm already worthy.

My value is not dependent on productivity.

I am allowed to take up space, be seen, and be celebrated.

I can be both growing and worthy at the same time.

My presence is powerful, even in stillness.

I am lovable without doing a single thing.

Rest is not a reward—it's a human right.

My energy is sacred, and I honor its natural rhythms.

Slowing down helps me hear what matters most.

I have nothing to prove.

My needs matter.

I honor what feels right in my body.

I can create success in a way that nourishes me.

Taking care of myself is how I stay in alignment.

Saying no is a powerful act of self-respect.

I am allowed to prioritize my needs.

It's safe to receive (support, resources, love etc.).

Asking for help is a sign of wisdom, not weakness.

I trust myself to discern what's right for me.

I release the pressure to carry everything alone.

I choose and deserve reciprocal relationships.

Support is available, and I'm worthy of it.

I find alignment when I am fully myself.

I am safe to be seen in my truth.

- My authenticity is my greatest gift.
- I don't need to shrink to fit in.
- I trust that the right people recognize and value me.
- My uniqueness is not a flaw—it's my special magic.
- I'm not everyone's cup of tea, but I'm the right people's special sauce.
- I lead by living in alignment with my truth.
- I trust the timing and unfolding of my purpose.
- I am here to create, to love, to thrive—not just to survive.
- My joy is part of my purpose.
- My path doesn't need to look like anyone else's.
- I don't have to force what is meant for me.
- I create impact by being who I truly am.
- I don't need to prove my worth through constant productivity

Resource Guide

Throughout this book, we've drawn from a wide range of teachers, research, and wisdom traditions. Some live in the realm of neuroscience and physiology. Some live in energy, quantum theory, or personal development. And many—like this book—live right at the intersection of both.

Here are some of the voices, studies, and resources that may serve you if you want to go deeper into the science, soul, and systems behind thriving beyond burnout and living into your true purpose.

Burnout, Stress, and Nervous System Regulation

Porges, Stephen W. (2011). *The Polyvagal Theory: Neurophysiological Foundations of Emotions, Attachment, Communication, and Self-Regulation.* W. W. Norton & Company.

Nagoski, Emily, and Amelia Nagoski. (2019). *Burnout: The Secret to Unlocking the Stress Cycle.* Ballantine Books.

van der Kolk, Bessel. (2014) *The Body Keeps the Score: Brain, Mind, and Body in the Healing of Trauma.* Penguin Books.

HUMAN DESIGN, GENE KEYS, AND ENERGETIC ALIGNMENT

Curry Parker, Karen. (2020). The Quantum Human Design™ Reference Manual: A New Paradigm for Understanding Yourself and Others. GracePoint Publishing.

Curry Parker, Karen. (2009). Understanding Human Design: The New Science of Astrology: Discover Who You Really Are. Hierophant Publishing.

Rudd, Richard. (2013). The Gene Keys: Unlocking the Higher Purpose Hidden in Your DNA. Osprey Publishing.

Uruhu, Ra. (2011). The Definitive Book of Human Design: The Science of Differentiation. Human Design America.

NEUROSCIENCE, SUBCONSCIOUS MIND, AND TRANSFORMATION

Chopra, Deepak. (2019). *Metahuman: Unleashing Your Infinite Potential*. Harmony Books / Penguin Random House.

Church, Dawson. (2018). *Mind to Matter: The Astonishing Science of How Your Brain Creates Material Reality*. Hay House LLC.

Davidson, Carey. (2020). *The Five Archetypes: Discover Your True Nature and Transform Your Life and Relationships*. S&S/Simon Element.

Dechar, Lorie Eve, & Benjamin Fox (2021). *The Alchemy of Inner Work: A Guide for Turning Illness & Suffering into True Health & Well-Being*. Red Wheel/Weiser.

Dispenza, Joe. *Breaking the Habit of Being Yourself: How to Lose Your Mind and Create a New One*. Hay House, 2012.

Elliott, Carolyn. (2020). *Existential Kink: Unmask Your Shadow and Embrace Your Power*. Red Wheel/Weiser.

Lakhiani, Vishen. (2020). *The Code of the Extraordinary Mind: Ten Unconventional Laws to Redefine Your Life and Succeed on Your Own Terms*. Harmony/Rodale.

Lipton, Bruce. (2005). *The Biology of Belief: Unleashing the Power of Consciousness, Matter & Miracles.* Hay House.

Panksepp, Jaak. (1998). *Affective Neuroscience: The Foundations of Human and Animal Emotions.* Oxford University Press.

Pert, Candace B. (1997). *Molecules of Emotion: Why You Feel the Way You Feel.* Scribner.

Schwartz, Richard C. (2021). *No Bad Parts: Healing Trauma and Restoring Wholeness with the Internal Family Systems Model.* Sounds True.

Wiest, Brianna. (2020). *The Mountain Is You: Transforming Self-Sabotage into Self-Mastery.* Thought Catalog Books

QUANTUM PHYSICS AND THE NATURE OF REALITY

Bohm, David. (1980). Wholeness and the Implicate Order. Routledge.

Capra, Fritjof. (2010). The Tao of Physics: An Exploration of the Parallels Between Modern Physics and Eastern Mysticism. Shambhala Publications.

Goswami, Amit. (2011). *How Quantum Activism Can Save Civilization: A Few People Can Change Human Evolution.* Hampton Roads Publishing Company.

Goswami, Amit. (1995). The Self-Aware Universe: How Consciousness Creates the Material World. TarcherPerigee.

McTaggart, Lynne. (2008). The Field: The Quest for the Secret Force of the Universe. Harper Perennial.

CULTURAL CONDITIONING AND NEW PARADIGM LEADERSHIP

Birdsong, Mia. (2020). *How We Show Up: Reclaiming Family, Friendship, and Community.* Hachette Go.

brown, adrienne maree (2017). *Emergent Strategy: Shaping Change, Changing Worlds.* AK Press.

Lahti, E. (2022). *Gentle power: A revolution in how we think, lead, and succeed using the Finnish art of sisu.* Sounds True.

McTaggart, L. (2017). *The power of eight: Harnessing the miraculous energies of a small group to heal others, your life, and the world.* Atria Books.

Walrond, K. (2021). *The Lightmaker's Manifesto: How to work for change without losing your joy.* Broadleaf Books.

Acknowledgments

There's no way a book like this could come into the world without a constellation of support, inspiration, and guidance—and we are deeply grateful.

To Karen Curry Parker, thank you for being the spark that set this journey into motion. Your whispered nudge at just the right moment was the domino that changed everything. But even more than that, thank you for your heart-centered teachings, your unapologetic devotion to this work, and your leadership that has made Human Design not just accessible—but sacred, livable, and embodied. Your impact and inspiration is part of the fabric of this book.

To each other—this collaboration has been nothing short of magic. Writing this book together, in alignment with our unique designs, gifts, humor, growth edges, friendship and deep respect for each other, has been the most easeful and inspired creative flow either of us has ever experienced. This book was built on mutual trust, aligned invitations, and an almost otherworldly synergy that we know is rare. We do not take that for granted.

To the team at GracePoint Publishing—thank you for believing in this book and walking alongside us to help bring it into the world. Michelle Vandepas, your initial invitation, trust and encouragement gave us the confidence to say yes to this journey. Tascha Yoder, thank you for holding the big picture with grounded brilliance. And to our editors, Anna Paradox and Laurie Knight—your thoughtful edits, care, and clarity helped refine our voice without ever dimming its essence. We are so grateful for your support, skill, and presence.

To our Beta Readers- Mindi Yeger, Kelly Hanson, Tom Boots, Michael Diettrich-Chastain, and Patrice Ludwig — your wisdom, reflections, and encouragement helped shape this book into what it was always meant to be. We cannot thank you enough.

— Meghan's Personal Acknowledgments —

To my son, Liam—thank you for being one of my deepest sources of inspiration. Your sensitivity, insight, and way of seeing the world give me so much hope for what's possible. It is my absolute honor to be your mom, and my deepest wish is that this book supports you in owning your unique brilliance so that it can shine fully and unapologetically in the world.

To my mom, Jackie—thank you for loving me so fiercely, even when you didn't fully understand the path I was walking. Your wholehearted support, especially throughout the writing and birthing of this book, has meant more to me than words can capture.

To Pete, my former partner—thank you for believing in this book, in me, and in the vision I've carried for so long. Even in the midst of the grief, complexity, and vulnerability that came with our divorce, you chose to support this project with generosity and care, and for that I'm truly grateful

To my clients—*all of you*—thank you. The work we've done together over the years has shaped me, stretched me, inspired me and offered me more insight and wisdom than you'll ever know. Your courage, your truth-telling, your willingness to show up in the most raw, courageous and tender ways—*that* is what makes this work sacred. Walking beside you on your journeys remains one of the greatest honors of my life.

To my community—thank you for seeing me, getting me, and loving me exactly as I am. For honoring my quirky, sensitive, intuitive, sassy, hip-hop dancing, good witch self. To be celebrated for the full spectrum of my humanity is a gift beyond words. This book may have been written from my heart, but it wouldn't have found its way into the world—or into the hands of those who need it—without your inspiration, encouragement, and active support. You remind me what belonging truly feels like, and for that, I am endlessly grateful.

To everyone who sat with me through the tears, the overwhelm, and the doubt—as I faced the bigness of my own purpose and soul calling—thank you. To those who reminded me of who I am and why I'm here, who held the vision with me when it felt too big or too scary to carry alone, and to the teachers, guides, and conscious leaders who showed me it *is* possible to live your purpose and create ripples of healing impact—you were embodied examples that helped me stay brave when parts of me wanted to hide, shrink, or run from the risk of failure.

This book is for the ones who feel deeply, dream bravely, and are learning to trust their own magic—especially when the world tries to make them forget it. May it remind you that your magic is real, your voice matters, and your authentic presence is the medicine this world needs now more than ever.

–Laura's Personal Acknowledgments –

To Patton—thank you for walking beside me through the many twists and turns of this journey. Your quiet devotion to our family and steady support behind the scenes made space for me to show up fully to this work. You held the edges when I needed to go deep, and that kind of support is rare. I don't take it for granted.

To my brilliant kids, Eve and Benni—you are the best parts of my story. Your curiosity, your honesty, your creativity, and your beautifully unique ways of seeing the world are constant reminders of what truly matters. You keep me anchored, laughing, and deeply inspired.

To my mom Mary Jane—thank you for being a soft landing and a strong foundation. Your encouragement has always felt like a north star, guiding me back to myself—even when I took the long way around.

To my siblings—Patrice, Leigh, and Kenny—thank you for your humor, your love, and your quiet belief in me across all the chapters of my life. You've helped me feel known and seen in ways that only siblings can.

To my in-law family—thank you for being generous with your support and encouragement. Knowing you were cheering from the sidelines gave me extra wind when I needed it most.

To my clients—working with you is one of the greatest honors of my life. Thank you for trusting me with your truth, for allowing me to walk beside you in your transformations, and for teaching me more than you'll ever know. The work we do together is sacred, messy, beautiful, and alive—and it's woven all through this book.

To my friends—you've held my hand (and sometimes my hair) through the hard and the holy. Thank you for the coffees, the calls, the texts that made me laugh inappropriately in public, and mostly the fierce reminders that I'm not alone. You've been lifelines, soul mirrors, and the kind of people who show up with snacks and love when both are desperately needed.

And to everyone who made space for this book to be born—thank you. This wasn't just a writing project. It was a healing, a remembering, and a reclaiming.

This book is for the ones learning to live in alignment—with joy, with purpose, and with just enough sparkle to remember they're made of both grit and stardust. A little mystery, a little mermaid magic, and a whole lot of heart.

About the Authors

Laura Cardwell is an Intuitive Business Coach, author, speaker, and expert in blending the science and soul of human potential. With advanced training in applied neuroscience, energy medicine, quantum concepts, and Human Design, Laura helps purpose-driven people, leaders, entrepreneurs, and creatives break free from burnout and build sustainable, joyful success that actually fits who they are.

She is the co-founder of *Embodied Leadership by Design* and the creator of *NeuroCohesion®*, her signature methodology that integrates Human Design, Gene Keys, Applied Neurology, and Traditional Chinese 5 Elements to create real, embodied transformation for coaches, healers, and heart-centered entrepreneurs.

When she's not teaching or writing, you'll likely find her by the water (any water), dancing hip-hop, learning something, or happily re-watching old episodes of *Murder, She Wrote*—because honestly, Jessica Fletcher never lets her down.

Meghan O'Malley is an intuitive embodiment coach, author, speaker, and former psychotherapist who helps purpose-driven humans stop settling for "fine" to create lives full of meaning, magic, and deep alignment. With expertise in somatics, trauma-informed healing, Human Design, applied neuroscience, leadership coaching and energy work, Meghan bridges the practical and the mystical to support real, whole-self and whole-life transformation.

She's the co-founder of *Embodied Leadership by Design*, where she guides leaders, creatives, and change-makers toward purpose-fueled lives that actually feel as good as they look. In addition to this work, she supports a small number of clients in her private practice—those ready to stop settling and start crafting relationships and lives that feel like practical magic.

Meghan's greatest joy is helping people reconnect with the wise, intuitive spark they've always carried—the part of them that knows they're here to live meaningfully, love deeply, and make magic in the everyday. When she's not coaching or writing, you'll likely find her at cardio hip hop class (or whatever new dance class she's excited about), belting out stage-worthy singalongs in the car with her teenage son, snuggling her intuitive rescue pup, introverting unapologetically (likely with a romance novel or journal in hand), or soaking in the inspiring and nourishing company of her incredible community.

For more great books from Human Design Press
Visit Books.GracePointPublishing.com

If you enjoyed reading *Unstuck Yourself,* and purchased it through an online retailer, please return to the site and write a review to help others find the book.

www.ingramcontent.com/pod-product-compliance
Ingram Content Group UK Ltd.
Pitfield, Milton Keynes, MK11 3LW, UK
UKHW020344080426